101ST AIRBORNE COMBAT MEDIC
TRANSITION TO DUTY

WITH THE
SCREAMING EAGLES
IN VIETNAM, 1968-69

Map of Vietnam.

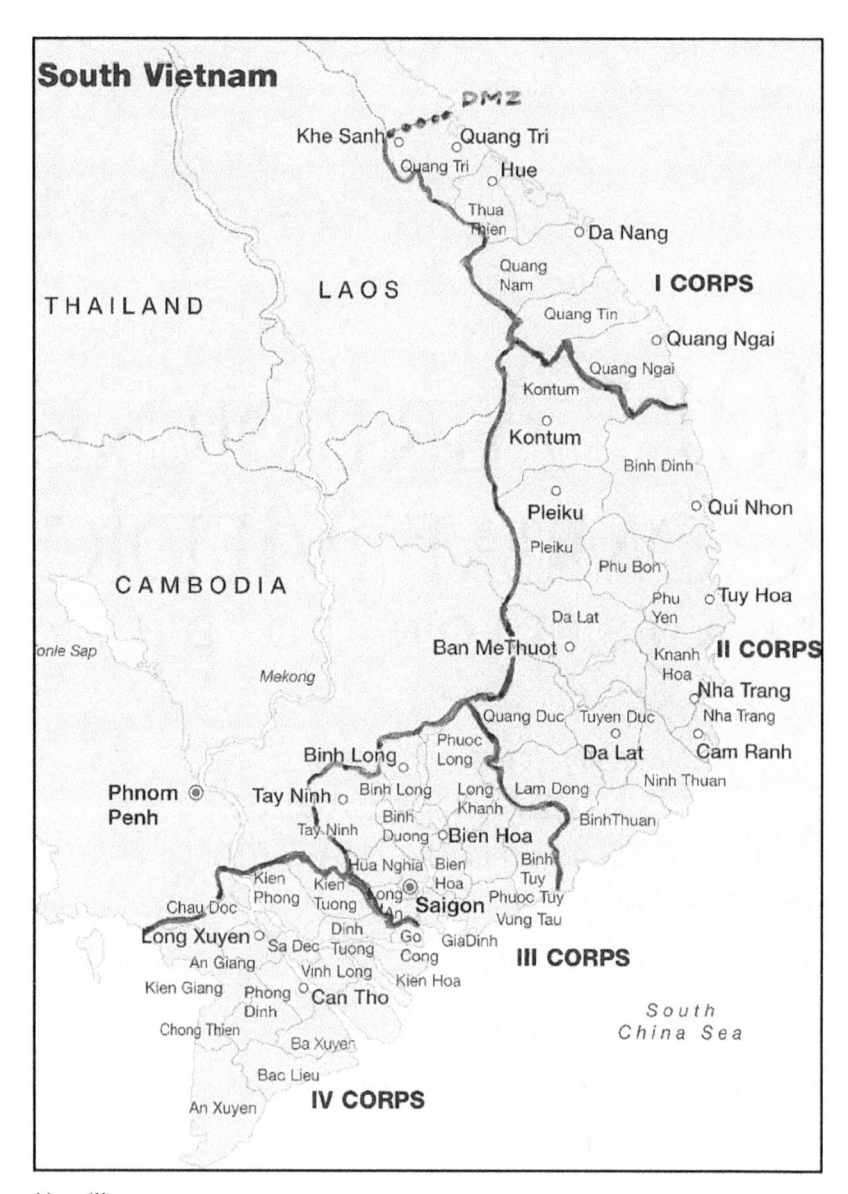

101ST AIRBORNE COMBAT MEDIC
TRANSITION TO DUTY

WITH THE SCREAMING EAGLES IN VIETNAM, 1968-69

LEO "DOC" FLORY

Copyright © 2023 Leo Flory. All rights reserved. No part of this book may be scanned, copied, uploaded or reproduced in any form or by any means, photographically, electronically or mechanically, without written permission from the copyright holder.

ISBN: 978-1-958407-14-1 (Hardback)
ISBN: 978-1-958407-15-8 (Soft Cover)

Previously published as *Transition to Duty*

The 101st Airborne Division and the 101st Airborne Division Association have not endorsed this book.

Cover photo: UH-1D Medevac Helicopter in South Vietnam, 1969.
National Archives

Book design by designpanache

ELM GROVE PUBLISHING
San Antonio, Texas, USA
www.elmgrovepublishing.com

Elm Grove Publishing is a legally registered trade name of Panache Communication Arts, Inc.

*For Robert Malecki, a man I never knew—
yet without whom this book would never have been written.*

*And for Dave Reinheimer, for his tireless effort in putting
B-Co. back together again.*

Contents

Foreword 9

Preface 11

Acknowledgments 16

1. Greetings from your Friends and Neighbors. 18
2. Induction 27
3. Good Morning Vietnam 33
4. Orders, B-2501. 37
5. Contact 49
6. Stand-Down 56
7. The Green Mission 66
8. In the Shadow of the Valley 74
9. Pohl Bridge 82
10. Rockets and More 88
11. Culco/Eagle Beach 103
12. Mountains and Monsoons 114
13. Firebases. 132
14. Just Another Day in the Jungle 153
15. Whip. 166
16. Hard Times. 183
17. Back to Pohl Bridge 210

18. Apache Snow 220

19. Firebase Airborne. 230

20. Eagle's Nest 239

21. R&R 250

22. Short-Timer at Sally 265

23. The First Ten Years 295

24. Reflections 306

Postscript to 2023 Edition. 316

Appendix

    I. A Chopper Pilot's Mind Pictures. 346

    II. "Justifiable Sacrifice" by Elizabeth Flory 352

    III. Robert "Uncle Bob" Malecki by Jennifer Gaines . . . 354

    IV. Statistics 357

    V. Unit Roster 362

Index 370

Foreword

In the late 1960's an entire generation of young Americans were presented by their country with a dilemma. The nature of this period in American History and the way the nation chose to deal with the "Challenge of Vietnam" resulted in a generation confronted with choices like no other before it. The spectrum of options available was indeed vast; from total commitment, no commitment, hiding from commitment, to maligning the commitment of some. No matter the choice this generation of young men made, it changed each of them irrevocably. In this narrative "Doc" Flory has effectively captured the experiences and perspectives of a young man in the late 1960's that were the result of the course he chose.

Many aspects of this story are shared by the 3,000,000 who served in-country. This particular narrative is about life in an elite infantry unit at the face to face level of combat. It is excellent work, a great memoir with some wonderful insights. It is very accurate as my memory serves, but I must admit Doc's is better than mine. Also, there are, of course, perspectives and views a platoon leader and company commander never realized and this book improved my knowledge, even 42 years later. I enjoyed learning the views of my former soldiers who did not share them with "The Brass." In addition, reading of their exploits made many of them live again.

Anyone who claims to be a historian or student of this period or "the war" and cites his studies from the "Pentagon Papers," "The Best and Brightest" or Vann's "Bright Shining Lie" must also have a work like this on his shelf or he has missed the personal experience and insights of the almost 10 percent of the 60's generation who chose to serve the nation honorably. Great work "Doc," serving with all of you made me a better soldier and this is meaningful work. Thank you, Geronimo and Drive on.

Pierce T. Graney Jr.,
Colonel, Infantry (ret.)
Former Commander, Co B 2nd Bn 501st Infantry, Airborne

Preface

On February 16, 2009, while checking e-mail, I found a message from a Ms. Jennifer Gains who discovered our military website, *www.b2501airborne.com*. For the sake of documenting that morning, I am including her first message and the subsequent messages relayed between us:

> *Hi. I found all of your e-mail addresses on a website and I am hoping that maybe someone can help me. I am trying to find any information that I can about my uncle, Robert R. Malecki. He graduated basic at Ft. Leonard Wood mid-July 1968 and went to Vietnam on November 29, 1968. He was in A-Co. 2-501 101st and was killed at FB Airborne on May 13, 1969. He was from Chicago and other than that I don't know much about him. I am trying to piece together his military life in hopes that future generations won't forget what a wonderful man he was. Any help would be greatly appreciated...and any suggestions where else to look would be helpful. It is all a bit overwhelming. Thank you so much from the bottom of my heart!*

Well, I knew that place and I knew that date and a flood of memories came pouring in. I sorted my thoughts for a while and decided it would be wrong not to answer Jennifer's request, even if I didn't know her Uncle Robert.

My reply to Jennifer:

> *I cannot tell you the rush of memories I felt when I read your request about your uncle. It is almost eerie to hear from someone about this event forty years later. I am not doing so well at holding back the tears right now as I sit at my office computer, but I've been here before.*
>
> *I did not know your uncle. Our companies traveled together only two times during that year, and it was hard enough to know all the men in my own company, as it was the nature of our work to travel in small platoon-sized elements. I was however on Firebase Airborne with B-Co. for several days prior to A-Co. taking our place in guarding the perimeter. B-Co. then made an assault to the opposite side of the A Shau Valley and were on maneuvers there.*
>
> *Jennifer, not knowing your tolerance for this kind of thing, I will keep it short. From our position, B-Co. had a visual to Airborne. In the morning of the fifth day of that maneuver, we suddenly became aware of the activity on the base. By daylight we had prepared a landing position for helicopters and were flown back to Firebase Airborne. I can tell you this in good faith, your uncle most surely was a hero.*
>
> *You must have found us at www.b2501airborne.com, and I have sent your request to David Reinheimer, our group president. He has been in contact with A-Co. and has gone to one of their re-*

unions. Dave will forward their contact information to you.

Meanwhile, you will notice on the B-site that we are having a reunion in Kalamazoo, Mich., this summer. You are very welcome to visit us there in person. What happened on that Firebase was a major event for all of us during that year. If you would care for more information from our perspective, I could probably let it out in small pieces.

God bless you for your effort.
Leo "Doc" Flory DRIVE ON AIRBORNE

Jennifer then replied to me:

Dear Mr. Flory,
Thank you for writing me back. I can only imagine how hard it must be to talk about everything that you all have seen and gone through. I have read so many dramatic horrifying stories...all I can do is thank all of you for serving your country and those in it with such honor. With that said, if you don't mind writing about what it was that you saw, then I would like to hear it. Whether or not that is a story you wish to share, I do not know. If it is, please write me about it- however long or short you wish to make it. I know your time is valuable and I would appreciate anything that you would share.

With many thanks,
Jennifer

I wrote back to Jennifer and explained that I copied our messages and showed them to my wife, Ann, and then explained some of the events surrounding that Firebase, some of which she knew. Hearing some of these stories in a new way gave her a different view and solidified that particular time better in her mind. Ann agreed that I should move forward if I wanted to and supply Jennifer with as much information as I could about the incident. So I started that night.

I remembered an article about Firebase Airborne in a recent *VFW* magazine, and found the issue, which was a very good account of what happened on the Firebase. I scanned the article and e-mailed it to Jennifer. It was the May 2008 issue, starting on page 34, and can be viewed on the VFW web site.

David Reinheimer, our veterans reunion president, had also answered her request and forwarded information about A-Co. (Alpha Avengers) web site to her. I survived the Vietnam War. Robert did not. I did not know Robert or serve with him directly, but while pondering Jennifer's request, I felt overwhelmingly obligated to tell her what I could, from my perspective with B-Co. It plagued my thoughts for several days. I shared it all with Ann, who listened more carefully than ever before, and my daughters, Rebecca and Elizabeth, who have begged me for years to write down some of the stories I told them when they were kids.

I resolved not to let it out one piece at a time, but to tell it all, the good, the bad, the ugly and all that pertained to Firebase Airborne. I will also try to reflect on a question that plagues me and any veteran who has experienced real combat or has been in the throes of what it takes to make combat happen and for anyone who has survived natural or unnatural disasters. The question that you learn to accept, but one that sticks with you for your entire life is, "Why did I survive?"

This collection of stories is about my experience with the US Military and a tour of the Vietnam War as a combat medic. I am dedicating these stories to a man I did not know, simply because, if it were not for Robert Malecki, Jennifer would have never made her request for information, and I most likely would have never written a single word of it.

My memory of events and conditions serves me well, but some of the events relative to the time and sequence, have been lost to me and many of my comrades.

However, Robert Malecki represents one of more than 58,000 men and women that died because of the Vietnam War. In this book, Robert represents all of them. I decided to take on this task of documentation for several reasons. The first is for Jennifer. Even if there is little information that I can provide her about her uncle, she may come to know a little of what his day-to-day life in the military was like. The second is for my wife Ann, who stuck by me in that first decade and through thick and thin ever since. The third is for my wonderful daughters so that they may understand their dad just a little better, and for my grandkids, so they eventually know what happened to their crazy old grandpa, and for my family, friends and relatives, for whom it is nearly impossible to convey my full experience.

I also welcome anyone, veteran or otherwise, to read it, and I do hope they like true stories.

For the record, this evolves around a war. A war in every conceivable way you can describe it, not a "conflict" or a "police action," as the politicians would have it. I do hope that these stories will cause you to laugh, cry—and wonder why.

Acknowledgments

First and foremost, I wish to thank Jennifer Gains for the unrest that she felt in her heart. She desired to know what she could about an uncle who she never met, but who died in a far away war. She not only had a desire to know of him, she put herself to work in finding what his military life was like. Part of her quest brought her to our B-Company website, and the subsequent request for information about him, which stirred me to write. I did not know her uncle, but I knew the circumstances of his death, and I could describe in great detail just what his day to day life would have been like in Vietnam. Thank you Jennifer, for the information and photos, and for sending me on a new and wonderful military mission.

I want to thank Mark Frazier for doing the exact same thing that Jennifer did, in regards to his uncle Michael Carl Sneed.

Now for the person that did all the really hard work, Denise Scurry. This amazing woman volunteered to work her way through over four hundred hand-printed (half scribbled) pages and typed them all. She then suffered through three of my own complete edits of the entire book and three more from Larry Massie, my editor and publisher. After that, she organized more than a hundred scanned photos, assigned labels for all of them, and sorted them all to my chronological order. With her mastery of the computer, she put it all in electronic documents and on disk for the publisher. She saved me an extraordinary amount of time and money, but she said all she wanted was an autographed copy of the finished book. We will see about that. I would like any reader of this book to keep in mind that she touched every single word in it. I stand at full attention and salute you Denise.

I thank my friend David Tate, director of Van Buren County Public Libraries, and his wife Carol, who directed me to Larry Massie.

I thank Larry and Priscilla Massie at Priscilla Publishing, Allegan Forest, Michigan, for publishing my book the first time around, and Deborah Neumann who designed the original edition.

Thank you to David Reinheimer for being the first B-Company veteran to read and critique the rough draft, and then providing so much help with proper names, photos and information. And for Dave's wife Lynn who also read the draft and was so willingly gave thanks and praise for the work.

Thank you Cathy Jimmerson (Cat) for all the assistance with the photos from the B-Co. website, and other assistance. Thank you Ann, for wandering into the kitchen at 2:00am to check on me at those times when the words were flowing.

Thank you to my daughters Rebecca and Elizabeth for your additions to the book and the belief that I would finish it. Thank you Jim Hunt, for reading the draft, correcting the helicopter terminology, and for your "Mind Pictures."

Thank you Jan Roeder, for giving freely of your time, your critical eye, and imagination.

Thank you to anyone else that I many have failed to mention, a great many people shared freely with whatever they could.

1.
Greetings from your Friends and Neighbors

What can I say? It was the 60's, with the second or third level of baby boomers acquiring driver's licenses at a time when factory-built muscle cars were growing exponentially and were often better than the street rods that the "gear heads" were building.

The 50's had given birth to new breed of rock-n-rollers and the fantastic, ever-evolving music was pouring in on the AM stations, and we just couldn't get enough of it. We had songs about cars, drag racing, beach parties, surfing, summer vacation, skipping school, brown-eyed girls and how the northern girls could keep you warm at night. It took a little longer for the new fads, dances and clothing styles to reach us in rural Michigan, but we caught on quickly when they did.

Most of our parents had felt the effects of the Great Depression, and all of them experienced World War II and the Korean War. Many families had both parents working, so there was a fair amount of money around. We teenagers were the recipients of an America with freedom for young people probably never felt by earlier generations. My father had become a welder in the Bay City, Michigan, shipyards during WWII, so was exempt from the military draft, as Uncle Sam needed his ships. He then became a pipe fitter and welder in the trades, working commercial construction around Kalamazoo and one season on the Mackinac Bridge. He made decent money for the times and was a "do-it-yourselfer" extraordinaire.

Mom was a multi-talented woman and very hard working, but by 1965 there were seven kids in the family, and it was all she could do to keep up with us. We were raised well, always having a parent at home. Dad's income provided us with all the basic things we needed along with a perk from time to time. However if you wanted anything extra, you needed to get it yourself.

Being the eldest son gave me an advantage as well as good experience. At ten years old, I could crank start Dad's Farmall tractor to keep the driveways cleared of snow, plow or disk the fields and weld parts back on if they broke off. From the time I was ten until I went to the service at 19, dad never needed to mow a yard or shovel a flake of snow.

By the time I was 14, I could drive a one-ton truck and just about any tractor, so I had no problem getting summer jobs with the local farmers. I spent about half my earnings on things that I wanted and saved half to get me through the winter, as winter work was hard to get if you couldn't drive a car there.

It was about that time that the Dutch elm disease was killing all the elm trees in Michigan, and Dad decided to burn wood instead of coal for heat in the winter. I became very proficient with an ax, sledge-hammer and splitting wedge. It was a daily chore for Mom, Dad and myself to keep the fire going. My task was to keep the chunks of wood small enough to fit through the furnace door.

I was taught a great deal about the trades from Dad, as the house was constantly being made bigger or improved. This prepared me for better summer jobs later on.

I always did every task that my parents asked of me, on top of working every job I could get my hands on. The only thing that suffered was homework once I started high school. I got my driver's license within 24 hours of turning 16, and my parents allowed me to drive the old pickup truck on a fairly liberal schedule, but with limitations. I did manage to take a few girls on dates with it.

In the early spring of 1965, before I turned seventeen, I plunked down cash for a 1957 Pontiac Star Chief two-door hardtop and secured a construction job as soon as school let out.

Things were a little different now. I had a very nice car, paid for my own insurance, gas and upkeep, a better job and more money. I completed all the chores my folks could assign me and did as many family things with them that I could, but otherwise I was hunting down a party.

That was the year I went to my first kegger with old "Flip" Dragon, and we both took up smoking. I managed to keep that a secret for quite a while because Dad was a smoker at the time, and the house smelled of it.

Schooling suffered, but in my junior year I managed to hold a "B" or better average and made the honor roll for it. The folks were proud but couldn't believe it. That was the summer I found a '57 Chevy two-door sedan that I couldn't live without and spent nearly all my money and time for the following six months, turning it into a candy-apple red street rod.

I painstakingly overhauled that 283 V-8 engine. When I put it back together, it was bored out over sized, had a high lift cam, over sized carburetor, and the car would flat out "run". I had an absolute blast with that car. The engine never failed me, but its power broke about every drive train part you could list, including a full dozen old three speed "trannies." I learned that you shouldn't race your primary source of transportation. But the girls loved riding in it, and the boys loved to race against it.

I worked extremely hard, kept up on all of my chores at home, then partied as much as possible. My parents could see the direction I was going and tried to intervene, but it was hard to tell a self-sufficient 17-year-old kid who owns his own car, maintains and insures it, to, "Turn over your car keys son, you're not going anywhere tonight!" That just didn't work anymore.

My 1957 Chevy, winter of 1967.

    During the summer of 1966, the Vietnam War was in full escalation and on the evening news every night. But I, and I suppose a great many people, paid little attention to it. It was a long way away and had little or no effect on us, with the exception that more and more upper class-men were joining the military.

    I picked up a construction job that summer, just before school got out. It paid double the wages I was accustomed to getting, and it doubled again before June ended. The superintendent quickly saw that I always knew exactly what was to be done next and would sweat blood to have the preparations ready for him.

    It was a fantastic summer of sun, sand, surf, dancing, parties, all-nighters, beer and drag racing. And I entered my senior year with a decent wardrobe, a stash in the bank and a good weekend job for the winter.

My senior year at Decatur High was absolutely wonderful, as well. For some reason, the class was very cohesive. There were cliques, as always, but when something needed to be done we would always pull together. We had a very mischievous class, girls and guys alike. We stuck together in that regard also, not destructive or anything like that, but always pushing the limits of the system and having fun.

I joined very few sports. My parents hated the thought of football, and I had no time to practice. I did, however, manage to get in two years of track and field and enjoyed it. We all had one hour of physical education each day throughout high school, and in 1966 and 1967, the coach conducted an all-school competition of physical fitness, where everyone competed for the best of about twelve different exercises, push ups, pull ups, sit ups, rope climb, etc.

Both years, I only won one event and that was push-ups. I came close in many events and lost badly in one or two, but when the total points were added up for each individual event, I won it both years. I was not a favorite of the coach, as I was physically able to play the major sports but just didn't. He was noticeably pissed off when he gave me the surprising news about winning. I think he thought one of his jocks should get it. "Don't mess with the skinny country boy."

We were all living the dreams of teenagers in the 60's, as our senior year was coming to a close. About May of 1967, a most disturbing message raced through the school. The 1966 graduate, Clarence Gipson, was reported shot and killed by a sniper in Vietnam. Everyone in school and the village was completely stunned by the news. I ran track with him less than a year earlier and had not known that he joined the Army.

Clarence was a black kid, an amazing athlete, scholar student, a heck of a nice guy, a square shooter that you just had to like and respect.

Later, when his funeral was arranged, the school all but shut down, allowing all the students who knew him the opportunity to attend. The Presbyterian Church could not begin to hold all the people who came to pay respect to Clarence. I stood against the back wall throughout the funeral proceedings and joined the line to view his body afterward.

Clarence's coffin was sealed with clear Plexiglas. He was in full-dress army greens, medals, accoutrements with a First Cavalry patch on his arm. Stories of bravery highlighted the funeral; how he volunteered to stay and hold off an enemy force while his comrades escaped. For the first time I began paying more attention to the news about the "police action" going on in Vietnam. I also became concerned but strangely curious about it. The draft was in full swing, and only a short time remained of school. My parents rightfully became very concerned, as they knew better than I what was likely to happen. They spent a lot of time discussing it between themselves and with me from that point on.

Graduation. Oh, what a wonderful and exciting time as a teenager—especially for me, who had many doubts that I could make it! Three days after that most memorable moment in my life up to then, I received a letter from the federal government stating that I was now of class "A" status for military draft, and a wallet-sized card to carry declaring the status. Every male in our class received theirs at about the same time, including my first cousin, Bill Flory.

I called the county courthouse in an attempt to find out my report status. All they said was, "You may get called this month, this year, next year, or never." So I headed out to find employment and was fortunate to pick up a union laborer's job as a mason tender building a new high school in Gobles, Michigan, about 20 miles northeast of Decatur. The work was extremely physically demanding, but fun none the less, and I could maintain a good tan.

I thought it was a good time to get rid of the old '57 and get something a little more reliable. I picked up a '63 Plymouth two-door sedan with a hemi six-cylinder engine and push button automatic transmission. I gave it a muscle car face lift, but enjoyed the improved gas mileage.

Fall of 1967, with 1963 Plymouth.

I and several of the guys rented an old cabin on nearby Lake Cora and used it as a party shack on weekends all summer long. But sometime in July, I and all the guys I graduated with got "the letter" that started with the line:

> *Greetings from your friends and neighbors, you have been selected to report to your county Selective Service Board on September 6th. You will be joining the U.S. Military.*

Many of the guys immediately went to recruiters and joined the service of their choice because we were told that the odds of getting a job you liked increased dramatically.

The rest of us were not interested in three or four years of service and opted to see what the two year draft enlistment would yield.

Now, the most difficult phase of my transition into the military was just beginning. Both of my parents were quite religious, Dad being Dunkard Brethren (similar to Mennonite) and Mom a Jehovah's Witness, different and often opposing sects. I had been pushed and pulled from one to the other, but went to church mostly with my father. There was one area of the two religions that was complementary, and that was the avoidance of military service (the opportunity to kill).

Mom and Dad truly joined forces on this issue and demanded that when I was called in I must go as a conscientious objector, and my mother made all the inquiries and collected all the information and forms to make it happen.

I knew that I was an absolute hell-raiser. I hadn't attended much church in several years, and had not even been baptized. I felt the status didn't fit me, but I loved my parents very much, and I was a dutiful son. I consented to submitting the paperwork.

The last week of August I left the construction job, drove to the U.P. (upper peninsula of Michigan) and visited some friends there as a short vacation prior to induction. While there I received a call from my mother. She said I'd received another government letter that looked important. She opened it to find that my September 6th induction was deferred to a later time. I cut the vacation short and made the trip back down state to see the document for myself. I took it to the induction office in Paw Paw where they confirmed it to be a temporary deferment.

I was very happy on one hand but on the other wondered what to do now. I could not afford college, construction jobs were winding down for the year and not hiring, and most of my friends had gone into the military. Oh well, their girlfriends were still here!

I finally picked up a factory job with Jessup Door Co. in Dowagiac, at half the pay I was accustomed to and just knocked around for six more months. One day in late February, 1968, the induction notice arrived again with a departure date of February 28. This time it stuck.

2.
Induction

The last day of February was cold, as my parents dropped me off near the county court house in Paw Paw, where a Greyhound bus was loading other inductees. After a short wait, the bus headed for Fort Wayne Induction Center in Detroit, where we stayed in a hotel for one night.

The morning of March 1st was a mad rush of physical examinations (in large groups) with educational and experience testing in the afternoon. For everyone who passed the testing phase, there was an immediate swearing-in ceremony. We exited the clean but very old buildings to board buses headed for Detroit Metro Airport. Through friends of my father I had flown on three different single engine airplanes but never on a commercial size plane. I had never even seen a large airport.

We were taken to an area separate from the main terminal and boarded the airplane that held about a hundred people. It was propelled with four internal-combustion gasoline engines, a dinosaur for the time. The plane departed promptly, and about two hours later we landed in Louisville and traveled by bus down to Fort Knox, Kentucky.

Having never been on a military base, this really looked like a military base to me. Nature offered a little color, otherwise, everything was painted white, including the WWII vintage two-story wood-frame barracks. Each barracks had a brick chimney exhausting the unmistakable aroma of burnt coal. There was no snow on the ground, but it was very cold.

We were put up on one floor of a barracks for the night and given instructions as what to expect the following day. The sergeant also asked if there were any special assignments in the group, like ROTC (Reserve Officers Training Corps) students, transfers from other services, OTS. (Officers Training School) or CO's (Conscientious Objector).

I was in the process of putting my hand up for the CO status but quickly recanted, thinking that from this point who would be wiser if I just ignored the request? So, I ignored it.

Day one in the Army began at 0600 hours. Jumping out of bed, we faced drill instructors already shouting out orders, "shit, shower, shave and do it quick." We were formed up outside the building, and drill instructors began training as they marched us to the chow hall and on to the quartermaster supply to be outfitted with fatigue uniforms.

Day two was more of the same, but now we were in uniform. They already had us marching much better, and I enjoyed trying to get the moves precise. Part of both days was spent at the medical facility where a regimen of shots was administered to everyone.

It was time for hair cuts, GI hair cuts. We marched to a building that housed five or six barber chairs and rough looking barbers in civilian clothing. The Beatles and other rock bands were sporting long hair, and the fad affected nearly everyone there. The barbers wasted no time in directing us into the chairs, and the hair started hitting the floor. The barbers occasionally left a patch of hair like a pony tail or a patch sticking straight up from some guy's otherwise bald head, long enough for everyone in line to laugh at him, then buzzed it off. Some guy must have had a mole on his head, and the barber buzzed it off too. The guy left the chair with blood running down the side of his face and a bit upset.

On day three, we moved to a different area and barracks to start actual basic training. I was in the process of packing my gear, when an orderly came to me and said I was to report to headquarters quickly.

"What's up?" I said, and he replied, "You'll find out when you get there. Report to the CO (Commanding Officer)."

I hoofed it down to his office, and he closed the door and asked if I'd entered the service as a CO? I confirmed that, but said that I was going to just skip it. Boy did that guy chew me out! He told me I could have put his butt in a sling along with the Department of the Army; that a CO status is granted by the governor of your state and would cause him embarrassment, and so on and so on! He said my test results would probably put me with an Army engineering unit, but he was making the decision to send me to Fort Sam Houston, Texas, to be trained as a medic.

I was moved into a holding station with several other guys with other assignments and waited for about two days before being taken back to the airport and flown to San Antonio, Texas, this time on a Braniff Airways passenger jet. This was more like it. The planes were painted multiple bright colors inside and out, and the stewardesses wore mod outfits with mini skirts.

Arriving at Fort Sam, I was assigned to a basic training unit with the first two days getting oriented and outfitted with GI clothing again (I had been ordered to turn in all the supplies I was issued before leaving Fort Knox).

Most of the men in this unit were of CO status. We lived in the four two-story brick barracks in the compound. Each held about one hundred men in different stages of completing the eight weeks of basic training.

The training was identical in all respects to any other Army basic training with one exception, no guns. There was rigorous PT (Physical Training) with copious amounts of running, marching and obstacle courses. Also, we attended classes in compass and map reading, military protocol, how the system of rank works, and we were constantly tested on all of it.

In lieu of firearms training, they offered optional classes of hand-to-hand combat, self defense and some judo-style techniques. I opted for all of them and learned them well.

Basic training included all day and all night bivouacs. We even killed, cooked and ate an armadillo. We went through the gas chamber, exposed to very strong tear gas, and last, but not least, conducted a night trip, low crawling through an infiltration course, under barbed wire obstacles, with artillery simulators exploding and live machine gun fire blazing away over our heads.

During basic we learned a few unwritten military rules as well, like how to deal with a guy that does not like to shower. A dozen guys would grab him one morning, carry him to the shower room, hold him on the floor and scrub him down with Ajax and scrub brushes. The problem disappeared quickly. Also, for a barracks thief, there is the "blanket party", but I will not go into that.

On Graduation Day we were ordered to march for review before some "High Brass." Since everyone knew the military drill quite well, it was fun, and we looked good, too. Everyone received a one day pass for Saturday, the first day off in over two months. On Monday we packed and moved a half mile away to the Army medical training area to begin AIT (Advanced Individual Training) as a unit. The month of May was already heating up in Texas. Very few of the buildings were air conditioned, which made it difficult to stay alert in the old wood-frame classrooms. But the training for the most part was very good. In finishing the 91-B-20 training, I was very well equipped to be a ward corpsman in a field hospital, but as experience was going to show me later, I sorely lacked field combat training.

We still had daily PT and occasional morning runs, but most of the twelve-weeks training was concentrated on class time. The military protocols were still in effect, but the atmosphere was definitely more relaxed and campus-like. We received weekend passes about twice a month.

About midway through AIT, I received a letter from my parents with very bad news. My first cousin on Mother's side, Stanley Campbell, had been shot and killed in Vietnam. I made phone calls home and learned his death was hard on the entire family, and it caused their fears for my future to intensify. My own concerns about having to go into combat were stronger now, also. But it was the same for all the guys, as we knew that the majority of men from previous graduating classes had received orders for Vietnam.

I was afraid, but I also had a curiosity about that country and the war. I never wished to go, but I did not hesitate when orders came down for Vietnam, one week before graduation from AIT. Nearly every man in our class received the same orders, including my good friend throughout AIT, Paul Pawlak from Chicago.

We flew back to O'Hare Field together but separated to begin an all too short 13-day leave home, before heading to the war.

The author and Pawlak at Fort Sam Houston AIT.

At Fort Sam Houston during AIT Training.

The toughest task for me was telling my parents. Coming home to Decatur on leave turned out to be a strange experience. All of my closest friends were gone, working, married or involved in some summer job to support them in college.

On the military base, I could go to a PX (Post Exchange) and have a beer on weekends. But back home, the drinking age was 21. I was old enough to go to a war and die, but not old enough to go downtown to a bar.

I stayed home most of the time and got plenty of exercise with my little brothers and sisters chasing me all over the farm every day. The night before I was to fly out, many of my relatives and neighbors stopped in to see me and say their good-byes. My Uncle Phillip and Aunt Donna, Stanley's parents, were there.

When it was time for them to leave, Uncle Phillip, with tears in his eyes, said, "I want you to promise me one thing,"

I said, "I sure will...What?"

He replied, "Just come back alive."

And I swore the promise that I would.

3.
Good Morning Vietnam

As I think back about it, my anxious curiosity to get over there, was seriously blinded by youth. But, on August 4th, I was on my way. Four days later I arrived at Cam Rahn Bay (pronounced Cam-ron-bay), in the II Corps area of South Vietnam.

The trip to Vietnam took a full 24 hours from Fort Lewis, Washington, through Anchorage, Alaska, and Yokota, Japan, and finally to Vietnam.

Cam Rahn Bay was on the coast of the South China Sea, at about the middle of the country. The landing strip at the airbase looked like it was on a long skinny sand bar that stretched out into the bay. When we landed on the PSP (Preformed Steel Plank) runway, I could see the water almost below the wings, the bay from the left side of the plane and the ocean on the right. Landing on the corrugated steel runway caused a vibration through the entire plane until we taxied to a stop.

We were all very tired and weary from the long trip and wanted to exit the plane as soon as possible. But we were ordered to stay put until further notice. With the engines shut down, there was no air conditioning. So they opened two side doors to let the 100° humid air in. We remained baking in the hot sun for nearly two hours before two Vietnamese military men did a walk-through inspection of the fresh troops in sweat-soaked khakis and on the verge of passing out. As soon as they finished, we were allowed to leave the plane. Some of the men were having difficulty from dehydration.

We then needed to hoof it for a mile or two to wood-frame, screened-in holding barracks that were painted white. White wooden sidewalks ran through the nearly white sand from building to building. That made it easy to walk, but what on earth was that weird bad smell?

Cam Rahn Bay was actually a beautiful place, tropical with palm trees and a nice breeze always coming off the ocean. If the remainder of the country were anything like this, I thought, everything should work out just fine. Besides, my cousin Bill had already been here for six months as a helicopter mechanic, and maybe I would be stationed nearby.

Within 20 hours I was in a C-130 transport plane headed for Tan Son Nhut (pronounced Ton-Sa-Nute) Airbase, near Saigon. We boarded buses shortly after landing and caravanned through the outskirts of the city to a huge base called Bien Hoa (pronounced Ben Waw) in the III Corps area. We joined many other men there at the airfield, and all were ushered into a large flat-roofed open-air pavilion. There were small "hoochs" (slang for house) on three sides, displaying signs with military insignias and manned by one or two men each.

Most of us were seated on plank benches, duffel bags in hand, listening to the speaker blaring out individuals names and which unit (hooch) to report to. In due time, my name and service number were announced (along with a strange surprise), "Report to the 101st Airborne Division."

"What the Hell", I thought to myself, "I am not jump qualified."

I had not been in the army six months, but I already knew

plenty about the airborne units, the 82nd, 173rd and the 101st airborne. Parachute school or jump school, as it is called, was even a prerequisite for Special Forces. "Why on earth would they be calling me to that unit? They are the most famous unit in the army! They have made a mistake!"

I made my way over to the marquee with the large painted symbol of the 101st Screaming Eagle patch and said to the attendant, "Sorry boys, you've made a mistake, I'm not jump qualified!" "It doesn't matter," he said, "you're property of the 101st now, so just get on that truck."

Next thing I know, I'm at the unit rear of the 101st Airborne Division, going through its five day version of "Welcome to Vietnam" they called "P" training (probably because you were quite likely to pee your pants at least once before they were finished with you). It was carried out by GI's who had already done hard time with combat units, and some were still recovering from wounds.

We were immediately sent to quartermaster supply and issued new jungle fatigues, boots, baseball cap, rucksack and most of the gear we would need for field duty. We were required to bring civilian clothing for a future R&R (Rest and Recuperation). That, along with our khaki uniforms and all other personal junk, was stashed in our duffel bags, tagged, recorded and put in a warehouse.

As we were in line playing follow the leader from one supply building to the next, I entered a building where M-16 rifles were being issued. It was my turn to the counter, and the attendant already had the next weapon on the counter with the barrel straight up. I quickly said that I was not qualified through the army to carry a weapon. He shoved it out closer to me and said, "You're in Vietnam now, do you want this f—king gun or not?" I left the building with a brand new M-16, serial number 704097X. I remember the number yet today.

By day two, the rigorous training started. All the items we

were issued had to be put in the rucksack and carried nearly everywhere we went. They ran us in the morning, in midday, in the evening and in the middle of the night, especially if it was raining. In between, we took classes on the M-16, shot up clip after clip of ammo, learned night firing methods and finally qualified on targets. They put us on trails, much like we might encounter in the field and set booby traps that would explode artillery simulators if we tripped them. They had ARVN (Army of the Republic of Vietnam) troops dressed like VC (Viet Cong) and ambushed us every chance they had. Everyone had to walk point (first in line) at one time or another.

Along with the tough physical training there were classes on the culture of the country, language, civil diplomacy and personal hygiene. Of course, we got more shots for disease prevention, and we were well warned of the dangers of venereal disease. They even had us go through a ten minute brushing of our teeth with some new chemical that was supposed to help prevent cavities. It was called fluoride.

Let me tell you, that was the hardest, most rigorous day and night, intense, true to life, miserable training I had ever received in the military. At some point, every day, they would end up shooting very close "At Us" with (live ammunition) in real jungle style survival. I was enlightened before "P" training was over, and I thank the unit and the individual men that put us through that week of hell, trying to prepare us for the true hell to come.

4.
Orders, B-2501

My next set of orders was to report to LZ Sally (Landing Zone Sally), which was about 40 miles south of the DMZ (Demilitarized Zone), and the battalion rear for Second Battalion 501 Infantry Brigade, 101st Airborne Infantry Division. (2-501's, 101st). Sally sounds tame enough, and it was for me, but not for the men that secured the area a few months prior to my arrival.

Traveling with the military in Vietnam turned out to be nothing less than hitchhiking. As long as you had orders, you could climb on anything with enough space going your way and ride along. I caught a C-130 to Da Nang then a deuce-and-a-half (26-ton truck) headed north. It was about 15 miles of rough gravel highway into Hue City (pronounced Way City), which had recently been liberated and had plenty of evidence of the battles. Then came another 15 miles of what you could call "mud bogging" in a 20-ton truck full of GI's with locked and loaded weapons.

Sally was a well fortified camp with good perimeter bunkers and lots of concertina wire, (huh, there is that smell again) lots of gun batteries, 105 howitzers, and even some track-mounted eight inch guns. The housing was tents in haphazard rows with dirt or pallet floors. I felt far less safe here, but was hoping this was home. That was not to be the case. I located headquarters for the

2nd battalion and was quickly assigned to "B" Company, which was in the field doing recon (reconnaissance) in the vicinity. I already had a rucksack, steel pot, M-16 and other field gear. I got my field aid bag from the medical supply hooch, and a veteran medic helped me stock it quite well. I spent the evening trying to make sense of all the gear, got it packed and tied down as best I could, then slept on a wooden pallet that night.

Next morning I had my first breakfast of C-Rats (C-rations) and got promptly put on "Shit Detail."

What's "Shit Detail," I asked?

"Why, all newbies get to do it," he said, and he had me carry two five-gallons cans of diesel fuel to the back of the outhouse area. I was instructed to prop open the back door, use a re-bar hook and drag out the sawed-off 50 gallon drums full of shit and urine, pour in some diesel fuel, light it on fire and stir it occasionally with a fence stake until the contents were gone. I soon found out where that weird smell came from!

Another interesting thing about sanitary control on almost every base is that in almost every conceivable place, you could find a "piss tube." They were made from aluminum canisters that held howitzer rounds. They had a rim at the opening that worked well at holding a piece of bug screen. Just knock a hole in the other end and bury it at a slight angle, about a foot into the ground. If you were on a base, you never had to walk very far to take a leak.

By noon that day, I was getting my first UH-1 helicopter ride out to B-Company along with a load of C-rations, water, assorted ammunition and a bag of mail.

B-Company was in a defensive position about three or four miles out from Sally, and was taking on supplies for a five day hike. I was assigned to third platoon and introduced to some of the guys. Shortly thereafter we were on foot and looking for Charlie (slang for enemy). Now, things were starting to get a little scary, and a taste of reality was stinging my palate.

Infantry (all divisions) have one basic job, and that is to "seek out the enemy, make contact with him, kill or capture him and take his stuff." It seemed, however, that the 101st had a reputation to uphold in this regard, the more ground you can cover the more likely you are to make contact.

Burning shit off the side of Firebase Vehgil.

Now, I was in extremely good condition. But after humping close to a hundred pounds of gear a good 6 klicks (slang for kilometers) through the rice paddies, thickets and bamboo, my butt was kicked at the end of the day. We dug in, had a hasty meal of C-rats and prepared for dark, always a "Scary Time."

I talked to a guy that night about our hike and asked if they did that very often. He said that today had been a short day because of receiving supplies and that tomorrow would be longer. "ten klicks a day, it's the Airborne way—Hurrah!"

The next day he got to me quickly, went through my pack and tossed out everything that I did not need. We gave the stuff a shallow grave, and my equipment was about 15 pounds lighter. The grunt who helped me was Danny "Snake" Wakefield, from Minnesota. He had joined the unit about 30 days before. He kept me under his wing for some time, and we have remained good friends to this day. As the days wore on, I met many other good and brave men, like: Gary Welch of Iowa, Jimmy Green of Texas, Mel Waite, Bob Baldwin, Larry Trask and Joe Hudson of Michigan, "Gap" (Dale Fisher, from Pleasant Gap, Pennsylvania), Pat O'Leary from Manhattan, Robert Butts from Detroit, David Krautscheid from Oregon, David Reinheimer of St. Louis, Missouri, Al Kontrabecki from Niagara Falls, Irvin (Moose) McCoun from Montana, Frank Hilley and Patrick Armendariz from California, Jackie Johns from Iowa and many, many others. All these men took their turns walking on point or humping the "60" (slang for M-60, the 30-caliber machine gun) also known as "The Pig."

The author reaching for a water jug during a long day in the low lands.

We worked the lowland rice paddies, small hamlets and farms, further and further away from Sally, from September to December, without making contact with the enemy. There was one exception to that. A Viet Cong soldier became a *Chiew-Hui* (Defector, pronounced Chu Hoy) and walked toward our NDP (Night Defensive Position) one morning with a white rag tied to a stick and gave himself up. We treated him well, humped him out to the nearest road, where we were met by an MP (Military Police) truck that took him to who knows where.

At that point in time, the area from Da Nang through Hue to Quang Tri was basically cleared of enemies, all the way west beyond the rice paddies to the foothills. We humped our 10-K per day, rooting through everything that showed promise, but found no Charlie. Of course, no one had a problem with that. We did, however, find several large caches of weapons, which gave us some notoriety.

I became accustomed to my job of making the rounds, and did what I could for the guys with cuts, boils, jungle rot, foot problems, bug and leach bites. Sometimes immediate action was required otherwise just the normal evening ritual. Once a week, after LOG (short for logistics supply) day, I passed out enough anti-malaria pills to each platoon sergeant for all his men at one per day. They were in tiny foil packets on a roll like raffle tickets, and I gave them out in groups of six for each guy. Also included in this was a large orange pill, as part of the regimen that I gave out personally every Monday. The guys would not take them otherwise, because it meant it was loose bowel Tuesday. These rituals never stopped during the length of my full field duty.

By now, my curiosity about Vietnam had waned a bit, and a little bit of a chip began to grow on my shoulder. I was drafted, I could be home making some good money and chasing the babes around town. There was some evidence of the hippie movement and anti-American tactics of academia in regards to the war, but we were isolated from most of it. The magic 60's were a spectacular time to be a teenager in America and well, what were we doing here? I could have been a better soldier at that time.

We "humped" (walking with full field gear) from early morning to evening every day, allowing just enough time to dig in, string up a quick hooch and eat a few C-rats. During these long reconnaissance missions, we were in and around many rice paddies, fording rivers and streams almost daily. The waters in these paddies and lowland areas were full of leeches, big ones. You could see them swimming like snakes towards you.

Hunting for Charlie, humping heavy packs, fighting the heat, leeches, mosquitoes, flies and muddy wet feet and clothes was our daily grind. The water was bad, too. Every canteen needed pellets of halazone added to decontaminate it. It was also my job to make sure the men had plenty of it and that they used it in their water. It tasted like shit, but it would keep you from getting sick.

We were in the field almost continuously, but occasionally we pulled perimeter guard duty on a Firebase. For us that was a good feeling of safety. We could sleep in pre-constructed sandbag and PSP bunkers, and sometimes they didn't leak much when it rained.

During one of these extended field tours, we met up with several of our sister companies along a canal that led into Hue. We set up a cordon line that stretched out, possibly a click, down to the waters edge. It was like driving deer at the end of the hunting season. We held a line while a sister company attempted to flush out any enemy in the dense vegetation on the opposite side of the river.

The canal was 50-80 feet across and fairly deep. We were on an ancient dredging along the bank, covered with short grass that looked like a pasturing area for water buffalo. The dredging sloped off away from the canal and into the rice paddies that were almost endless. It was easy duty for a couple of days, almost like being on a picnic. It didn't matter if we made noise during the day. I was introduced to a model 1911, 45-caliber automatic pistol, and several of us wasted some ammunition plunking anything we could see across the river.

Further downstream, either at the end of our company or the beginning of the next, the guys pulled concertina wire across the river to stop any sampans (boat) and search them. The third platoon was at the far upstream end of the line, and we were not aware of what was happening at the barricade until we saw a Medevac helicopter fly in, set down for a moment then leave again. The word filtered down to us eventually that one of the GI's stringing the wire had decided to cool off when the work was done. He dove off the borrowed sampan into the canal but did not return to the surface. He became tangled in wire that had sunk to the bottom at some previous cordon. The four minute grace period had long passed before his comrades could pull him free and get him back on land.

After three months hard pounding without one man lost to enemy fire, and some unwitting grunt tries to escape the heat, drowns and becomes our first casualty. We were all sick in the gut for some time after that.

The second day a sampan was spotted navigating down the river toward Hue with a very old man and woman on board. A four striper (staff sergeant) I'll call Sergeant DA flagged the old handmade craft to shore. They had one large sack of rice with them. Sergeant DA started yelling at them, interrogating them in English and pointing at the bag of rice. He directed them off the boat by waving his 45 pistol toward shore, climbed in, slit the bag of rice and dumped it in the water. It was easy to see the complete and utter fear and disbelief in their eyes as they climbed back in the sampan and retreated slowly back the way they came, having never uttered a sound the entire time.

I asked Sergeant DA why he did that? He explained that they were most likely trying to get the rice to the VC. I replied that they were headed into Hue where any VC could get all the rice he wanted. I wasn't a military strategist, but I would have been more skeptical if a sampan were headed upstream deep into the bush.

What I think we did was dump out their means of subsistence for the next six months.

(You are free to decode the meaning of DA!)

Another time we NDP'd (Night Defensive Position) around a small, very old and decayed pagoda. It had enough space inside to hold the CP (Command Post), and we slept on the smooth stone floor.

My guard duty came in the middle of the night. It was quite moonlit, and I sat on the edge of the open air pagoda because the raised floor made a good place to sit. It was everyone's job to pull night watch for one to two hours, with the "Pric 25" (radio) mike in hand. Every 15 minutes or so you would quietly say "1st squad, sit rep negative, break squelch twice" and so on for 2nd and 3rd platoons.

As long as the platoon guard depressed the mike key twice, causing a small audible sound, all was well.

Mosquitoes ruled the night, and flies took over for the day shift. As I sat in the quiet moon light, I could hear mosquitoes buzzing ever more intently, but I couldn't see them. This went on for a while, becoming more and more noisy!

I had my legs held close together, supporting the radio mike, and at some point I grabbed the mike to make a "strep request." I spread my legs and a cloud of mosquito poured upward into the moon light that they must have been trying to avoid, or it was warm, under my legs. The tiny mystery was solved, and I kept my legs spread wide.

I continued to sit quietly on guard, almost enjoying the peaceful night and the strange old religious icon we were in. Then from the corner of my eye, I saw movement, not in the perimeter but just at the edge of the cut stone slab I was setting on. Rolling my eyes down slowly I spied a giant snail that was at least 4" across the shell and 6 or 7" long slowly moving toward me.

He was a great distraction for my last hour on guard. Now I understood why the French eat *escargot*, because this sucker would have fed four people. My guard duty over, I slept good the remainder of the night.

By November we had worked into the foot hills and made our first company helicopter lift into the edge of the northern highland, to a Firebase called "T" Bone. We had a great east visual to Sally from the Firebase.

We spent about a week pulling perimeter guard at night and made sweeps further and further out from the base during the day. The terrain was quite hilly with occasional trees, but mostly low underbrush.

One morning movement was spotted about two klicks down the hill, five or six people were moving around down below. The artillery guys had binoculars, and we glassed them for a while.

A squad (me included) led by Sergeant DA was dispatched down the hill to see what they were doing. The squad traveled very light, but I always needed to carry a full pack because the aid bag was heavy and secured well to my back pack frame. As we approached, it became evident that they were old women with small chopping knives working their way across the hill and gathering a local weed-like willow tree that would grow four or five feet stalks slightly larger than a pencil in diameter. I had been in a few small villages by then, and recognized that it was the fuel that all the rural people used for cooking. They dried out bundles of the stuff, hung on or inside the homes. When broken up by hand into pieces six to ten inches long, it made a nice hot fire they controlled by adding sticks as needed. It also had a very nice aroma when burned.

It was also easy to tell that the area had been "farmed" for this resource for many years. None the less, out comes Sergeant DA's 45. He waved it at the women's heads, screaming *"Dedie-mow Dedie-mow"* (Go Away). These women actually looked pissed off, but again, not saying a word, they picked up their meager collection and headed home. God only knows how far away that was. We were at a great visual advantage point from T-Bone, and I couldn't see any villages from there. Sergeant DA happened to be a black man, which had no bearing on what he was doing, it was just the way he was, "Old army."

I learned to dislike the guy. The issue was not prejudicial, but I will touch on that matter later.

While on Firebase T-Bone, I was chewing gum one day and managed to pull out an old filling from a tooth. There were regular flights back and fourth to Sally, and the platoon leader gave me permission to see if I could get it fixed. I jumped on the next "bird" along with one other guy. Sitting on the empty floor, we leaned against the back wall of the ship that divided the cargo area from the door gunners and relaxed for the ride. Most Hueys had the doors removed, and there was not much to hang onto inside. You just relied on gravity and a little "stick-shin" to stay in the craft.

Neal Salsbery at Firebase T-Bone.

The pilot cranked her up, lifted off as normal, flew off the base a short distance, and put the bird in a steep dive down the side of the hill. Ooowwweee, that bird gained speed fast. Down the big hill, over several foot hills, flying too close to the ground for my comfort, the pilot, laughing his butt off, held the bird at full throttle across four miles of rice paddies, straight to Sally. We were actually leaving a wake in the water as he cranked that bird all the way to the perimeter, then jerked the collective back hard as he could, making a near straight up climb until the bird nearly stalled.

The pilot then made a couple of nice easy circles down to the PSP landing zone and softly touched down. As the pilot and crew continued laughing, I am saying "Holy bat shit," (famous Danny the "Snake" Wakefield quote) what a ride!

I found the dentist hooch along with his hydraulic chair and foot pedal operated drill, but no dentist. I caught a nice uneventful ride back to T-Bone that evening and never got that tooth fixed until I was back in the states.

The author with Jimmy Green on Firebase T-Bone.

Bob Baldwin had a camera while on T-Bone and took lots of pictures. He took one of me and Jimmy Green standing near the perimeter. Jimmy was a year or so older than the rest of us and must have had a dozen girlfriends. He always received more perfume-soaked letters than anyone, good care packages too. At our 2009 reunion, Bob presented me with a framed copy of that photo, which I had long forgotten about, and I am so happy to have it now.

5.
CONTACT

We were sent to guard Firebase Birmingham for the first time. It was about 14 miles southwest of Hue and had road access from Route #547, which eventually led through the A Shau Valley and into Laos. Birmingham was in a fairly secure area with very nice bunkers and a few wood frame barracks that the Arty (Artillery) and Engineer guys stayed in. Some weeks earlier, while out on mission, A-Company came across a 16-foot python. They caught it, put it in a mail sack and humped that thing on a pole until they had perimeter duty on Birmingham.

The engineers built a very nice chicken wire cage for that serpent and supplied it with ducklings (big as small chickens) to snack on. Well, me and old Danny (Snake) Wakefield had a few extra beers one day and decided that the python needed to eat one of the ducks. Dan got the python's head while I caught a duckling. Dan found that if he squeezed the snake's neck hard enough, it would open its mouth, "Holy bats, what a mouth!" I made several attempts at trying to stuff the frantic bird into the python's mouth when I noticed (wits dimmed by the beer) that the majority of the snake body was sneaking out of the cage and gently beginning to hug old Dan.

Dan's eyes got pretty big when he realized what was happening. I quickly returned the duck to the cage and began the fight with Mr. Wiggly. Those suckers are far stronger then you'd think. We had a heck of a time getting him back in the cage.

As we were guarding another Firebase called Boyd, A, C and D-Co.'s managed to score the first contact with the enemy since late summer. They were on top of a high jungle ridge farther south and west from Firebase Boyd, and they didn't just make contact, they stirred up a first class hornets nest. The radio traffic was heavy for several days. They were taking casualties, a lot of them.

It was late November or early December, when orders came from the commander, Captain Hallums. I do not remember him, as I did not have many opportunities to travel with the company command post in those early months. And that also was about the time that the command was taken over by Captain Graney, who I grew to know fairly well as time passed.

"Saddle up B-Company, we're going to help our sister companies." Our cream puff times in the field were coming to an end.

On day one of this mission, we all knew it was likely to get more serious as we headed out in six-bird sorties, taking one platoon at a time out to their hand chopped LZ, which was on a very high and continuous ridge that divided the highlands from the lowlands. I don't remember which lift I was on. There were a lot of guys in the woods all around the LZ when I arrived. With a new and unfamiliar look on their faces, they were slump-shouldered and hollow-eyed.

Men from these units were boarding the birds as we were getting off. We were quickly mustered up and headed south, along the ridge line where much of the action had taken place. We learned that a Huey had been hit the day before, crashed through the canopy and caught fire. We came across two pairs of grunts with poles over their shoulders, ponchos tied to the poles, and the charred remains of two crew members in each one. There were morbid looks on the men whose duty it was to dig out the over-cooked remains of their bodies from the burnt out fuselage, after it cooled down through the night (I think my gray matter has blocked out any memory of the smell that permeated the area that day). Two of the bodies were fused together. It appeared that a door gunner made a heroic effort to free one of the pilots. He made it to the door, opened it and tried to free him, but they burned to death together.

B-Company made its way far beyond the other units, using a new found form of stealth. The afternoon was uneventful, and we dug in for the night on that razor-back ridge. We were headed out of the NDP early the next morning, reconnoitering the ridge, slowly moving forward. The guys were on their toes and spotted movement ahead. They brought a M-60 gunner to the point position. Sure enough it was a "Gook" sneaking along the trail toward our position, and the machine gunner took him down. The remainder of the day was uneventful, but B-Company had a body count for the first time in five months.

Day two of that mission took us down a steep crevasse, deep into the jungle. With extreme stealth and cautious point recons, we moved down into valley. We were into triple canopy jungle for the first time now. Mid afternoon the company came to a halt. The point men had discovered an area full of thatched huts. We cased the area carefully, then moved in to scout each hooch, 10 to 12 in all. About 30 minutes passed, when someone shouted out "Booby traps in the doorways!"

Everyone came to a paralyzing halt, then pulled bayonets, prodded the ground at the entrances and, sure enough, there were 60 mm mortar rounds buried at the center of each opening. Fortunately for us, the enemy had neglected to remove the safety caps from the explosive devices.

We spent the remainder of that day and all of the next day sweeping the area around the enemy camp. We found that the hooch farthest down the hill was a cook shack. It had a rather elaborate dirt hearth with a large aluminum bowl of rice still on it and still warm. The rice, mixed with some sort of starchy tuber, was quite good, by the way. We discovered that they dug a trench from the hearth up the hill and under the floor of most of the hoochs. They covered the entire length of it with thatch and dirt to prevent smoke from rising up and marking their location. They had a small hatch door in each hut that allowed a little smoke to filter through the thatch roofs. All of this was made from jungle materials. One hooch was, no doubt, a briefing pavilion, with a place to hang maps or whatever on the wall and even a piece of Visqueen fixed into the roof as a skylight.

There was a small tumbling stream working its way down through the camp, and the guys eventually found the entrance to a cave dug 40-50 yards back into the hillside. The NVA (North Vietnamese Army) piled the dirt into the stream, which washed it far down stream so there was no mining slag left to be seen by the allied forces flying over.

There was a small but significant cache of weapons, mortar rounds and ammunition in the cave, which we hauled out and packed along with us. It was raining when we left the camp on day four, and I was given a 20 pound sack of 7.62 rounds (standard bullet for the Russian built AK-47) and told to scatter them as we made our way slowly up the hill via a different route. Like Johnny Appleseed, I scattered the rounds through the jungle until the sack was empty.

The drizzle continued, and about midday the column came to a halt with the hand signal given to be very quiet. Movement was spotted on top of a knoll, and the 60 gunner was once again deployed to point. He maneuvered to a vantage point and killed two more NVA. The dead NVA were dressed in khaki uniforms, had fresh haircuts and crude rucksacks with about six 60mm mortars rounds in each and one AK-47 rifle.

We formed a perimeter around the dead men, searched them, divided up their weapons and ate some C-rats before moving on. We worked toward the ridge we had originally come down four days earlier, but did not make it to the top that day. On day five, we reached the top, but in that area it was nearly sheer cliffs. Recon teams searched in both directions until we found a reasonable place to climb down with the assistance of repelling rope. It took some time for every man in the company to "half-ass" repel down the first 100 feet of that hill. How the last man untied the rope, I don't know. For the rest of that day we slowly made our way down an extremely steep wooded area, hanging onto anything we could to keep from falling. We stopped at a point where a huge rock projected out from the face of the slope, big enough for the entire company command post, led by Capt. James Hallums, to form a night defensive position on the top. When the downward movement stopped, each man had to try his best to find a place to hang on and sleep for the night. We felt fairly safe because there was no logical reason for any enemy to be there.

It was getting dark fast, and I found a nice cradle-shaped place on a projected tree root and called it good. There were 30 or 40 men above my location at the bottom of the big rock, and debris was occasionally tumbling down the slope and flying over my nest and on down the hill. All was well until I heard a large rock coming down, bounding off anything in its path, and men hollering, "Heads up! Heads up!"

It was pitch dark, couldn't see shit, as that rock slammed into something directly above me. All was silent for a second and wham that frickin' rock landed square on my gut and drove all the air from my lungs.

I went brain dead for a second and pushed the rock off me, only to send it tumbling down past the rest of the company farther down from me. It didn't hit anyone else and is probably still going down that hill. I foraged around in the dark until I found a small tree jutting out well under the big rock but out of the line of falling stones. I hung my sore gut over the tree and dangled there. When you're tired enough, you can sleep even like that.

On day five there was no way to fix a meal, so we continued to head downhill for several more hours. We abruptly reached the bottom and in short order found a very nice 30-foot wide stream. The company commander had us form a perimeter on each side, and everyone got a chance to lie in the stream and clean up a bit. After about an hour we rucked-up and started a force march across the rice paddies that lasted about six or seven hours. We arrived at FB Boyd (some referred to as Panther II) before dark.

You could probably call this luck, but when we came through the perimeter of the FB a small USO (United Service Organizations) show was about to start. It was a five piece Korean rock band doing American 60's music. We were an unshaved, raggedy, mean-looking rabble of infantry dudes, who had just come from a tough and fully successful mission, as we somewhat impolitely took over all the good seating positions and enjoyed the heck out of that 3rd rate show.

Doc Summers, Unknown and Sargeant Dennis enjoying a USO Show.

The perimeter bunkers were already under guard, so after the show we had a little free time. Several of the guys sneaked into the back of the supply tent and made off with several cases of C-rats. We stripped them of the good stuff, like peaches and pound cake, then just sacked out where it looked comfortable and slept well.

6.
STAND-DOWN

We didn't stay at Firebase Boyd very long. The brass must have thought the battalion needed a break, as deuce-and-a-half's showed up the next morning, picked up all of B-Co., and five trucks headed for camp Sally for our first, and what would be our last, Battalion stand-down during my tour.

We had just completed a very successful mission, no KIA or WIA on our side, and had logged in about four months of continuous field duty. It was unfair to our sister companies because they took the heat on that last mission, and we took the notoriety. Well, no good deed goes unpunished. From that time on, every time the proverbial shit hit the fan, it was "Send in Bravo Company!" and we eventually took our chewing.

Our ride back to Sally took us through Hue City, which was surprisingly restored and bustling from the first time I saw it. Captain Graney must have been in a really good mood. He sent word through the troops that he didn't want to find a single smoke grenade on any man when we came out of the city. Oooweee! We turned Hue into a carousel of colors. It may have pissed off a few civilians, but no one was hurt, and we were happy troopers.

Camp Sally had grown! It now contained a wood-frame mess hall, a barber shop, a church and—oooweee—an NCO club

Hue City.

with 25 cent beer! The place was a neat and orderly military camp now. A large open spot to the north of the main housing area had a multitude of large tents set up for the entire battalion (grunts still got dirt floors). But I got lucky and was able to hooch up in a barracks that was quarters for the aid station. Outdoor showers were set up near the perimeter. "Oh sweet showers!" Tripods held the rows of shower heads with hoses connected to 500-gallon black rubber blivots full of sun baked water. Naked GI's made their way through a line into the showers, then walked away on old wooden pallets, trying to keep their feet clean.

Cathloic Church in Hue City.

Party time during Battalion stand-down at Camp Sally.

Al Contrabecki, the author and Wilfred "Doc" Jackman. Party time during stand-down at Camp Sally.

Someone had the foresight to have enough beer on hand for an endless supply for four companies of men, and by nightfall the entire place was like a carnival. The music was fantastic in the '60's, and all of us were "jonezin" to hear the jams, drink beer, play cards and feel just a bit normal.

The author in rear, and unknown GI who had broken his ankle jumping from a helicopter, Camp Sally stand-down, 1968.

On the subject of playing cards, we never received pay in the bush, not even on forward Firebases. So at Sally everyone received about two months of their salary, and I had another opportunity to observe a phenomenon about certain GI's. That first evening, if there was an enclosed barracks with a table and a light, there were smoking, beer-drinking GI's with pockets full of cash, all fully willing to try their hand at blackjack. This was serious gambling, with piles of paper money in the center of the table and young GI's crowded around, with looks of stern intent on their faces.

Dan Wakefield and Gary Welch facing forward, serious card game. Stand-down at Camp Sally.

This didn't happen very often with us, as the opportunities were few and far between. But when it did, the majority of the gamblers ended up borrowing money from their buds the next day just to purchase a 25 cent beer.

During the day, I had been looking for one of our guys, and going from tent to tent I made eye contact with a familiar face. I stopped in my tracks, looked at the guy and said, "Do I know you? Where are you from?" He said,

"Lawrence, Michigan."

Oh my God, we knew each other!

We exchanged hugs and talked for half an hour. As it was, the last time we met was at a Lawrence High School dance, and the two of us were in the back parking lot going fisticuffs over some girl. Well, that didn't matter now.

The next morning I got up about 8:00am, took a look outside, nearly went into a state of shock, then laughed my butt off. There were bodies everywhere, draped over sandbags, on top of bunkers and with their faces down in the dirt. The poor bastards had forgotten how to hold their liquor. Oh, what a night we had. The aid station was busy handing out aspirin for hangovers all day.

We were going to be there for four days. So on day two, most of us dug into rucksacks and purged all the old or worn-out battle rattle. Sally was where all our supplies came from, and we all took advantage of the opportunity to get new gear. I went completely through my aid bag with help from "Doc" Summers, who had been a well seasoned grunt medic and was spending his last days in-country here at Sally. The medical supply shack had one nice new item, vials of iodine about the size of a cigarette. You removed the cap, held it upside down and it would not run out. You just touched the opening on your skin, and iodine leaked out exactly where you needed it.

I packed about 50 of the vials, and later they became very handy. Doc also gave me a vial of weight loss pills with about 40 capsules in it.

"What the heck would I need these for?" I asked.

Doc shrugged his shoulder and said, "Who knows, someone may need them."

So, I am packing all my fresh aid supplies as Doc Summers

got another knock on the supply room door, and the next medic is ushered in. It's Paul Pawlak from AIT! The hugs and how-did-you-get-heres were traded, and we just talked as Paul and Doc Summers replenished his supplies.

Paul was with the A-Company and talked about some of the firefights that he had been through, along with the grunts he patched up and Medevaced out. There was an entire section in A.I.T. that was devoted to sucking chest wounds, and Paul talked about having his first one and how he responded to it. "Enter the Paradox." I am listening to his stories, feeling guilty that my tour had not been traumatic this far, is that crazy or what? In order for me to have equal experience to Paul, some of my friends would need to be mortally wounded. But yet, I almost hated to tell him that jungle rot was the worst condition I'd dealt with so far. Paul and I would have more encounters in the future.

With all the supplies available at Sally, I could not beg, borrow or steal a boonie hat (soft cloth hat with a full brim, that could be wadded up into a rucksack). But what was far better, I finally acquired an air mattress! It was like having a three star hotel for the jungle. Rolled up smaller than a loaf of bread, it added weight, but I could hump anything by then, and it was worth it.

It was also a great time for me as a medic. The 101st had a well equipped aid station with a doctor and several corpsmen. I was free of the daily routines, and the guys who required extra care had experts at their disposal.

Day three was planned for a USO show. In mid-afternoon at least 1,500 men crowded in around a stage with no seats, got comfortable on anything they could find, and the show began. The band was from Australia and they started cranking in with all the latest rock songs. The lead picker used a six-string flat top, hooked through a fuzz pedal, Good God that dude could play! An older guy, 50-ish, would take the stage from time to time and belt out all the best crooner love songs and—oh yes—the scantily clad dancing girls had a captive audience that day.

Fall of 1968, Austrailian USO Show stand-down at Camp Sally.

Crooner with USO Show at Camp Sally.

This show was a very good class "B" event. Everyone fully enjoyed it, and it was a terrific start to the third day of partying.

A Bob Hope show is what I would call a class "A" event,

but it would be a rare case indeed for a pack, grunt, ground pounder or line doggie, (field infantryman) to attend one of his shows. One of his shows came as close as Da Nang one time, and there was to be some kind of lottery throughout the battalion so, a few field troops would have a chance to go. At Christmas, 1968, Dave Reinheimer, Don Ogelvie, and one other were chosen to represent B-Co. They had a wonderful time. Look for *Bob Hope Show* at *B2501Airborne.com*.

USO Show at Camp Sally.

Our time at Sally was terrific for receiving and sending mail, but I really wanted an opportunity to call home. I invested some time inquiring about making telephone calls home, but found that it was nearly impossible. I was told that there was a base near Da Nang that had a place a GI could make a call to the states using a radio communication link through a satellite, called a "Marz Link" or something. We had no way of getting a pass to go there in the first place, and if you did, there were long lines, mostly officers or GI's with emergency family problems.

On day four, it was time to ruck up and get back to our jobs.

The brass had done well in giving us the reward of badly needed rest, entertainment and re-supply. In retrospect, I think the brass had a fair idea where we were headed, and the stand-down was also a going away or a "good luck party!"

It was now late fall, and I had been in-country for nearly four months during stand-down. The exact date is lost to me now. But we do know that a young man by the name of Robert Malecki from Illinois was navigating his way north to LZ Sally on November 29, 1968. Robert had assignment papers for A-Co. 2-501, 101st Airborne, as an infantry rifleman.

A-Co., its sister company in the 2-501, along with the 1/501, all the 101st Airborne Infantry and the other airborne units, were commanded in an extremely aggressive manner, regardless of environment. Robert would have ample time to become a hardened, keen-eyed, reactive, point- walking, fighting man. A-Co. would be fully engulfed in the highland missions that took it from one mountain to the next and one end of the A Shau Valley to the other.

7.
THE GREEN MISSION

The entire battalion was deployed in an area around the south end of the A Shau Valley. The valley was well known to us in the I core area, probably the worst possible death trap a GI would ever want to enter. We knew we were close to it, but thank God we weren't in it.

When leaving Sally we assaulted into an area of very big hills and began hunting for the enemy. On January 20th, we were working our way down a hill, stopping to recon every 10-15 minutes. Going was tough, as it was an extraordinarily steep hill and under triple canopy. I remember coming to a place where the trail turned a hard left, followed the slope horizontally and made a nice flat place to walk for about 50-60 feet. The sun came through a large opening in the canopy above the flat area, then the trail turned right again and dropped at nearly 70 degrees downhill. I worked my way down another 100-200 feet, when the line stopped again for recon, and I pushed off to the right 20 feet or so to guard our flank.

Ten minutes passed, with little or no noise other than that of nature. "Bang," the rifle report that rang out back up the hill, drilled all of us in position. Muffled voices came from above, then a message whispered from man to man, came to me as "medic needed." Nothing like this had happened before. The look of raw question appeared on the faces of the men as I passed them one by one, their safeties off, fingers on triggers, wishing they had x-ray vision. I began moving back up the trail, trying to be quiet but as quick as I could. As I reached the horizontal section of the trail, it was almost like climbing a wall, and as I peered over the edge I could see GI's with their weapons trained toward the opening in the jungle.

A GI lay on his back, only three feet away, when I climbed onto the ledge. My heart was already working hard from the climb, but went into high gear when the reality sunk in of seeing my good friend Jimmy Green with a large amount of blood oozing from his head and onto the ground.

"Sniper," I thought, and now I am vulnerable!

"Goddamn it boys, keep your eyes open," I said, as I jerked off my pack and simultaneously tried to figure out what to do first. Our training at Fort Sam was designed around three basic principals, stop the bleeding – clear the airway – prevent shock. Jim was taking raggedy breaths with long pauses in between. Still on my knees, I maneuvered to his side, got hold of his shoulder, slid my left hand into the blood under his head to roll him over far enough to see the wound. As I did, my fingers sunk deep into the back of Jimmy's skull, and I knew that Jimmy's condition was fatal. I grunted out, "He's gone," and laid his head back down.

Having come from a rural farming and livestock area, where the slaughter of animals was commonplace, and loving the sport of hunting, on those terms I knew death. I knew I was right about Jimmy's condition.

A flow of tears came, and I went into some kind of chant, like a broken record – he's gone- he's gone – he's gone. It stopped when Lt. Pue said sharply, "Stop it Flory, do whatever you can for him. The Medevac is on the way." I had forgotten about the sniper who had done his work for the day and apparently left.

I pulled a few appropriate bandages around his head as

Jimmy's body continued to do what the involuntary muscles and nerves are supposed to do. He breathed with very long pauses, even though I couldn't find a pulse. Meanwhile the guys were trying to mark our spot by popping smoke, all of which just drifted down through the forest. They finally bent down a small tree, tied a smoke grenade to it, pulled the pin and let it spring back up into the opening. In minutes the Medevac was there, deploying a jungle penetrator (a cylindrical device with a folding seat and harness that fastens to a cable, and is lowered from a helicopter through the opening in the trees).

Jim's involuntary breathing had stopped, and I was on my own to move him 25 feet or so to align with the penetrator. I needed to figure out the mechanics of the device, then fold down parts that created the seat that a rider could straddle. I had one hell of a time getting Jimmy's limp body on that thing and strapped in. But, extraction began with Jim's arms hanging down and his head hung back as we began to see the shadowed side of him heading toward the opening above. When a vine found its way across his neck halfway out of the canopy, the pilot and crew (God bless those guys) lowered the cable again, maneuvered and freed him from yet another insult before clearing the top of the jungle and pulling him on board. The chopper left, but the radio began barking at the brass, as these Medevac missions are extremely dangerous for the crew when penetrators are used. We were not supposed to use them for KIA's (Killed in Action), but at the same time, it would have been extremely difficult and dangerous to sling a body in a poncho strung up on a pole between two guys, navigate the mountainous country and hunt for Charlie until the next LOG day.

Medical training at Fort Sam was very good, but sorely lacking in preparing us for the rigors of combat. We had never seen a back pack aid bag, nor had been shown how to stock one. Knowing how to operate a jungle penetrator would have been handy about then. We were also taught nothing of the psychological effects of dealing with traumatically injured and dying men.

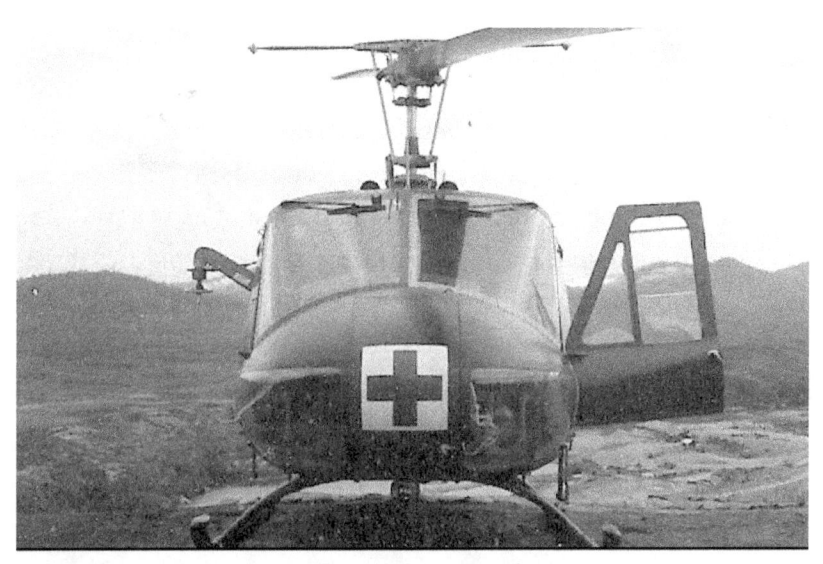

Typical Medevac chopper with Penetrator Winch.

Things changed for all of us that day, I think especially for me, when our first WIA (Wounded in Action) became KIA by the time he hit the ground. I was still a shit head kid with an attitude about being there, but Jimmy taught me what my job really was, and I resolved to do it better from that day forth and to be a better soldier. Jimmy Green from Dumas, Texas, was the ice breaker for B-Co.

The mission continued.

For the most part, us line doggies had no clue where we were at any given time while in the jungle, but when air assault missions took us from the places we normally frequented to fire support bases like Firebase Boyd, Birmingham, Bastogne, or Vehgil, as we could see they all lay in a westerly direction from Hue, with the A Shau Valley beyond them.

FB Boyd, was a big round knob of a hill maybe 1,500 feet high. A single company could guard the perimeter. It and the others were all accessible by road. At the base there was the remains of an old air strip that was almost part of the road, but no buildings or tarmac.

There had been little or no enemy activity in the area for some time, and we could relax a little while we were there. A USO show came to Boyd one time, a small Korean rock in roll band with some female singers. They were quite good, and we enjoyed the heck out of it. Another time at Christmas, most of us received care packages from home. Pat O'Leary received a small plastic Christmas tree, complete with decorations. He assembled it all beside his bunker, an area we all gathered in to eat and shoot the bull, and the little tree from home was enjoyed by all. Firebases were good places to receive LOG and good places to add on new recruits.

Christmas on FB Birmingham – 1968. Pat O'Leary.

By now, many men of the original unit were finishing their year and heading home. We picked up a new recruit on Boyd one time. A tall, slender Native-American named Clyde Crossguns. He was shortly thereafter observed slithering around and through the rocky perimeter, peeking out here and there.

We said, "Clyde, what are you doing?"

He replied, "Looking for snipers!"

We said, "Good idea," and let him go about his business.

Later, Clyde earned our respect when he became one of the many good point men, and we all relied on him.

Vehgil had what looked like a man-made ridge through part of the camp, with bunkers built thirty feet or so down below the narrow, flat-topped ridge. Helicopters used it as an LZ and could land anywhere on the length of it. On a clear day a Loach (small pumpkin seed shaped helicopter that seated two crew and two passengers) carrying two high brass, landed on it and stayed for an hour or two. Later, the original occupants climbed back on board, the little chopper fired up and prepared to take off. When the bird was warmed up, it lifted up as normal, transitioned sideways to begin flight, but apparently lost lift as it moved away from the ridge. I and others were on top of a bunker down below and in line with the craft as it lifted off. We were watching it when it disappeared over the opposite side. "CRASH" echoed back over the ridge! At about the same time a steel pot (helmet) flew over the ridge and rolled down the slope to our bunker. It was totally smashed! My aid bag was in the CP hooch, but we all scrambled to the crash site as fast as we could go. The Loach was lying on its side atop a bunker, rotors twisted and bent, a little smoke drifting up, and it was already covered with GI's pulling the occupants free.

Amazingly enough, no one was seriously hurt on the ground or in the chopper, only cuts and bruises. I had always wanted to ride on a Loach in the worst way but never got the chance.

Part of our Platoon CP was put into a rather nice, almost totally buried wood-framed bunker with a wooden floor. I had an idea of constructing a raised bunk and scrounged the base for enough lumber scraps to build the bed off the floor. I laid out my poncho and poncho liner neatly on it and headed out to see if the guys needed anything. On my return I found that a black guy named Wooten, who was an RTO (Radio Transmission Operator) at the time, had decided for some reason that I was below his pecking order. He had given me a great deal of shit over the last several months, and now he had thrown all my gear into the corners and was laying out on my freshly built bunk, his hands behind his head. As a big grin came up on his face when I stepped in, I looked at what he had done for a second, and all the crap he had given me over several months came out all at once. Before he could blink, I spanned the 10 feet between us. I crossed my arms into the position for mounting a rucksack, grabbed his fatigue jacket just below his collar, then jerked him off the cot in a choreographed spin, ending with him over my back in rucksack position. With everything a 145-pound Michigan farm boy could put forth, I lunged forward, bending over at the same time and throwing him against the wall some five feet away. For a split second he looked like he was standing on his head, his eyes big as barrels. He then slid on his back out onto the floor.

Wooten got up, grabbed his things and looked at me, sputtering and stuttering. Finally, he said, "You in trouble, you in trouble white boy!" and headed off to another bunker. I worried about it for a while. But that stopped his harassment. I think he decided not to "mess with the medic" anymore. Aside from constantly harassing me and trying to make life more miserable than it already was, Wooten was a whiner. He probably whined to another black guy named Sgt. Battle about what the mean old medic did to him, and after that Sgt. Battle began giving me constant problems.

Battle was different, more of a tough guy who had been in the Army for a while. He was the artillery forward observer for our platoon, therefore always with the Platoon CP He never missed an opportunity to try and make my life harder. It would not have been wise to go after him physically, so, I just endured, hoping he would leave the unit soon. But, it's also my nature to look for another way to return a favor.

Vehgil was a rough muddy knob with one or two batteries of artillery and some sort of communication unit. Someone on that base had the clout to have a refrigerated trailer, stocked with meat and frozen vegetables, and a makeshift cook shack provided the base inhabitants one meal a day, and it beat C-rats big time.

The trailer had a gas-powered refrigeration unit that ran automatically to control the temperature. On the second day I had a great idea and crawled under the trailer and hooked one end of a claymore wire to the battery, then buried the wire slightly as it ran into our bunker. After removing a taillight from the trailer, and a little handiwork with medical tape, we had an electric light in the bunker. It made a great place to write letters home.

8.
IN THE SHADOW OF THE VALLEY

Most of our missions would last from one to six weeks. Some lasted two to three weeks before returning to a FB for "line doggies," time passes in a strange way. There are no Sundays or Tuesdays, no TGIF's, no holidays except Christmas and the 4th of July, and for some guys, not even that. Months blended together and trouble me now as I write these lines, trying to put things in chronological order. I can remember the events, but when? The only thing a pocket calendar was good for was to cross off one more day closer to going home and, of course, for marking the seven day intervals between handing out the big, orange malaria pill.

Most missions would begin with a full company assault, which then split into three platoons of about 30 men each. Sometimes we would meet for an NDP, then head out in separate directions again.

On occasion 3rd Plt. was given a dog handler with a German Shepherd. These guys were always more than willing to walk point and did so. We were encroaching closer and closer into Charlie's supply routes. We saw paths being obviously used along with other clues of human activity.

We broke camp early, as usual one morning, and, for whatever reason, we headed back out in the same direction we had come into the NDP site the night before. The dog handler moved out about 200 feet, while the rest of us were rucking up and slowly moving into the line.

As he told the story later, a gook literally jumped out of a thicket, took a quick bead and shot an RPG (Rocket Propelled Grenade) directly at him. He had one split second to dodge the rocket, but in the process his right forearm, cradling his M-16, caught the rear fin of the rocket, cutting a deep gash from his wrist to his elbow. The RPG deflected into a bush and exploded. The sound of the detonation marked the start of the ambush, as one or two AK-47's cut loose in our direction.

Almost instantly, the men in the point line returned fire, and in a few seconds those that were remaining in the NDP had jumped to the perimeter and opened fire to protect the flanks. Seconds after that, an M-60 was pounding the area the ambush came from. They lit up the area fairly well, then several men charged the spot. But the gooks must have immediately turned and ran behind a berm and down a gulch that protected them from the onslaught.

When I got to the dog handler, he was shook up but laughing at how close he had come to his end. We didn't carry sutures in the bush, and he needed stitches bad, but we were not going to head for an LZ for three more days. I used about 20 butterfly bandages to close the wound, a few good compresses, a roll of ace wrap, and he was back on point.

There was no body count on either side, but it may have been on this same mission that the dog sniffed out and discovered one hell of a cache of weapons. Just covered up with thatch were 100 or more long guns, AK-47's, old bolt action rifles, 60 mm mortar tubes, a couple old light machine guns and a small amount of ammunition. The entire cache was divided up between all of us and carried some distance to location where we chopped out an LZ, and the weapons' were flown back to Sally.

Days turned into weeks, and big hills turned into mountains as the jungle canopy grew thicker and thicker. I knew we were somewhere west of Hue, in the Thou Thin province, but that was about it.

It would happen from time to time that conditions would prevent us from finding a good NDP. The recons would continue until the point of darkness before we would stop, form the rough semblance of an NDP, crawl off the trail a short distance with a buddy or two and try to catch a few winks during the long night.

Any condition outside the confines of an established fortified base calls for as much silence as possible, especially at night. But on one of these more desperate NDP nights, one of the men let out a muffled screech and cursing ensued along with thrashing in the bushes. The man was only about 20 feet from me, and I could hear him crawling in my direction, whispering to anyone in ear shot as to my location. I was up on my knees by then, couldn't see my hand in front of my face, and guided the man with low tones to my spot. I recognized the man's voice as Sgt. DA, mumbling curse words and something about, "A freaking rat bit me."

"What the hell," I thought. First time for everything.

Finding my flashlight, I held it under my helmet to shade the light as he explained that it bit him on the forehead. I had him lay on his back and took a look. Blood was coming from two small gashes. As I cleaned them up, I asked him how he knew it was a rat. He said he grabbed the son of a bitch with both hands and tried to crush it before flinging it into the jungle.

I dressed the wound as he repeatedly asked if he would get rabies. I assured him he would not, and that I would change the dressing in the daylight. I chuckled to myself as I turned to get comfortable on the foliage of the jungle floor thinking, "I wonder why that rat chose Ol' Sergeant DA?"

On extra dark nights like these, I noticed tiny bits of something making a phosphorescent glow on the forest floor. I saved small sticks and leaves that I found, some brighter than others. Retrieving them the next day, I looked for the source of the light, but there was never anything to be seen. The only common clue was that the foliage was always dead and decaying.

I learned over time to use the phenomenon to move around at night if I needed to get to the radio for night watch or whatever. I found that I could distinguish objects 25 to 30 feet away.

If my memory serves me correctly, Wooten was still with the platoon. He hated the ground I walked on but no longer bothered me. Sergeant Battle, on the other hand, picked up where Wooten left off, keeping the harassment pressure on day in and day out. Why the two of them did this I will never know, but again, we will return to that subject in "Reflections."

On one of these pitch-black nights near the Laotian border, I had to pee. There had been no time to dig in or hooch up, just enough to roll out our poncho liners and cover up. I sat there for a minute and let my eyes adjust to the dim glow on the ground. I could make out a tree trunk here, a fern base there, and GI's causing large black spots on the ground where they lay rolled up in their liners. I knew where each man in the CP was lying, including Sgt. Battle. I pondered certain consequences as the Devil took over my common sense. I stood up and walked with stealth through the ink-black night to Battle's resting place some 20 feet away. I could not figure out which was his head or feet, so I pulled out my weapon of revenge and hosed him down from one end to the other. I was nearly relieved, when he woke up and figured out what was going on, so I concentrated the remainder in the direction of the noises.

Of course, in those days I could shoot six feet away. I figured that he would never know who it was, as I slowly crept back to my own black spot, with Battle making more noise than he should, thrashing about and cursing in low tones. He crawled about the CP, finding others and interrogating them as to his misfortune. Soon enough, I could hear and actually see his path of travel in my direction! I lay silent until his groping in the darkness finally located my spot. He grabbed and shook my liner and in a low growl said, "Flory, did you piss on me?"

Acting like I was waking up, I said, "Oh-Oh—shit, I'm awake—I'm awake. Is it my watch?

Where's the radio?" He repeated, "Doc, did you piss on me?" I said, "What!?"

He said, "Forget it," and continued his mission hunting for others, until a crisp low report was heard from the platoon leader.

"Battle, cease and desist now!"

Within a few weeks, Sgt. Battle, DA and Wooten would be leaving the company, as they were original members of the unit, and their time was up in the field.

They survived the war and went back to the "world."

During that last couple of weeks, however, Battle must have had some inkling that it may have been me that hosed him that night. I got the evil eye from time to time, but he finally left me alone (He had messed with the medic far to long).

Chaplains were assigned to most military units. In our case, they made visits to us field troops while on fire support bases and sometimes on LOG days. They would form groups or talk to us as individuals. They performed various church services, such as, Mass for the Catholics. They became the closest thing we had to psychological advisers or counselors and were just plain good morale builders.

One day a new chaplain showed up, but played the game totally differently. He was in full field gear and stayed with us for weeks in the bush. He rotated from platoon to platoon and from company to company. He was an extremely gung-ho Airborne trooper who carried a bible as he humped the jungle. He went with recons, with dog handlers, and he walked with the point men on a regular basis. Chaplain Corbin Cherry was a captain, and he was a terrific morale builder whenever it was our turn to share him.

Chaplain Cherry did not carry a gun unless it came from a cache of enemy weapons. He conducted himself no differently than any other grunt and shared the extra loads of C-4, belts of M-60 ammo or whatever. He was always first on the scene, assisting the

CALENDAR FOR 1968

No Promotion Psalm 75:6-7	Dischargitis Hebrews 11:1	Out-Ranked Psalm 3:1	Reply by Indorsement 2 John 12
"Digging In" Psalm 7:15	**TESTED SOLUTIONS FOR TRYING SITUATIONS** Second Geronimo Battalion 101st Airborne Division Chaplain Wm. W. Erbach		Chewed-Out Psalm 39:2
Lost at Cards Prov. 1:19			Drunk Prov. 23:29,2
Bad Chow 1 Cor 10:27			Worried Romans 8:28
Reveille Prov. 20:13			Sick Call Luke 5:31
Restricted Psalm 55:6	No Furlough Luke 22:68	Overworked John 9:4	No Mail Prov. 25:25

A Chaplain's calling card.

medics with the dead and the wounded. He was a very intelligent, motivated and clever counselor who was on a never- ending quest of reminding us of our origin and responsibility to our Maker. He was a jokester, a prankster, fun to be around, a person you do not forget. I recognized him immediately when he showed up at our 2005 reunion at the Duke Ranch in Tulsa, Oklahoma.

Chaplain Cherry, leading in prayer and bayonet throwing.

By late January or early February 1969, I had been in-country nearly half of my tour. I was living life as a hardened infantry soldier, and 95 percent of the day-to-day talk was of military matters, from the flavor of your last C-rat to the last mission, the next mission or the whereabouts of the platoons or sister companies. We didn't forget about our civilian world, it was just more like a dream. Then a letter from home would arrive, oh those precious letters. My family and extended family did a wonderful job of keeping a steady flow of letters and the occasional care package coming my way.

They were fun letters, funny letters, informational, of concern, good news or bad. My sister June, then a senior, explained how "dead" it was in the halls of the school now that the class of '67 was gone. Mom always included a quote from the scriptures or a pamphlet from her church (mentoring her black sheep son). Mother did the writing for Dad, as he just didn't care to write much and probably didn't pen more than twenty words during my 730 days in the service. Mom wrote about everything, including the exploits of my Dad who had started construction on a full-sized pontoon boat, along with his week-by-week progress, including pictures.

My cousin Bob Flory's wife, Joey, wrote to me and cousin Bill on a continuous basis. Bob had purchased an old cable crane, and I read of the blow-by-blow action as he restored it to working order, including a new paint job. He began earning extra money digging irrigation ponds for local farmers, and he is still digging holes.

There were a few old girlfriends who corresponded, along with other classmates stationed in Vietnam. I was told that Jim Sowa, class of '66, was stationed near Da Nang. I got his address, but the very next letter announced that he had been killed by the rotor of a helicopter while volunteering to unload wounded men from Medevac at the field hospital. A sudden gust of wind tipped the helicopter sideways as he and others carried the litters away from the LZ.

I also received care packages from women and men with familiar names who were involved with the VFW back home. Words of encouragement came from veterans of previous wars.

I kept a note pad in the liner of my helmet and used it constantly to record notes for my next opportunity to write letters home. It was unfortunate, but 95 percent of the letters and photos we received needed to be destroyed shortly after receiving them. It was impossible to pack very much of that sort of thing and no way to get it to the rear.

Another mission ended and we flew to a defensive guard position called Pohl Bridge.

9.
Pohl Bridge

Third Platoon pulled guard duty at the place called Pohl Bridge on two occasions during my time with B-Co. It was good duty and always hard to leave when it was time to return to the jungle. The bridge was quite new, built by US Army engineers, and it crossed the Perfume River just southwest of Hue, between Firebases Birmingham and Camp Eagle. It was built on steel pipes at least 16-inches in diameter that were driven into the riverbed to support the flat wooden deck that went some 300 to 350 feet across.

The deck of the bridge was probably some 20 feet above the natural waterline, wide enough and strong enough to easily drive a tank across. Bridge traffic was primarily military, but civilians used it as well. The bridge provided access to Route #547, the road that traveled past our Firebases and headed west into the highlands, eventually connecting to the A Shau Valley, in the Thua Thien province.

A contingent of Navy CB's (Construction Battalion) operated a large water purification unit at the southeast side of the bridge, with their bunkers built from the very edge of the river to the edge of the road some 30-feet away. A road followed the river and intersected with the bridge road just a hundred feet to the east of the CB's station. The remaining three corners were filled with bunkers, and, in the evening, wire fences were pulled across the road at the bunker perimeter line. They opened again every morning by 0700 hours to allow the mine sweeping trucks and crew to pass on their way west.

If I recall, with the help of the CB's it took two platoons to guard the bridge and the CP was on the west end. Four of us in the CP shared one of two command bunkers which were fairly roomy and of stud and plywood wall construction. They were buried about halfway into the ground, the upper half being completely sandbag covered. Ours had a guard's bunker built on top for night watch, and the main room had a gun portal about a foot high and four-feet-wide just above ground level and facing the river.

Standing position would be required to use the portal. The opening did add some daylight and fresh air, which helped reduce the foul swampy smell that came from the soggy dirt that was under the loose board floor.

On our first night in the bunker all went well until about 1200 hours when a really weird screeching noise began echoing through the bunker every few minutes.

"What the heck was that?"

"Don't know."

A minute later, "Screechfpfpfp" again.

"There is definitely something weird in this bunker."

"Yeah, we better try to find out what it is."

Out came the flashlights and we looked in and under everything, but couldn't find the source of the noise. Whatever it was kept us up most of the night. I do not sleep well anyway and vowed I would find the culprit the next day.

There were four bunks framed from 2x4's and plywood on one side of the bunker walls, and the bottom bunks were only a few inches above the clapboard floor covering the mud. I went on a vendetta the next day to discover what had been making the noise and pulled out anything that would come loose and took it outside.

I nearly depleted the flashlight batteries before finally spotting the culprit far back in a dark corner under a bottom bunk. It was a cricket—a really big cricket—probably three inches long. You could troll for muskies back home with a bug like that.

It was just out of reach, and I needed to remove some floor boards and dig out under the bunk to reach it. In the process I discovered the bunker had a plywood floor under about six inches of half dried mud, but did not let that distract me from my mission of capturing the noise maker. It was only a small trick to catch him, as he only had one rear leg. He could catapult himself a good distance, but he had no control of which direction he wanted to go. I lodged him in a poly-bag and showed the guys our nemesis. He was blond color, old looking, his one missing leg probably the result of previous less fortunate occupants of the bunker.

The next day Dan and I found a five-gallon pail and spent eight to ten hours nonstop removing all the mud from the bunker and reinstalling the fine furniture—*Ha!* Next day the floor was dry and the smell was better. We relaxed and swam in the Perfume River, which we did every chance we had.

I made good friends with the CB's by helping them fix up a very old and rusty 45-caliber Grease Gun. My payment was the opportunity to shoot it into the river when it was finally operational. They really were good guys but, on one visit to their bunker, the cricket somehow slipped out of my pocket and into the dark corners of their hooch.

"Oh damn..." The medic messed with them—just a little!

While doing the gun smithing for the CB's I met a young girl about nine years old. Her name was Hoha, and she had a fair command of English. I knew a few Vietnamese words along with established French slang, so we communicated really well. She was very smart or street-wise and made money by selling blocks of ice to GI's. Where she got the ice, I don't know.

Bunker at Pohl Bridge, late summer, 1969. Dan Hefel, Dave Sullivan, unknown. Gun portal is visible behind the men.

    She would take me to her parent's house in the evening. I would bring them sundries and candy bars, and Hoha would interpret as we asked each other questions. They were wonderful people, but so poor. Their house was typical of any along the river road. It was maybe 20 feet long by 16 feet wide, and made of poles, with a thatched roof and corrugated tin tied to the walls, and no door to close the entrance. The floor was dirt, but everything was as neat and tidy as possible. It was about 50 yards from the CB perimeter, so I could stay there until dark.

    Stepping through the door there was a large wooden table to the right. The legs were sawed off so the table was only 16 inches high On the opposite side were two beds built of tightly stretched woven reeds, 6 feet by 6 feet, 20 inches off the floor and attached directly to the walls with a woven partition between them. They were like wicker, stretched as tight as a trampoline. Wicker shelves above held a few blankets and a meager supply of clothing.

    To the far right a partition divided the house from the cooking area. The kitchen was the width of the house and 5 feet wide, with no tables or counters. Aluminum and porcelain pots and pans hung from the walls. A dirt and stone hearth in one corner with a cast iron tripod above hot coals held a cast-iron kettle, 20 inches in diameter. Bundles of willow switches hung from the round pole rafters, ready to become fuel for cooking. The opposite side contained wicker shelves with tin cans and bags holding whatever.

There was no refrigeration and no electricity, only candles for light at night. When *mama san* cooked, she propped a stick under a tin flap just behind the hearth to create a draft and keep the house (hut) from filling with smoke.

Hoha invited me to her house in the evening a time or two. Their neighbors would come over and all of them stepped up onto the table, formed a circle, assumed the *kimuchi squat* (sit like a dog) position and played card games for hours.

They held cards in their hands and between their toes, chatted quietly, briskly and happily between themselves, paying little attention to me as I sat on the corner of the table, as there were no chairs in the house.

In turn, Hoha and several kids were allowed inside the military perimeter. She would find me, sit down beside me and crack betel nut seeds and feed me the meats. They were very good, somewhat like sunflower seeds. Some older Vietnamese women chewed betel nut leaves, and, in time, their teeth would turn red and eventually a glossy jet black. They loved to smile at everyone, showing them off.

One day an old woman came up the street, an "idiot stick" (GI slang for shoulder pole) over her shoulder, suspending heavy articles for and aft, and leaving behind a trail of smoke.

Hoha said, "Would you like to have lunch?"

The old *mama san* was a traveling restaurant. Hoha flagged her to the side of the road, and the lady set her wares on a level spot, then laid the shoulder pole to the side.

The rear portion had a hardened clay hearth with an area

molded in to fit a small kettle and teapot over a bed of hot coals. It also supported other pans and utensils. The front portion contained the dishes and cups, along with a supply of vegetables, fruit, seasoning and extra water.

We had a nice pork-based soup, a salad topped off with orange slices and hot tea. I paid the lady what Hoha suggested, plus a tip, and she was on her way. I estimated that the weight of the mobile restaurant was equal, or more, to the weight of the woman.

Back in our bunker, we awoke one night to intense gun fire on the opposite side of the bridge. We bailed out of our sacks and looked through the gun port for answers.

A Quad—four 50-caliber machine guns mounted on the back of a deuce-and-a-half—was parked near the water. It had a spotlight mounted to it, and we could see the shadowed side of a sampan floating down the river toward the bridge. The men had been ordered to destroy it, fearing it could be loaded with explosives. The 50-caliber is an impressive gun as it is, but when you mount four of them together on a turret, all cranked up on full automatic, you do not want to be on the business end. The sampan was shredded to pieces in less that a minute, as tracers could be seen hitting the bridge pilings.

The excitement over, we went back to our bunks. Tomorrow we would be making an assault on the next mission.

This one had a name. I believe it was called "Operation Jeb Stewart."

10.
ROCKETS AND MORE

I believe that all of our missions at this point, took us on one side or the other of the A Shau, as we prodded further north on each new assault. The terrain was getting rougher, and good LZ's were harder to find. A couple of times the choppers could get in close to a open spot, but the ground was too steep to land. The pilot would hover as close as possible while we jumped to the ground. This is a dangerous time for the pilots, because sudden weight loss affects the controls of the craft. We would take our primary rucksacks off, stand out on the landing rails and, at the signal from a door gunner, drop our packs to the ground, then jump off. Poor old Danny failed to get the instructions on our first jump of this kind and bailed out with his ruck on his back. His legs held up just fine, but something tore loose in his shoulder. He needed a couple of Darvon pain killers that night, and he complained about that shoulder the remainder of his tour.

On one of these missions we were once again assigned dog handlers, and like our chaplains, they rotated from platoon to platoon and company to company. This time it was two dogs and handlers. Again, these guys were brave men and worked the point.

The company was split into the three platoons as usual, and we were working different approaches to a hill. The dog team was with 1st or 2nd platoon and making recon up a steep path. At some point, the dogs detected something ahead, but it was too late. The NVA ambush killed both handlers and one of the dogs.

We (3rd platoon) were several hundred yards away and, of course, went into code red alert. When we heard shots fired, we began guarding the flanks. As the platoon in contact started trading volleys of gunfire with the enemy, we began to move in their direction. In due time we joined up with their platoon. The ambush and firefight were over with, and we aided with the aftermath. There were no immediate LZ's available, and the KIA's needed to be carried on makeshift litters through tough terrain. If I recall, it took more than 24-hours to get the two dead men to a place where their bodies could be choppered back to the rear.

Tasks like that are dreaded, and nearly every man takes his turn carrying the bodies.

Revenge may have come later, while making an NDP on a very high and steep sided ridge. The platoon was dug in, night had just fallen, and a few of us in the CP were chatting quietly. At the spot where we stopped, the sky was open to the east because of an old landslide that took a 100-foot swath of jungle down the side of the ridge. The sky was like a giant movie screen full of stars and the outline of nearby hills, with just enough light to see some detailed terrain.

The view was beautiful, and we were, most likely, enjoying a clear sky, when suddenly we saw a flash of light and a spark trail streak into the sky, arc to the southwest and disappear.

"Wow! What the hell was that? Rocket—it must be a rocket."

Then came another.

"Holy shit it's got to be gooks shooting at Da Nang or Camp Eagle."

Captain Pierce T. Graney, our company commander at the time, jumped on the radio and begun calling in warnings to those areas – "Wow," number three just went off and our red leg (slang for Artillery Forward Observer) had his map laid out, locating our position and orientating the map to the terrain.

"Keep an eye peeled on that spot," he said, "then we will locate it on the map. I will direct artillery to the area and walk it in."

Captain Graney was busy on the radio, trying to find out if there were any friendlies in that area, and the answer was no. By then two or three more rockets had launched, and we had the spot marked quite well on the map. The red leg could have been Bill (Tiny) Kaufmann, I no longer remember, but he was very good! The first round from the artillery looked like a perfect hit, then the red leg ordered the gun battery to "Fire for Effect"! They pumped fifteen or twenty big ones in and blew up everything on the side of that hill.

A marine unit close enough to the vicinity was directed to scout the target the next day. We learned later that it was a good strike, and that guns, rocket launchers, equipment and bodies were found.

Lord have pity on the NVA soldiers who were trying to rocket one of our bases. If there were any survivors they are probably still wondering how anyone knew their hiding place. We never found out where the rockets landed, however.

It was more dangerous now, and more caution needed to be used as we set out each day to do our job. We were on another ridge, not unlike the one just described, inching along a trail that followed the razorback. Many of the point men truly seemed to have a natural instinct for discerning trouble. As we came to a saddle in the ridge that was 150 – 200 feet across, with an open sight line straight through, we thought "What a spot for an ambush." It was midday, hot as usual, and the point man took great caution making his way down the saddle and up the opposite side to reconnect with the ridge. David Krautscheid told the story, as he was the point slack man (next behind point or last man in a group or last squad in A-Company etc.) that day. When the point crested the saddle, he spotted an NVA lying on the ground off to the side of the trail behind a bush. He froze for an instant, then realized the perpetrator of what could have been a very successful ambush was sleeping!

The point man took aim and shot the NVA where he lay with his RPG launcher in hand. At that moment, a second NVA stood up quickly between the trunk of a split tree, but before he could collect himself from the surprise, the point man once again responded with his M-16, and the two NVA both lay silent.

We searched them for papers, collected their weapons, which always made an additional burden for someone (that includes the medics). We were never immune to packing extra M-60 ammunition, an axe, Charlie-4 (Composition-4, plastic explosive), det cord (clear plastic tubing filled with Composition-4), or weapons collected from the enemy. It also seemed to be an unwritten necessity for the medic to have a look at the bodies, "The coroner effect." But from their wounds, anyone could deduce a zero survival.

We proceeded down that ridge for some distance, then made our way back the same route to the NDP from the previous night. On the way back, trip wires were set up coming and going on the trail from the location of the bodies, and the red leg marked the coordinates of the spot.

Sure enough, late that night the booby trap was tripped. The red leg had already called the coordinates into the nearest artillery battery, and the deadly 105-howitzer rounds pounded that spot hard.

One of the jobs I feared the most was night ambush. There were various reasons for using them, but typically they were used when the company was in full force. We would rendezvous at an NDP spot, then send out a five or six man squad back down the way we had come in. We moved to a predetermined location, got off the trail just before it was too dark to see and guarded the trail. The idea was to give early warning to the larger group if enemy were sneaking up.

These were times when you rarely slept at all, you didn't make shelters, no digging in, and there were no ponchos. You didn't dare try to feel at home. I accompanied these ambush squads ten or twelve times during my tour. The company as a whole was at less risk if one medic was lost, and I was always an extra gun on the ambush until someone needed me.

It rained on many nights, but on one occasion while on ambush, we were in a small hole in the earth. A very large vine encircled the hole several times. I was able to take comfort in the wee hours of the morning while bridged between the loops of the vine. The rain became very intense and eventually filled the pit. There was no choice but for all of us to stay there, half submerged, until there was enough morning light to safely join the company. It's hard to describe just how miserable you can feel.

One thing about the 101st, (maybe all field units) is that you are required to be "standing tall" (as possible under the conditions) every day. We would be in the field for ten or fifteen days, half of them raining, humping 6 to 10 kilometers per day up and down mountains, sweating and stinking badly in the 100 degree plus, steaming jungle. After sleeping and crawling on the jungle floor in the same uniform you started with, you were filthy and had a brackish odor. But, by golly, you needed to shave every other day, no matter what.

Once again, you just did not pack anything you did not need. Guys would form coalitions of three men. One packed a mirror, one packed the aerosol shave cream, and the third packed the razor. Now keep in mind, water was often rationed if it hadn't rained or you couldn't get any morning dew off your poncho. If shaving was required during that time, we would first each pour a little water in the cap from the aerosol can, then use some method of drawing lots for who got to use water first, second, then third. The shave cream went on a dry face, let it soak in for a minute, shave a swath and spin the razor in the cap to clean it. By the time the cap got to the third man, well, we won't go there. The real airborne dudes (jump-qualified) always said that it was much easier to pound the whiskers in with their gun butt and bite them off from the inside!

The AO (Area of Operation) we were in during the early months of 1969 was fairly active with enemy. It may be hard to think about it this way, but we could take solace in knowing that if something moved in front of you, just shoot it. There were *montagnard* (native aborigines) people out there, but they always knew where we were and stayed away. It was NVA soldiers, American soldiers and jungle animals, period.

Things were much tougher for the troops in the lowlands, where there were farmers, villagers, kids, Viet Cong and NVA that looked and dressed like everyone else. Where we were, there were only NVA, and most wore khaki shirts and shorts.

So anyway, one day we were inching our way up some ridge and took an abrupt turn down into a deep draw. It took nearly half the morning to reach the bottom. By mid-afternoon we were getting back close to the summit on the opposite side. We were moving through the jungle, but not on any established trail.

Reconning for hours on end is tedious work for everyone, not just the point man. Silence is truly golden, and hand signals are used a great deal of the time. Up ahead a right arm goes out slowly, forearm vertical, fist clinches, then opens again, and waves left, then right. Behind you someone else picks up on the signal and repeats the command, and so on it goes down the string of men that are 20 – 30 feet apart. The men sink low, ease 10 – 20 feet off to the side, seek cover if they can, but watching the flanks carefully, quietly, and the line of men nearly disappears.

Time passes slowly as the points probe forward into the unknown until they are satisfied. Then the remainder of the men can safely move forward.

The "slack man" bringing up the rear of the column has a very tough job as well. He not only needs to watch where he is going and watch his flank, he needs to study the terrain as it moves away, making sure no one is following. The best "slack men" always seemed to be short guys, and they loved to carry a single shot M-79 grenade launcher. They kept a buckshot (beehive) round chambered and a M-79 grenade round in the other hand, at the ready.

Meanwhile, I had no idea how close we were to the summit, and, for whatever reason, I was about the sixth man back from the point. Usually I ended up around 16 – 18th in a platoon of 28 to 30 men.

We were moving forward (and upward) at a steady pace for a while, and the usual signal to sit tight and watch the flanks came through the line. I moved off to the right this time and sat down 15 to 20 feet off the projected line of travel. It was a nice quiet day under the triple canopy that was letting in just a little more light then usual.

Time passed, and I noticed a rather large bat flying through the second layer of trees and taking a perch upside down on a limb some 75 degrees up from my horizontal sight line. I was looking at it, thinking, "Oh that's a big sucker, nothing like that in Michigan."

As my head was cocked back, I noticed movement closer to me. I was sitting on the ground, under a giant fern, my feet pointed down the slope. Some of the ferns are huge in the rain forest, with six or eight branches jetting out from a single stump, a single leaf fixed to the rhubarb-like stalk, some four to six feet in diameter.

I looked up slightly higher at the connection of the leaf and stalk, and there was a brilliant green bamboo viper, his head and the first 12 inches of his body hanging straight down, looking directly at me and sticking his tongue out quickly (bamboo vipers are highly poisonous).

"Oh crap!"

I am sitting there, the butt of my M-16 between my legs and already pointing straight up. I moved the barrel directly in line with the snake and thought about pulling the trigger. Heck, we weren't on any kind of a trail, maybe no enemy would hear the gun's report and mark our position. Well, on second thought, I decided I can't take a chance on that. Even if everything was fine, I'd be in big trouble with everyone including the platoon leader. I chose to move five feet closer to the line of travel, and catching the attention of a few men around me, pointed to the viper's location.

The signal to move forward came once again, and we progressed forward (and up) for another 15 or 20 minutes. I was looking up through the men as we were catching up to Sergeant Wayne Carrara, from New York, who was first man out on point. It looked like we were reaching the top, when Carrara, while stepping over a log, stumbled, caught himself on a tree, swung partly around the tree before stopping and yelled at the top of his lungs—"Gooks! Gooks!"

He righted himself, stepped back in shock, tripped backwards over the log he just went over and cartwheeled backwards down the slope toward us.

Sure as shit, two gooks who were sleeping on a thatch bunk jumped up, racked shells into their AK-47 and started spraying the area with bullets. All of us dove to the ground, seeking the nearest tree, and swung into position to return fire. The NVA definitely had the upper hand for the first clip of ammunition.

There were red tracers headed uphill from every direction, green tracers headed downhill from every direction, and, despite the noise of all the automatic weapon, I could hear the bolts of the

AK's slapping shut in rapid action. The volley quit as abruptly as it started. A signal to fall back was given, and I hunted for casualties but found none. Lordy Momma, that was a tad too close!

Later on I took a bit of an ass chewing from our platoon leader, Lt. Pue, for being too close to point.

We hustled back down the hill a short distance and formed into a DP as Lt. Pue called in gunships. I'm not sure how the birds marked the target, other than the prominence of the hill, but Pue placed them correctly over the target. They must have been sitting ready to take off or already in flight, because it was only minutes before they arrived and begun pouring "piss and skunyen" all over that ridge, with rockets blasting, the rumbling blatttttt of mini guns, then more rockets. (The sound of a mini-gun, firing at a rate of thousands of rounds per minute, reminded me of fog horns on the big ore boats making their way on the St. Marys River back in the upper peninsula of Michigan).

The gunships approach most always, from behind us, flying at high speed, passing our position, then pouring their ordinance into the jungle, taking turns circling around, and doing it again several times, until their weapons are empty. We got a glimpse of the birds as they maneuvered above. They were Cobra gunships and had such incredible fire power that if anyone was in this field of fire, they were in big trouble. Our enemies knew it and usually didn't stick around long.

When the Cobras finished their work of chewing up the hilltop, it was our turn once again to head to the top. We moved in quickly as the birds were leaving, hoping that if any unfriendlies were remaining that their heads would still be down.

Upon reaching the summit, we found two things right away. One was a trail unlike anything we had ever encountered previously. It was three to five feet wide and packed down hard from foot travel. As we explored the trail later, we found that the enemy had created steps in the steep areas and made improvements of other sorts to allow foot soldiers, their equipment and supplies to move quickly through the forest.

At the spot where Sergeant Carrara tripped, there was a nice two-man thatch bunk with a thatch roof bridged between two trees, and it was all well used. More interesting, however, were hand-hewn rungs lashed with vines and bamboo to one of the two trees. The tree was quite large and leaned out over the edge of the hilltop. It went out through the canopy to a perch, and from that point the NVA could watch for aircraft. That spot was the pinnacle of a ridge coming along in one direction. At the high point, the ridge and the trail took a sharp turn and began descending again. This seemed the Holy Grail of trails, and we were all amazed by the sight of it. We now knew the location of a serious supply route, which was good, but on the other hand, the NVA were not going to be happy we knew about it. We were guaranteed to find enemy if we stuck to this path long enough.

The CP stayed close to the lookout tree as the platoons split up to recon a distance down both directions of the trail. Meanwhile, I had time to study the effects of mini-gun and rocket fire while the aroma of the explosives was still in the air. A rocket trajectory was limited to the direct flight of the gunship, but the pilots could direct the war birds about anyway they wished. The mini-gun, however, is turret-mounted and could be rotated left or right, up or down.

The jungle, for the most part, was unaffected, but upon closer observation there were shards of iron frag, plastic, steel and aluminum everywhere. It was surprising how many bullet holes could be found in everything. It would have been a very unhealthy place to be when the Cobras were in action.

It seemed that no one was around, but after about 20 minutes shots rang out down one direction of the trail. Then came a short volley, followed by silence. A radio report documented one enemy body. As related by the point man, this was one time that the NVA dress code didn't apply. The gook stepped out into the trail, his AK at the ready, wearing a blue Mickey Mouse sweat shirt. The gook didn't know he was stepping out in front of "Snake," a man who had grown up as a very successful hunter in the backwoods of Minnesota, and he was a very experienced point man.

The gook died from lead poisoning. (Dan told me recently that this event was November 25, 1968 at 3:15 in the afternoon.) That night, sleep came hard, as we knew this was Charlie's backyard, and the tension was high. As I tried to sleep, my mind drifted back to the viper and how terrible the day might have been if I had pulled the trigger, alerting the two NVA lookouts that we were coming.

Weeks had passed by now, and it was time to go back to a Firebase. We found a good site for an LZ on a very high razor-back ridge. Again, it was an area where the land had collapsed from the side of the steep ridge, carrying everything down the side of the hill and creating a huge, very steep washout and leaving the ridge open on one side. All we had to do was open up the other side, a great idea and a great spot. But there were very old, very large trees in the proposed LZ that were four feet in diameter and over 100 feet tall.

Well, we couldn't chop or saw them down, so out came the "C-4." We had rendezvoused with a sister company at this spot, so there was plenty of the explosive. It would have been difficult for the enemy to assault our position other than from the top of the ridge. The sister company guarded one direction and we the other, with the proposed LZ in the center. The axes stayed busy on the smaller trees, as some of us performed as demolition "experts." A few days earlier one of our guys found nearly a bushel of Polish dynamite in a hollow tree, yes that's right, Polish dynamite. It was old and wet, but we packed it along anyway.

What the hay, why not use up this old dynamite too?

So we held a wad of Polish dynamite sticks against a tree trunk, placed two or three bars of Charlie-4 against it, wrapped demolition cord tightly around the tree, shoved a blasting cap in the end of the det cord, strung a detonator wire as far away as possible and touched her off.

This needed to be repeated several times on two of the trees to blow then in half. Eventually a treeless gap through the ridge appeared. The last tree that went down fell across the high point of the washed out landslide, blocking some of the approach. It had one large limb sticking straight out from the trunk and into the proposed flight way. We called in a Huey to test the opening, and the answer was "negative." The limb had to go.

"Snake, Doc (we had a reputation by then), Get that limb off there."

Dan shinnied up first with me right behind toting the ax. Dan worked his way into position, wrapped his legs around the trunk like riding an old bull and tried to make good swings at the 16-inch diameter limb. Dan was no quitter, and I did whatever I could to brace his position. But through prior experience, both of us quickly came to the conclusion that the limb would not yield to this approach.

"Screw it, blow the sucker!"

We shinnied back down the trunk, which was at least 40 feet above the crevasse, and falling off would have been very bad. We climbed up the trunk, this time with me in the lead. Dan packed three bars of C-4 and det cord. I placed them around the crotch of the limb, held them in place with det cord, shoved in the blasting cap, and we shinnied down the trunk. The view, by the way, was quite spectacular from the height of the leaning tree. It would have been nice to stay for a while and look around.

The demolition was successful, and the limb came crashing down and tumbled nearly to the bottom of the crevasse. Another chopper was summoned to retest the LZ and was en route, as men walked back and forth through the gap in the ridge that probably looked like a reverse Mohawk haircut from the air.

"Bang!"

A shot rang out from far below in the washout. At this stage of the game in our on- the-job-training, at least 95 percent of us could tell without question the difference between an AK-47 report and an M-16!

In about the time it took to make that distinction, I was already diving for the dirt and hollering "Sniper!"

I swear it wasn't five seconds before someone on the opposite side of the gap was shouting, "Medic-medic!" Visions of Jimmy Green raced through my head as I scrambled for my aid bag.

"Was that sniper waiting for a new shithead to go prancing across the gap?" I thought.

Carrying my ruck in one hand and with a 15-yard head start, I breached the opening like a sprinter on speed, reached the other side and skidded to a stop like a baseball player at home plate. There the guy was, just five feet away, with another head wound! But this guy was acting just fine. I began to work on him and found that the bullet had carved a path through the tissue of his scalp about three inches long, a half inch wide and a quarter inch deep, with his skull almost visible. It was as if you used a large round rat-tail file and ground a kerf into his head. The wound was hardly bleeding, but I cleaned it and applied a compress.

The only way to hold it on was to wrap an ace bandage around his head, under his chin and so on. He looked a bit like a mummy, but trust me, he knew just how close he came to having no head at all.

For whatever reason, the sniper didn't harass us any more that day. He probably knew we could have made it rain lead into the trees at the base of the washout.

The chopper arrived the second time and made a careful approach. This time there was enough room, but barely enough. Hats off, once again, for the pilots and crews of those helicopters. If it could be done, they would do it.

Keep in mind, the jungle floor had been undisturbed for hundreds or even thousands of years in this remote place. When that first bird took off with the wounded man and five others GI's, the rotor wash sent everything that was lying loose sailing into the bush on either side. I stood behind a large tree for cover, and as the chopper made its exit, I felt a terrible burning sensation at the top of my right boot.

"Good Lordy, Momma!"

It got worse very quickly, and I realized something was biting me! I stomped my foot down repeatedly until, *voila,* a centipede about the size of an Old Dutchman cigar hit the ground. He was using all of his hundred legs to make an escape when my leg, now on automatic pilot, came down again and turned him onto yellow goo.

I don't know what toxins are in those bugs, but I do know I spent the next 45 minutes reeling in pain, my leg half paralyzed. Even today, I can still find the scars of the two holes where that thing sunk his fangs at the very top of my boot, through my army issue socks and just below the taunt blousing string of my jungle fatigues.

It was always good to leave the jungle. But this time there was a little added anticipation in the air as the Brass said we were taking an in-country R&R at a place called Culco Beach.

I can't recall if sister companies were replacing us or not, but as we boarded the H1's and flew "precariously" out of that dangerously narrow LZ, I was just glad to go. We flew to a Firebase, where we boarded deuce-and-a-halves once again and headed for the east coast, this time just south of Hue City.

Highway One appeared to be in very well-maintained

condition, widened and raised—*huh?* A nice ride. It was also bustling with people, ox carts, mopeds, motor cycles, cars and bicycles, as our convoy made its way to the port village on the Gulf of Tonkin.

11.
Culco/Eagle Beach

Culco Beach was actually on an island, about a half mile off shore and covered with palm trees and greenery of all kinds. The island was large enough so that you could barely see the ocean at either end, making the bay look more like a river.

There were civilians coming and going from the small port, some debarking on the US military barge, others from sampans. Most were women with "idiot sticks" over their shoulders heavily loaded with produce and fish. Most civilian women wore black silk pants and long sleeve shirts and typical oriental hats, round, pointed and hand woven from reeds.

The culture was so different in Vietnam. The people chatted to themselves quietly and paid little attention to us. They would smile, show their glistering black teeth and move on. One woman heading down the dirt road with her load, had gotten 25 or 30 yards away from the dock, when she set her cargo on the road side, stepped slightly off the road, rolled up her pants legs to the top, arched her leg and took a nice long pee. Yup, things were different there.

The trucks pulled onto a very large barge, with an open pilot house and—Holy moley—the biggest outboard motor I had ever seen! It must have been a Cummins diesel hooked up to a huge angle drive, all of which were mounted on a turret that could pass as tank parts. The pilot operated it from remote control, first spinning the engine 180 degrees to the push position. He hit the throttle and away we went. The island was not much above sea level. Arriving at the dock, the trucks drove off the barge, and headed through a small village, agricultural acreage and onto the camp at the opposite side of the island.

On the Barge to Culco Beach.

    It was quite a well-kept camp, and its purpose began to make sense, as we could see very large fuel storage tanks inside the confines. This was a large CB facility, a fuel pumping and storage area. Tanker ships moored offshore could hook up to pipelines that ran across the Gulf seabed for a half mile into the island and unload their cargo.

    The base had very nice buildings, brick and steel along with wood frame. The bunkers around the three-sided perimeter were still bunkers, but nice ones with bunks. It was still our job to pull guard around the camp, except there simply were no enemy here, and many civilians worked within the perimeter. We could truly take a breath and relax at this place.

    An entire R&R area was divided off from the working portion of the base, all directly on the beach facing straight out to sea. The buildings were made to look like Tiki huts with thatch roofs. It had an open air pavilion with an NCO club that had movies at night, trinket shops and an outdoor bandstand attached to the pavilion. But the thing we liked most was showers. Oh, what delicious showers—hot water and all! Or, was it the Navy mess hall, with chairs, tables, tile floor and food trays. This place was like heaven.

Once again, duty was fairly easy for me. As the Navy maintained an excellent aid station, and I was mostly duty free. I observed a phenomena that took place here and became apparent in the days and weeks after returning to the field. We were at the beach about four days. My guess is that all of us spent several hours each day in the salt water. Swim suits and surf boards were provided, and we all gave them a go. Most of us took time to catch the rays as well, and it felt good after being in the shadowy jungle for months.

Back left to right: William Christenson and David Reinheimer. Kneeling left to right: Dave Kissell and Frank Duchow.

When we arrived at the beach, most of us had jungle rot infections somewhere on our bodies. It only took a scratch or a bug bite to get it started, and curing it was slow. But when we returned to the jungle after the salt water and sun, all the infection was healed, barely leaving a trace.

Above: Gary Welch wth the author, Culco Beach, 1968.

Above right: Fall of 1968, the author (with unknown fellow surfer) at Culco Beach.

Right: Walt Bouman, Wayne Carrara and Dave Testerman, Culco Beach, 1968.

The author in front, Louis Johnson sitting on picnic table in Culco Beach. Fuel storage tank in the background, 1968.

We had a great time lying about, drinking beer, watching movies, listening to music and—oh yes—food! The Navy knows how to lay out the grub: broccoli, cauliflower, green beans, apples, oranges, bananas, pork, beef, chicken, fish, bacon and fried eggs.

Oh my God, we were in heaven!

On our first day there, we found our quarters, pulled off all our battle rattle and stored it in the bunkers. It was noon by then, and we all headed to the mess hall. We were a filthy, stinking battle-hardened rabble, deprived of good food for months. A group of us settled in at a long table with CB's on the opposite side and we were busy eating, with not much time for chatter. One of the CB's says "Pass the salt," (even condiments were on the table!) "this crap tastes like shit, gotta cover it with something."

Well, that was the wrong thing to say. Before he got the shaker, I stood up quick enough to shove the chair five feet away to the wall behind and looked at the guy. He returned a bitter look, like he's going to jump bad on me, and the other guys near me start getting up too.

I said "Look, you f—ing REMF (Rear Echelon Mother

F——r), we've eaten C-rats for six months straight. You say anything bad about this food, and you're going to find your portion pounded up your ass!"

I think he got the point. Looking quite sober by then, he mumbled, "Well, maybe it's not so bad after all."

Don't mess with the Medic!

That first night, as I lay on the bunk, my thoughts went back to the LZ I wondered if that sniper had been working his way into position as Dan and I were like sitting ducks out on that tree.

We all needed haircuts badly, and there were several barber shops on the post. I found one in the confines of the R&R area, between some of the buildings, nestled in the palm trees. Wood sidewalks led through the sand to most places, and one led to this small round Tiki hut made of poles, wood, thatch roof and woven reed walls. It was open air for about 4 feet up and just big enough for an old-time barber chair to do a 360 degree spin.

A little old Vietnamese man was the barber. Dressed in regular civilian clothing, he spoke a fair amount of English. With the small bits of Vietnamese I knew, French slang and hand gestures, we carried on a quite nice conversation. He lived on the island, had a family that he supported, and was happy that the Americans were there (this guy truly understood free enterprise). He gave me a buzz cut, then used a razor to make a very neat line around my ears and neck. He did a thorough job of cleaning up the shaving cream and applied aftershave. He then pulled out a tiny set of tools, doused them with alcohol and told me he was going to clean my ears.

"Oh—uh—okay," I said, and he spent all of five minutes gently scraping my ear canals.

Boy that was weird, but it felt great. Then he proceeded to massage my neck, shoulders and upper arms and concluded it by placing his hands together tightly, spreading his fingers out in a fan and with a chopping motion begun striking my neck and shoulders at high speed. Each strike was only millimeters apart, and when his little finger struck all the others fingers would subsequently snap down against the next in succession, creating a ratchet sound. He worked each arm to the wrist and back again several times. Then, he removed the cape, folded it, made a polite bow and said, "Two dollars."

He received a substantial tip along with his fee, and I headed back down the boardwalk with a slight stagger, maybe a little drool from the corner of my mouth and a dreamy smile on my face.

I learned a lesson in marketing that day, and again, that the Oriental culture was quite different, mostly good.

Viewing the ocean and swimming in it were new experiences for me. I could see it when I arrived at Cam Rahn Bay, and of course, flying over it at 30,000 feet, but now I could touch it. The creatures that washed up on shore and that dug their way out of the sand at night were much more interesting than anything on the shore of Lake Michigan.

The author at Culco Beach.

Jimmy Green and Dan Wakefield cleaning their M-16's at Culco Beach.

    This place was beautiful and peaceful, the sea shore was open in either direction, and the civilians had their fishing fleet of what looked like very old wood sampans and junks pulled far up on the beach at high tide. It looked like art work, mixed with palms and white sand. It was a great time to write letters home. Several days passed and reality kicked back in.

    We went through our gear, cleaning, trashing out, refreshing, finding ways of harnessing things higher and tighter on our ruck frames.

    Every man took these opportunities to thoroughly clean his weapon to it finest, the LSA (Lubricant, Small Arms) gun oil flowed by the case. Every clip was emptied, cleaned and reloaded, primer cord was unrolled, straightened, rerolled and packed away carefully, ready for the next time to set a claymore mine.

    It may have been day two that I purchased a cheap bottle of Vietnamese rice whiskey. I couldn't read the label, but it had a full picture of a tiger on it. The REMF that I bought it from said every one calls the stuff tiger piss and to go easy with it. The contents were clear for the most part, but had tiny bits of white stuff floating around in it that looked like bits of rice. Well, throw caution to the wind, I shared the bottle with three or four other guys. Before the night was over, we were all drunken slobs puking all over the nice white sand and hung over bad the next day.

This in-country R&R was a good thing, and I still remember it that way. But we knew all along that this was not our job, and we would be returning to the real thing soon. The nighttime chatter would include, "What's up with D-Company?"

"I heard A-Company hit the shit today."

"Poor bastards, I hope they can come here next."

Like the others, I went through my gear with a fine tooth comb. When you do not know if you will be out in the bush for five days or five weeks, you need to be certain you are carrying the things you need and nothing you do not need.

Irvin (Moose) McCoun, Human Flame Thrower. Culco Beach, late 1968.

Our equipment provided us with many places to carry things. My jungle fatigues had ten usable pockets alone, and I used most of them on a regular basic. The pants had six, the big thigh pockets worked well for reading material, especially comic books. People back home sent lots of comic books in their care packages, unfortunately, most of them were "to be continued" issues, and we didn't have a fart in the wind chance of getting the next issues.

In the left front pocket was my nail clipper and a pocket knife (pen knife) that I had to smuggle into the country (does that make sense?). The right front carried my Zippo lighter, car keys (not), and a P-38 (can opener), but the rear pants pockets were mostly useless to me except for a comb.

The jungle fatigue shirt had four pockets. My wallet and a little black book full of addresses, both wrapped up inside two separate plastic bags to keep them dry, were lodged in the left breast pocket over my heart (hoping it would be bullet resistant). That pocket also held a sawed off toothbrush, made to fit inside the pocket with the flap buttoned down.

The right breast pocket held cigarettes for daily consumption and candy bars (lifer bars) that came in some of the C-rats (we will talk about C-rations later). I could also fit a pen, a pencil and a vial of iodine.

The bottom front of the shirt had large button down pockets on each side, and I kept one or two clips of M-16 ammunition in each one. As a medic, three to five clips at the ready, proved to be enough ammunition. To keep the metal clips from making unnecessary noise, I kept lots of TP (toilet paper) poked between them.

So, at any one given time, I could smoke a cigarette, start something on fire, light a heat tablet, manicure my nails, gut out a critter, cut clothing away from a wounded man and give him a tracheotomy, or whittle a stick as a center post for a poncho hooch. I could entertain myself with reading material, write letters to my friends and family, perform oral hygiene, identify myself, purchase things, have a snack, load a M-16, blow my nose, make a land leach do a break dance, comb my hair (what little there was) or wipe my butt—all without adding any extra gear.

The entire ensemble, including jungle boots and socks, also

served as my pajamas every night while in the field. Even on some Firebases it was advisable to keep your boots on. The exception for night wear was the steel pot (but not always).

The fun was over. We were headed back to the field, and the old timers were complaining that the monsoon season was coming up fast.

"What's a monsoon season?" I thought.

12.
Mountains and Monsoons

It was about the end of February when we made our next assault into the highlands, near the well-used supply trail we had found two weeks earlier. Our sister companies were deployed into the area as well. The AO was probably divided up in sections with single or multiple companies working an area together.

This was high country, rough, rugged rain forest you could not call hills anymore. They may not be mountains, but they were at least junior mountains, at 2,000 to 2,500 feet above sea level.

On the peaks and high ridges of some of the mountains we were on, the air was decidedly cooler, the canopy thinner and no mosquitoes, flies, centipedes or land leeches. There was a different species of spider roaming around up there that looked like a granddaddy long leg. In Michigan their bodies were about the size of a dry pea with a leg span of two or three inches. Here, their bodies were about the size of an acorn, with a leg span of six to eight inches. They seemed to be blind and harmless.

We rarely found evidence of the enemy in these high places, but they apparently needed to be checked out regardless. However, in the lower hills, ridges and valleys we were finding plenty of evidence. This happened to be quite close to the Laotian border, and at times we were patrolling directly on the border. Several days into the mission, a sister company, just a few clicks from us, found an active NVA base camp the hard way, and casualties were taken.

They called in air strikes, artillery and gun ships into the area, and we made our way to rendezvous with them. When we arrived they were just starting to clear the bunkers, and we joined in on the process. You cover each other while approaching a bunker, get beside the opening, pull the pin on a grenade, take one split second look to gage the trajectory of your throw, then pitch the grenade. Grenade explosions are really loud when you're that close, but a split second after it goes off, you jump down in the cloud of dust, empty out half a clip of M-16 ammo onto the bunker and jump back out. You stand guard for a while as the dust settles and peek in cautiously with your flash light shining down the side of your M-16.

I had the opportunity to "clear" one of the 12 to 15 bunkers built from jungle materials, dirt and rocks. They were well-built, fairly large, maybe eight feet by ten feet. There is definitely an adrenaline rush in doing this. Ironically, I found and cleared the bunker of a medical area. It was crude, but possibly the NVA medic took off with his primary gear before the area was bombed. I found a few medical pans, glass syringes and vials of medicine that were not broken in the blast.

My prize for the risky work was an old-fashioned, lunch box-sized, heavy canvas medical bag with a heavy shoulder strap and a faded white circle and red cross symbol displayed on the flap. Inside were some medical supplies that were useless to me and several personal items, including a post card from North Vietnam and one piece of paper money with Ho-Chi-Minh's picture on it. I had an idea for the use of the bag and kept it (I still have the post card and paper money).

A short time into the raid, when our sister company cleared

a bunker and the grenade went off, there were cries from inside. They were women's voices! An interpreter coaxed three women out of the bunkers. They wore black silk pants and blouses and sandals made from car tires, as did many Vietnamese, north and south. They had no hats, rings or jewelry, no underwear and no identification.

They were, however, peppered from one end to the other with grenade shrapnel.

The author in the jungle with "catastrophe bag" (found in bunker).

North Vietnamese Currency found in the bag.

I began working on them, patching up the worst wounds and using my iodine vial on as many of the small punctures as possible. We held them in custody until an LZ was created near by. We treated them well while with us, then put them in a H-1, and they were flown back to who knows where in the rear. A great many weapon and equipment caches were found at this site, confiscated and flown to the rear as well.

It was in February that my good friend Robert Butts, from Detroit, Michigan, left B-Co. during one of these helicopter flights, as his one year tour had come to an end. Bob was a black guy, an amazing man that was well liked and respected by everyone. He was also a very good soldier and had already won a Silver Star for his bravery in the taking of Hue in the spring of 1968. Bob exposed himself to enemy fire and then fought them off to protect the men in his squad.

In the summer of 2008, Bob and his wife Audrey, my wife Ann, my daughter Elizabeth and I, met again for the first time since the war at Bob's home near Detroit. It was a wonderful reunion. We met again in Kalamazoo at the 2009 B-Co. reunion and continue to stay in touch.

Robert L. Butts crossing bamboo bridge.

Only a few bodies were found, so most of the occupants of the base had moved into the jungle before the artillery hit. I am quite sure the word went out that we were in the area! We reconned around that spot for several days, running into what the high brass call "light resistance." Light resistance is when the NVA plot our direction of travel through the jungle and find an ambush site on a knoll just ahead of a draw leading into a valley. They wait for the point man and one or two of us to move into range, then try to shoot the point man and maybe one or two others. As soon as their clips are empty, they head down behind the knoll and run down the draw into a valley. You can shoot back all you want, but now there is earth between you and them. If the point man or others are wounded or KIA, the platoon is disabled until the men or the bodies are taken care of.

This was happening to us every few days, and we all became extremely sensitized to gun fire.

Working along a ridge one day, shots were fired from the point position. Before you could hit the dirt, the entire platoon had their weapons on rock-n-roll, chewing up the flanks with M-16 and M-60 fire. Some of the men instinctively dove left or right off the line of travel before opening up with "Recon by Fire." I had turned to the right and had only taken two or three steps off the trail, when a guy behind me also spun to the right, but stayed on the trail, and started firing his weapon, fanning the barrel left and right. Another guy who was 15 feet in front of me, had already moved to the right quickly and realized he was in the path of fire from the guy behind me. He had flipped over on his back and was digging his heels into the dirt, trying to evade the bullets.

Like in a film directed by Sam Peckinpah, I witnessed his left knee come up to make another stroke at the ground, and his fatigue pants popped open at the knee revealing the gnarled white flesh of his knee cap, shattered from a M-16 bullet. You could yell at the top of your lungs, but in a burst of intense fire, no one could hear a damn thing. I leaped back toward the shooter, grabbed his arm and pointed to the wounded man he had just shot.

I was at the side of the wounded man as the blood started flowing, cut his pant leg off and bandaged him up. He had a free pass to America that day, but I kept some of his blood on my pant legs for several weeks to come. I remember well who the shooter was, as well as the tall, skinny, wounded GI named Freaman Tunnell, from Tennessee.

We moved away from that area and continued the hunt. We were following a high ridge trail one day, when it came to an abrupt transition and headed down a steep hill. I believe we were doing recon as a platoon-sized element that day, and we had all been making our way down the steep terrain for a while when the point man came to a dirt pit in the trail.

It looked like animals used it as a wallow after a rain. They must have rooted up a booby trap and exposed it. The point man spotted it, removed it and spent some time working across the twelve-foot spot with a bayonet, hunting for more of the "Toe Popper" explosives. He then foot printed the exact steps to take for a safe trip across. Another man was dispatched up through the line to explain the delay and how to pass safely through the danger zone.

Man after man, crossed the spot carefully and proceeded down hill. When the spot came into view for me, I watched carefully where they were stepping. Booby traps are horrible. Any man who set foot off a military base worried about them.

At the point I was about 12 or 14 feet back (and up) from the pit, and with four men ahead of me, a man who had only been in the field a month or so, started to cross. He suddenly turned to the left, away from the marked path, and begun walking slowly clockwise around the berm of the wallow.

Several of us yelled, "Hey, what are you doing?"

One step, two steps, three steps, "BOOM."

My eyes were fixed on each step he took. When the mine went off, the guy's right leg flew out behind him, bending at the knee and nearly hitting him in the back. He toppled off the side of the berm, and at the same instant some big dude who was standing five feet behind him was knocked backward and fell into the jungle.

Shock held everyone locked in place for a split second as the guy, now on his back holding his leg in the air, reeling back and forth, hollering for help. I jumped down to the edge of the pit and froze there. It occurred to me that three of those poppers had been removed by the point man, this grunt found the fourth, were there more?

Several seconds passed as the big dude had regained conscious and was standing up, shaking himself off and touching his dirt-covered face where a deeply depressed boot print now resided. Then 30 or 40 seconds into the event, Lt. Bohdan Kopystianskyj popped up above the rim of the pit to see what was happening. I learned a lot about bravery that day. While I was looking for an alternate route around to the wounded man, Bohdan climbed into the pit, walked over to the guy, scooped him up in his arms and carried him 20 feet away into the jungle.

I was ashamed of myself for hesitating after seeing what our platoon leader did, but there was no time to pout about it then. I had a good look at his leg by then and was planning my approach to patch up his injury. When Lt. Bohdan laid him down, my pack was off, opened up, and I was digging out items I might need. I grabbed a towel first and covered his foot so he could not see it. I started calling him by name—Lee Shapanka—and repeating, "Dude, you are going back to the world, you lucky dog."

It was fairly easy to die doing what grunts do there, and this was like a million dollar wound.

I knew his foot was gone by the time Lt. Bohdan picked him up (pack and all). It was held on to his upper ankle by two tendons that come down from the lower shin and out to the top of the arch. There are many small bones that make up the heel and ankle, and they were all missing, including the skin around them. The middle of the foot forward was intact as if nothing had happened. I wanted badly to sever the cords and make it easier to bandage the stump, but his morale was bad enough already. I was hoping that seeing his foot was as good as believing it could still be reattached. I hope the philosophy worked, and I can meet him again one day to talk about it.

I compressed and ace bandaged the wound tight enough to stop all bleeding, but not before it soaked my same blood-stained pants once again. I ace bandaged the towel in place as the Medevac approached. We moved him to a small clearing several hundred feet away, where a jungle penetrator could extract him out.

The mission immediately continued. The event was like a blip on the TV screen, except for several of us who were left cleaning off the dirt, bits of clothing, boot and human flesh that had been splattered on us from head to toe from the explosion. The side of the big dude's face was beginning to look normal again from the blast that sent the wounded man's boot directly into the big guy's face (the bruises lasted several days). We resumed our descent down the trail. (I discovered at our 2011 B-Co. reunion in Branson, Missouri, that this incident actually occurred in late March 1969.)

Rain was becoming more and more persistent. You learn to be wet 24/7. We found that if you removed your towel from around your neck, you could flip it over your shoulders and pack, with the edge just behind your helmet, and let it soak up the rain for a while. In time, you removed it as you passed by a sapling, flung one end around the sapling, caught the ends butt to butt and wound it up like a mop, squeezing the water out. You could do this in a matter of seconds and have the towel back in position.

This did not keep you dry by any means, but it did keep you

from being totally saturated. The only part of your body guaranteed to stay dry was your head, as those steel pots just did not leak. If you wanted to keep something dry, you put it above the webbing of your helmet. I always kept a pocket-sized (Short-Timers) calendar and a small note pad tucked in behind the webbing. Funny thing about helmets, when you wear one for 10 to 15 hours every day for six or seven months, it's like an old friend. It felt good to take it off at night, but if it were put into a pile of helmets, I think I could have found it on a dark night, just by the way it felt on my head.

Wakefield and the author in a foxhole.

The more time we spent wet, the more health problems occurred. Jungle rot would start from a tiny scratch and spread. Some men were more susceptible than others, and I needed to make rounds every night to change dressings on them. Daily, I would stress to everyone, "Use the iodine vial often!" But the rain diluted the iodine quickly.

Foot problems increased, and there was almost nothing that could help. I kept an extra pair of socks tied to the outside of my rucksack, and if the time and place allowed, I wrung them out dry as possible and made a change. I encouraged all the men to practice this and many did. If nothing else, it felt good.

The author in the jungle with Aid Bag open.

    C–rations are designed to provide a fairly balanced diet, and I believe there were additives in them for extra vitamins and minerals. We rarely had fresh fruit or vegetables when on maneuvers. As I mentioned before, we might be out in the field for three weeks at a stretch. Once, the mission lasted over five weeks.

    Whether it was weather conditions, C-rats, lack of fruit and vegetables or all of the above, boils were another problem. Some men would have a new one coming on just when the last one was going away. I acquired one just above my right hip and in perfect alignment with the bottom support web of my rucksack. It can take up to two weeks for a boil to go full circle and begin to heal. They are extremely sore and painful, worse yet if you touch them. I had a constant reminder that it was there during the day, as my ruck support rubbed it constantly. Boils are basically untreatable until they become "ripe." I developed an eye for knowing exactly when to pop them. Then the hideous pain starts when I must squeeze them intently to remove everything from the core and then pack the core with a strip of gauze and a healing concoction. A day later, I removed the packing, dressed the spot again and hoped jungle rot did not set in.

One of the guys, Ed Wick, a good soldier and a good point man, was complaining of a boil. In checking it out, I found it to be in the early stages and in a fairly tender spot. It was his first boil, and I explained that they take time to form a head and it would become much more painful as it did. Ed came by nearly every night with the, "Is it ready yet?"

I'd give it a quick check and say, "Nope."

About a week later he repeated the scenario and, "Oh yes—it's ready!"

Ed was suffering with the thing, you could see it in his eyes. I instructed him to return in ten minutes and we would take care of it. Ed was just as tough as any man there (except maybe "Moose" McCoun), but for whatever reason I feared he might not follow through with the treatment because of the location of the boil. So, in his absence I prepared everything and instructed three guys to stay close so when I had him prepped and in position, they were to hold him down until it was over.

Ed was surprised when the guys politely grabbed him and held him down, but he did not protest when I began the process of cleaning out his boil. At our 2007 B-Company reunion he questioned why I had him held down? It was a memorable event for each of us, I guess, but I didn't have a good answer for him.

Every possible aspect of carrying out a war like this was just one more thing to add to the misery of the job and your day-to-day life. GI's are tough, however, and can always find a way to laugh about it before the day is done.

Unknown in front, Al Kontrabecki in rear.

The rain stopped for a while one day as we were patrolling on the Laotian border. I'm not sure whose idea it was, but we took a turn down a mountain stream and headed into the country of Laos. I don't know why, but we all felt more scared than being on Vietnamese soil. What's with that? Nothing worse could happen to us there with the exception of no air support.

We plodded three or four klicks in, turned around at an area where the trees thinned out (looked like ambush country) and headed back. It was an uneventful day.

On one of these later missions, we were working our way up a valley, and found a place almost breathtakingly beautiful. We reconned along a small tumbling stream working its way down a mountain pass in a hot steamy jungle with large roots twisting around rocks in the bed of the stream and growing off to the side where they sprouted into huge ferns. You just can't recreate a botanical system to match the sight of some of those places.

We came to a spot in the pass when the ground leveled out a bit, and a small ridge became part of the landscape. An active trail crossed the stream there, so the platoons split up, one leading out to follow the trail and the other following the stream. Our platoon stayed at the point of intersection until the recon was complete.

Twenty or thirty minutes passed when all hell broke loose somewhere up the creek. The captain got on the Pric-25, and the radio traffic was bouncing back and forth fast. It seemed that both platoons had hit an ambush at exactly the same time. The captain realized quickly the impossibility of the situation and screamed into the radio, "Cease fire, cease fire!"

All the gunfire stopped at once. The commander's instinct was correct, the two platoons were shooting at each other.

The trail followed a ridge, thirty to forty feet above the bed of the creek. It led away from the creek at first, but gradually reconnected to the area further down stream. The men did not realize it. The point men reacted immediately upon seeing movement and begun spraying their respective targets with automatic fire. These men were so sensitized to the possibility of ambush that in the twinkling of an eye, half of each platoon was pumping lead in all directions.

I think that the difference in altitude of the two platoons must have saved lives that day, but the initial fire took the life of a man that everyone called "Gap" and ruined the ankle of another man named Bob Tenny. Gap, was a big man, six-foot-two or more. A broad-shouldered country boy with a freckled face and blondish red hair. He was a quiet guy normally, but had an extraordinary gift for dry humor and one-liners. You just had to like the man.

Please think about this. We all were miserable, were not home, not with our girlfriends, were fighting a war, fighting the elements and bugs, with lack of showers, ringworm on our crotch, jungle rot in three places on our legs. We've been soaking wet for the last two weeks and scared to death for eight months. We truly were miserable.

It's hard enough to lose a friend or comrade to enemy action. You should feel what it's like and see what it does for morale when it happens from "friendly fire."

What really bakes your noodle, however, is all of that is nothing compared to the burden laid out on the mind of the man who pulled the trigger first. He was doing his job at point, as professionally and carefully as a man can. He is sensitized to a razor edge, sees, perceives, and knows the threat of the enemy. He responds with force, exactly as he should, then learns he has killed one of his friends.

What level of misery should that be listed under? For this man or men, could not just go home that day and cry in their beer or be consoled by their loved ones. But their duty never ceased, even for a minute. The sound of gunfire could alert the enemy of our whereabouts, and they could be laying in wait, only a hundred yards away.

Thirty-three years later, the "Moving Wall," a scaled down replica of the Vietnam National Monument, came to our VFW Post in Decatur, Michigan. I looked up as many names as I could remember, but ran into a problem when it came to "Gap."

I had no clue what his real name actually was.

Many men developed nicknames, either for themselves or by the men around them. There was Snake, Skinny, Red Leg, Moose, Tiny, Gap. They called me and all the other medics "Doc."

That went away when I returned home, but since my first reunion in 2003, the guys still say "Hey Doc." It gives me a deep feeling of brotherhood to hear it from them again.

I went to the manager of the traveling wall and explained my problem. He was called "Gap," I explained, because he came from Pleasant Gap, Pennsylvania. The data base for the men and women on the wall is fairly extensive. He sorted the data base on Pennsylvania, then Pleasant Gap. It turned out that the town is small and there was only one man from the town who was KIA. His name was Dale Fisher.

Dale Charles "Gap" Fisher, (KIA).

Back at the site on that ridge, the dead and wounded were dealt with as quickly as possible, and our mission continued. The CP was getting reports of a typhoon heading onto land from the South China Sea, and that it could have an effect on us within 30 – 48 hours. We would have been ready for LOG by then and headed for lower ground and a good LZ. It may have been on this mission that we came across a rather unconventional way to make the travel a little easier—an elephant trail. We could hear monkeys, we could see tiger's tracks and now the rumor of wild elephants roaming Vietnam became true. The animals were rarely seen, but this thing was doing us a favor. Elephants can plow a clean path through the most dense jungle foliage. Just watch what you are stepping on along the way.

We found the brush covered knoll that was picked out for

our extraction point, but it was too late. The torrential rains were already upon us, and chopper travel was impossible. We formed a defensive position around this knoll and tried to dig in. There was a lot of exposed earth, and it was already turning to mud.

Typically, two men constructed a hooch together. One used his poncho for a roof and the other for the floor. A branch was bent over and tied to the center of the roof poncho and cords run out from the four corners and tied off tight. The roof was usually set at about twelve inches from the ground to keep most of the weather from getting under. Our gear and weapons were stashed underneath, if at all possible. Then we'd roll up in a lightweight poncho liner, with our GI towel as a pillow and tried to sleep.

This hill was different. There was not much to tie a poncho off to, the wind was already at 25 to 30 knots and it was raining like holy heck. A conventional hooch just didn't work for anyone. I ended up somewhere in the middle of the knoll near a small thicket, struggling for hours, as we all were, trying to get a shelter built. It took several alterations and damage control over the next twenty hours or so to end up with a sturdy, nearly dry, place to stay.

My shelter took on a shape like an old-fashioned pup tent, with a ridge at the center and two sides sloping directly to the ground. My rucksack and gear were stuffed in at one end, while I could crawl in and out from the other. I put my soaking wet poncho across the rucksack, stuffed about half of it into my helmet, put my butt on the padded helmet, laid back onto my ruck, almost as if I were wearing it, with my towel for a pillow. I pulled the poncho liner across from the left and right. My legs were uncovered and my feet were near the open end of the shelter, my face and body only being a few inches away from the peak of the shelter. It was too low to the ground to sit up in, but finally, I was out of the rain.

That storm lasted for three full days. Me and all the others were lodged in these unusual positions for the entire time. Some had their shelters wrecked multiple times when the winds began to reach fifty to sixty knots late in the second day.

Strangely enough your body heat will eventually dry out all your clothing and even the poncho. If the storm calmed for a short while, we crawled out and dashed to the other hoochs to find something else to read. Cooking was impossible, so cold C-rats were the only thing on the menu. No one wanted to eat too much or drink too much water because it would result in leaving a raunchy but dry space to be drenched again while relieving yourself.

Typical jungle hooches from ponchos.

Food was getting very low by day three, and the miserable boredom and cramps from being in the position for so long was taking its toll.

Then, like flipping a switch, the rain slowed, then stopped, then came sunny skies. There was enough time remaining in the day to form our evacuation, and we were extracted and dropped onto Firebase Birmingham. The monsoon rain continued, but the storm had passed, and having good solid sandbag bunkers to live in was a true luxury for the next several days.

13.
Firebases

Boyd, Bastogne, Birmingham, and Vehgil, as I mentioned earlier, were fire support bases that we returned to several times each during my tour. The bases were connected by the same road, #547, running west from the south side of Hue City, passing Camp Eagle, crossing the Pohl Bridge and out toward the A Shau.

Over the years, my memory has blended them together along with events that occurred on each of them. Some had other purposes besides fire support and seemed to have something to do with road construction and engineers. They were medium-sized bases that took two or more companies to maintain full perimeter guard. One had mining equipment for gravel, a rock crusher and huge dump trucks. Another had a river at the base that was being dredged for washed gravel.

The enemy had been pushed out almost completely, and the bases were fairly safe. Mine sweepers cleared the road early every morning, and everyone could come and go as needed. On one occasion, me and the other two B-Co. medics took residence in the Birmingham aid station where a doctor was on duty full time. Captain "Doc" Cook was a great guy and a good doctor, and we enjoyed the experience of working with him while there.

The aid station was a military tent on a wood floor and

fairly well equipped. The front half was the aid station workroom. The back half was fortified with sand bags. It had canvas cots and some furniture and was a great place to write letters home. The aid station was beside an embankment that went up about 15 feet to a plateau where a battery of 155 howitzers sat. At the back side of the station, a three-sided, clap-board shower stall was framed up to hold an Australian canvas shower bucket. We would fill 5-gallon water cans, climb up the bank to a board that crossed over to the top of our bunker and set the cans on top of the bunker during the day to warm up. If it was sunny weather, the water was perfect for a shower.

Shots fired! Dave Kissell, far right and Bill Matelski, receiving shots.

Returning after the typhoon and weeks in the jungle was a great relief. It was so nice to change clothing and get rid of the fatigue pants that remained bloodstained from the mission. It was also time to go completely through my gear, and it was a good thing I did. The first thing I found was a small colony of sugar ants taking up residence in the food storage area. Apparently, during the three days storm it was jammed into the dirt, and they migrated in. The second problem was the back pack aid-bag, which was quite water-resistant but not waterproof. It had leaked, and most of the compresses, gauze and ace bandages, and anything that had a breach in the packaging, were contaminated with water and starting to mildew.

The author in the shower behind the Aid Station at Firebase Birmingham.

I removed everything from the ruck frame, cleaned and dried it, then made arrangements for a jeep ride to Camp Sally for a complete replacement of all the med supplies. I added one additional task for the trip, to design the medical contents for what I called the "Catastrophe" bag. I would use the NVA medic's bag I gleaned from their bunker for light recons and ambushes the remainder of my field duty.

The round trip was great. I rode with a driver who was dispatched for another purpose. We wore helmets, packed our M-16's and made the one-hour cruise safely to Sally. We headed out at about 0800 hours, and the old dirt road we traveled on months earlier was now a highly improved gravel road. Passing over Pohl Bridge, it wasn't long before we were in the rice paddies on the way to Highway One. It was early spring and time to begin filling the paddies with water for the next rice crop. We passed a woman standing in the canal along the road, scooping water from the canal and throwing it over the bank into a paddy. The scoop was made of bamboo, about five inches in diameter and four feet long. A good handle was fastened at the mid-section and at the opposite end from the tapered scoop. She swung her arms back and forth like a clock pendulum. As she swung to the top of the arch, the water would fly out from the tube, over the bank and into the paddy. The back stroke would extend the scoop far enough above the water to build momentum before making the next scoop and subsequent toss.

We reached Highway One, and to my surprise, it was paved, striped between the two lanes and with wide gravel shoulders on each side. The traffic was like a major highway with mini-buses loaded with people and cargo so heavy the tires should pop. As we traveled through the city, the improvements were quite noticeable. The people seemed quite happy, were very busy and commerce was flourishing. GI's were walking down the streets, unarmed, but MP's could be seen quite often.

It was nice to be back at Camp Sally, which had a church with a spire for the chaplains now, a large mess hall with a concrete floor and totally wood frame barracks. We did our work, took advantage of the good food and headed back to Birmingham. But before leaving, I checked the supply hooch for a boonie hat, and still none were available. I enjoyed the sights on the return trip. Highway One from Sally to Hue was gravel highway, but had huge improvements, with bridges and better side roads improved as well.

Just south of Hue, as we turned off Highway One and onto the road heading west back to the Firebases, there was an old steel trestle bridge at least a quarter mile across. It was only one lane wide for vehicles, and we needed to have the flagman signal to cross over. However, there was enough room to allow walkers, small carts and bicycles to cross at the same time. We were about halfway across the bridge, when I spotted an ARVN soldier on a bicycle heading toward us on the passenger side of the jeep. As he was about to pass, I noticed that he had a very nice American-made boonie hat. I don't know what made me do it, but my arm just popped out, and I snatched it off his head. We were rolling along at about 30 mph. By the time I turned around to look, he had stopped the bike, climbed off and was jumping up and down hollering out something I didn't understand—but could pretty well figure out what it meant!

As we traveled on, I inspected my prize and found it had been customized by trimming about one inch away from the perimeter with the bead neatly sewed back on. It fit quite nicely, as well, and I have it to this day.

As we were passing back through the rice paddies late in the afternoon, the woman "water pump" was still standing in the same place in the canal, her pendulum motion still at the same rate, and the paddy was nearly filled with water. I tell you, again, the culture there is much different than the U.S.

As you can tell by now, life with a hardcore infantry unit, especially one with a reputation to uphold, can be very dangerous, very demanding and, most of the time, miserable duty. For us, being placed on perimeter detail on some Firebase was good duty, but even then, supporting a war had its hazards.

Birmingham was large for a fire support base. It had one or two pieces of track armor for defense, and one was a twin 40. It had two landing pads, with a cobra stationed permanently, ready for missions, on one.

There were enough people to keep the aid station active a fair amount of the time, with bumps, bruises, rashes, plugged ears or ingrown toenails. On one occasion, I was assigned to prepare and administer a penicillin injection for a permanent party guy who managed to acquire a venereal disease in a nearby village. I showed little mercy with a large needle injection in the right rear cheek.

The author with Cobra Gunship, Firebase Birmingham.

The author with Track Twin 40mm at Firebase Boyd.

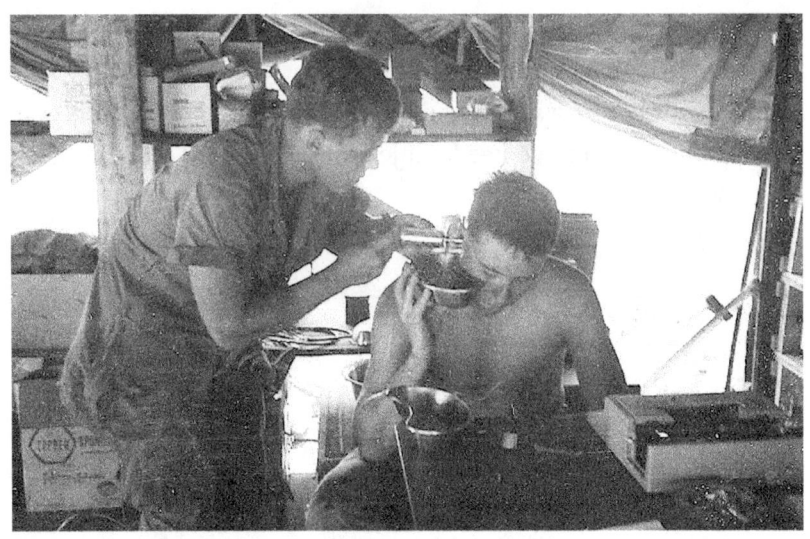

Ear cleaning at Aid Station on Firebase Boyd.

Once, an artillery man came in complaining of trouble with his ears. Doc Cook took a quick look, laughed, and said, "You got a little build-up there fella, going to need to get it out."

Captain Cook, me and one other medic spent a solid hour injecting soapy water into the guy's ears with a syringe about the size of a grease gun to get the wax plugs out. The guy had coke bottle glasses that were so filthy you could hardly see his eyes. While the others were working on his ears, I spent all of thirty minutes getting his glasses clean. I used a few harsh chemicals to do it, but by golly they were clean, and he walked out of the aid station with two of his major senses working again. Dr. Cook also sent him off with a few instructions regarding personal hygiene.

One day we heard a ruckus develop outside and stepped out to see some GI walking slowly toward the aid station. Two or three of his buddies were at his side, several feet away, shouting, "This guy needs help!"

As we got closer, we saw blood coming from his right hand and quickly ushered him inside.

"Oh crap—!"

The guy was missing three fingers on his right hand.

"What the hell happened?" we asked.

"Blasting cap," he squealed.

Doc Cook and the other medics began cleaning him up as I headed out at a dead sprint to see if I could recover any good parts of his hand. It was mid-day, with plenty of light in his bunker, but I could not find one piece large enough to sew back on his hand.

Back at the aid station the doctor had already administered a dose of morphine, and the guy was relaxing. He was a grunt from a sister company that was guarding the western portion of the perimeter. Like all of us, he was going through his gear, cleaning and re-packing. He said he was unrolling his claymore blasting caps and wires (both connected together), straightening out and re-rolling the wires, which were about 30 inches long, by holding the blasting cap in one hand and pulling the wires briskly through the other to remove the kinks. He had the wire pinched tight with his thumb and first finger (which survived) with the blasting cap sticking out the back side of his fist.

Apparently, the stroking action of the wires created enough static electricity to detonate the blasting cap. Word of his experience handling the caps spread far and wide among the troops. A six-by-six truck was summoned, and we loaded him into the back. He was taken to the field hospital at Camp Eagle and probably went back to the real world after that. I wonder where he is today?

Earlier, I mentioned the aid station was just below a battery of 155 howitzers. I had a great chance to watch these men manning the guns do their stuff. Everything about these bigger guns, the weight of the projectile, measurements of powder, gradations of the windage and elevation mechanisms, was designed and built with extreme precision. The crews were very well-trained. When a potential target is surveyed, a projectile can be shot to a given coordinate and the round will burst within a few feet of the target, up to 20 miles away. The rounds for the bigger guns are assembled each time with a prescribed quantity of gun powder relative to the distance they intend to shoot. Often a round is fired first which is rigged to burst in the air directly over an intended target. Then an FO (Forward Observer) can determine the accuracy of his coordinates relative to his map. He can determine it by seeing the white cloud from the explosion or by the direction and distance of the sound of the explosion.

If an FO is satisfied with the intended target, he will usually have one live round shot to the target. If that one is good, he can direct subsequent fire any direction he wants from the original site. When the FO orders fire for effect, the fire team may have two or three guns positioned at the same intended target.

Like ants, the team starts loading rounds, carrying them to the gun breeches, firing, opening up new canisters and pitching spent brass into a pile. They will work this regimen for five to 20 rounds, depending on what the field FO wants. This would happen during the day or at night, if a field unit had reason to think that the enemy was trying to breach their perimeter. The FO would call for a round to hit some distance from their NDP, then "walk" the next round closer to the perimeter, readjusting the coordinates so the rounds explode as close to his perimeter as possible.

We used this technique on many occasions. We needed to have extreme faith that the FO knew what he was doing as well as the men manning the gun battery. Just one extra click of windage on a howitzer, and the next round could be in our lap. Accidents have happened like this in all wars, so we just hug the ground and pray that it is not this time.

Another problem occurred while in the jungle. If a round made a direct hit into the trunk of a big tree, it would explode high in the air, sending shrapnel everywhere and causing the explosion to be louder yet.

Battery of howitzers above the Aid Station on Firebase Boyd.

For field troops, in the jungle 80 to 90 percent of the time, nighttime was typically very quiet. Being in the aid station when a howitzer went off at 0100 hours in the morning would shock the bejesus right out of you. The noise was not as bad as the shock wave, which could nearly compress the air out of your lungs.

Down the south side of the small mountain that Birmingham lay on, a substantial river wound its way out of the highlands and to the coast. It was about a half mile drive down to the river, and if the weather was nice, guys from the camp would make the trek down to the water on mules, jeeps or six-by-six trucks to take a dip in the evening.

The river at its normal depth was about three to four feet deep, at least 100 feet across and there would be thirty or forty naked GI's coming, going or submerged in the water at any one time. The engineers had been at work there, dredging a deposit of some special gravel from the bed of the river, and there were various spots in the bed that suddenly got very deep. We would work our way out along the edge of these dredge pits so only our heads were out of the water, then just stand there as the current brought copious amounts of cool water past our bodies.

The author at the river below Firebase Boyd.

One evening, me, another field medic and Captain Cook were doing exactly that, chilling in the river and talking about the day's work. Dr. Cook saw some guy moving downstream with the current and fixed his gaze on him for a moment. The conversation stopped, we looked at what he was looking at, and the captain said, "That guy looks like he is drowning."

So, now, all three of us are watching him closely. I don't know how big that dredge hole was, but that guy was out in it. I doubt that ten seconds passed from the time the captain spoke until I realized that the guy was truly drowning!

The man was twenty-five feet away and drifting fast. I dove out into the pit, and being a good swimmer, I reached him in a matter of seconds. They say a drowning person will try to climb on top of you, taking you down with them, but this guy was completely out of gas. I grabbed him under his left arm and around his neck and begun swimming back toward the two others. The guy was limp as a noodle. As I kicked my feet and pulled at the water with my right arm, I realized that the current had already moved us another fifteen feet downstream from where I made the interception. At this stage of my life, I was no slouch, and I put my strength against the river.

Slowly, the distance between me and the guys was closing, and I kept up the pace until I was about six or eight feet from them. I was completely exhausted and knew I could not close the gap dragging him along. So I took a breath and yelled at the two men, "Grab him!"

As I pulled him around in front of me and pushed him toward them with all the strength I had left.

Well, where there is an action there is an equal and opposite reaction. I was back out in the pit, very close to the condition of the guy I just pulled in. I had both arms free now, but my pace was barely faster than the current. I kept stabbing my foot down toward the bottom, searching for dirt, and finally got a toe hold on the gravel bed. My comrades had pulled the man in and were supporting him as he coughed the water out of his lungs.

It took me a while to recuperate as my chest heaved out of my control. I think the two of us may have revived at about the same time, as the three of us began scolding the man about going into the deep water if he could not swim. The victim made his way back upstream, and we went back to the conversation we were having prior to the interruption.

It's lights out at dusk on the Firebases, and since Vietnam is fairly close to the equator, that made night and day close to 12 hours each. Days in Vietnam were slightly longer, but it still made for very long nights.

In the dark of the aid station that night, the three of us sat around chatting about the events of the day.

Dr. Cook said, "Flory."

"Yeah," I answered.

"You know, you saved that guy today."

The other medic chimed in and said, "You sure as hell did."

I said, "Huh, I guess you're right, I never thought about it that way."

Deep in my mind I was haunted by another thought. I was a very good swimmer, I was in very good condition, and I was fully aware of my physical limits. I also knew that if five more seconds had been required to push that man to the others, or if my foot had not touched bottom on that last try, it would be unlikely that I would be writing this. I do hope the man that nearly drowned reads this one day and contacts me.

Birmingham was a small mountain, and the FB was on an irregular top which caused the engineers to create several levels with as much as ten to twenty feet from one to the next. It was on a sunny morning, when, once again, men came screaming to the aid station. Dr. Cook was not on the base, so the other medic manned the tent while I ran back with the frantic men. I kept pace with them for about two hundred yards to an embankment that dropped down about 20 feet at the bottom. The problem soon became clear; a group of men were gathered around a bunker that had just been flattened by a deuce-and-a-half.

Two men who seemed to be in charge were clawing at the sand bags and boards in an attempt to dig out one of their comrades they knew was inside.

At least two minutes had already passed by my arrival. Everyone joined the two men and tried to untangle the pile. But from things I learned from my father, the type of work I was accustomed to back home and a dose of reality, there was no way of freeing the man within his remaining two minutes. There was a two-and-a-half ton truck on top of the flattened bunker, and if that truck was not moved quickly we would never get him out in time.

I was concerned for his oxygen supply first, but God only knew what other problems he may have, and I began screaming, "Fire up this truck and drive it off this bunker."

I was abruptly hushed by the other men, because moving the truck might further injure the man buried underneath. At this point, all the material that could be removed had been removed. All remaining lumber, and whatever else, was pinned down by the tires of the vehicle. Someone decided to try and lift the truck off the bunker with a helicopter and proceeded to make it happen.

We were at the four minute mark, and I knew what that meant for sustaining life. I was looking at a deuce-and-a-half with a net vehicle weight over six tons. It's on top of a bunker laid as flat as you could possibly make it. I am sick in the gut, because I know this man is lost.

It took another ten or twelve minutes to assemble the snatch straps to the truck, as we continued desperately to pry debris out of the way to get to the man. Eventually someone spotted a bit of clothing through a gap in the boards, and I quickly put my arm into the opening to see if I could tell anything about the victim, but the only feedback I got was that he was still warm.

The H-1 chopper arrived and hovered over the truck as one man stood on top, fighting the rotor wash and flying dirt, to make the hook up. The rest of us moved back to a safe distance. Reality kicked in again. This was like watching someone trying to pull a Cadillac out of a snow bank with a shopping cart. The pilot made several attempts to move the truck, but could barely make it wiggle. So it was unhooked and it flew off.

Finally, a driver climbed in the cab, started the truck and drove it off. Within several minutes, we dug our way down to the man. As his body was revealed, it became obvious that he died quickly. His brothers mourned him as we removed his body from the rubble.

There was a row of deuce-and-a-halves backed up to the edge of the upper level. Whether the earth gave way, allowing the truck to roll backward down the bank, or a driver failed to set the parking brake, no one knows. But, if it were the latter, the driver would have known that it was his truck. May our good Lord be with him if it was, because he will be bearing that burden yet today.

We were on FB Boyd one time when an entourage of jeeps pulled in through the gate. All the vehicles came to a stop, as a blond "round eye" (American or Caucasian girl) climbed out of the jeep, along with an aid or two, and began talking to GI's as she moved along.

Okay, the curiosity was too much, and I joined the group. We all noticed the long blond hair and the distinct look of an American woman. Soon enough, I had my turn to say "Hello!" as she handed out photos of herself and autographed them for whoever wanted one.

"Oh Baby—it's Chris Noel!"

Chris Noel arriving with troops.

Signed photo of Chris Noel carried by the author and safely brought home.

    The rather famous (in Vietnam) and welcome voice as a DJ (Disk Jockey/radio announcer) on the armed forces radio station. We couldn't help but recognize her voice, but no one knew what she looked like. Well, let me tell you, she was downright cute!

    She hung around the FB for 30 minutes or so then headed on to the next base. But she was a great diversion for us that day.

    I have no idea how I managed to preserve her photo through the months to come but I did, and brought it home with me. Thank you Chris Noel for making our day.

Chris Noel.

    On the subject of photos, I can tell you that it was extremely hard for "packs" to carry a camera. If you were willing to bear the extra weight and forego the space, the next task was to try to keep it clean and dry. I carried two instamatic cameras during my time in the field. One was crushed and one could not swim, even though I kept it inside two poly bags.

    So, if you have a camera and it is in working order, where are you going to purchase film? During my first ten months in-country, I had only two opportunities to purchase film at the Sally PX. The same went for all of our guys. We all wrote home asking for film, but it took four to six weeks to make the turnaround from request to care package. Now you have fresh film, and you take a bunch of photos of your buddies. Now what do you do with the exposed film? Just drop it off at the local RX, right. A lot of film went into the small military issue envelopes supplied to the troops, but often enough, they never arrived home, having been crushed, exposed or torn from the envelope and lost.

    Photo quality, as a rule, was very poor, also. It is obvious when you look at the albums that show up at reunions and even on the internet these days. All the grunts had the same problem. True grunts just didn't end up with many pictures, and those of the actual jungle were few and far between.

My entire album consists of only about fifty pictures. Some were sent to friends and family members and are now lost. Mother, however, kept all that I sent back and put together an album that I still have today. In looking through it now, I realize that if it weren't for a guy named Neal Salsbery, my pictorial record would only be half the size that exists. Neal must have been a photographer for the Company, because he carried a really sweet 35 mm camera in a nice military case, and seemed to have some special privileges. He was an infantry "pack" just like the rest of us, with all the hardships. Except I do not recall him walking directly on point. He hung out with the CP and would disappear on LOG birds once in a while.

To everyone's dismay, Neal left the Company in January or February. He was a really great person just to know, and he kept that camera of his snapping photos of everyone every day and in many places. If we happened to be guarding some Firebase for a few days, he had some way of having boxes of photos sent out. He opened them up for all to sort through and find pictures of themselves or something they liked. He charged two bucks each for nice high-quality pictures. Thank you Neal for packing that camera.

On Firebase Boyd and every other Firebase or camp we were on, it was always a good time to write letters home. It was also a time when the post office back on Camp Sally would release all the care packages to the field troops. We happened to be on Firebase Boyd at Christmas 1968, and care packages came to us in a truck. Not every man got a box of goodies from home, but every man shared what he received with everyone else. I ended up with a fifth of Jack Daniels that was hidden inside a Quaker Oats box, sent by Aunt Joey, along with lots of canned fruit, nuts, candy and reading material.

This box had a quart of canned sweet cherries. They were so good that I ate the entire can in one evening, which had a downside the next day, but it was worth it. Most of the food items needed to be consumed before heading back to the jungle, anyway. But we all packed anything that would not spoil, take up too much space or add too much weight. And, of course, this was the place smiling Pat O'Leary received his Christmas tree.

Cake from home, Wayne Carrara, Walt Bouman, David Testerman and Lt. Jim Julien.

On Birmingham, probably in late January or early February, we got a new platoon leader who would be assigned to 1st. Platoon, replacing Lt. Jim Julien, who was moving to 2nd Platoon and replacing Lt. Walsh, who was to become the new XO back at Sally. Jim had been with the "B" since December.

As it was recalled by Sgt. Jim Duke of Oklahoma at our 2009 reunion, the company had just grounded packs on the middle level of the terraced base and was waiting for bunker guard assignments. Only a few minutes had passed when he saw a jeep coming through the gate down on the lower level with four occupants. When the vehicle stopped and the men jumped out, he recognized three of them as our Capt. Graney, Lt. Walsh and Lt. Pue, along with one unknown Lieutenant.

Jim was a squad leader in 1st Platoon, and he had not always gotten along with Capt. Graney. Duke was a hard-charging, hard-working Airborne trooper, but he liked to keep things a little laid back. Graney was all of the same but insisted on calling things right to the letter. Duke caught hell even if he used too much slang on his radio transmissions.

Pat O'Leary and Wayne Carrara, 1969.

The battalion commander's jeep driver enjoyed getting under a guy's skin and thought he'd put a burr under Duke's saddle. He told him a change in command of 1st Plt. was going to be coming soon. So, Duke was on edge but had a heads up when the four brass walked toward the next level, almost in a huddle. Capt. Graney stopped, pointed up the incline directly at Jim and continued chatting with the other men, looking back up from time to time.

Eventually the officers made their way to the company area where they performed a quick changing of the guard for 1st and 2nd platoons. Sgt. Jim Duke met his new leader, Lt. John Cecil Driver, for the first time.

Lt. Driver wasted no time in ordering the platoon to ruck-up and board a deuce-and-a-half headed down to the extreme lower level for their area of bunker guard. The truck driver, wearing a boonie hat loaded with patches and pins, was standing by the vehicle door while leaning on a walking stick that had a shiny 50 calibre shell casing fixed to the top. As the men were trying to climb up and over the side racks, Duke asked the driver to lower the tailgate for the men. The driver completely ignored him.

Well, that didn't go unnoticed by the new lieutenant, who promptly got straight into the face of the driver, put him in the "leaning rest" and told him he would be lowering the tailgate for his men "NOW!"

The trucker promptly obliged. The new lieutenant's actions did not go unnoticed by Duke or any of the men in 1st Plt. They began to respect and like him from the get go.

For the next several days, the platoon built or rebuilt bunkers as the new lieutenant worked right alongside. On the last evening before heading out on the next mission, they gathered in one place, sharing C-rats and stories. Lt. Driver said that he had heard about some of them being afraid to die.

"Well," he said, "Let me tell you, you are most assuredly going to die. But most of us will have gray hair and be long in the tooth before that happens. If my name or some of yours ends up on the shit house wall, well, that is just the way of things. Tomorrow we are going out there kicking some ass."

Driver quickly earned the respect of everyone.

14.
Just Another Day in the Jungle

It's now March 1st, and operation Nevada Eagle has ended. The next major assault on the area around the south end of the A Shau, called "Massachusetts Striker," would last until May 8th.

From the time I joined "B" company, there were rumors and stories about the A Shau Valley. They were all bad, some were horrible, and we were convinced that not even the Green Berets could survive for very long in the northern end of it. Even though our operations skirted the valley on one side or another for several months, we had not actually seen the floor of the valley first hand, and none of us had ever heard of Hill 937.

March 1st was also the day that engineers and heavy equipment were being dropped on a mountain top to begin building another forward Firebase by the name of Whip. It was on the southwest end of the A Shau. We had not heard of it yet, but would be making its acquaintance soon.

We were back in the bush somewhere in the southwest end of the valley. The monsoon rains seemed to be slowing somewhat. We found activity very quickly in the mission, and extreme caution remained the rule.

We had seen evidence of *montagnard* (we pronounced

mountain yard) people in the past, but this time there were huts, places for live stock, fire pits, crude utensils and neatly carved bamboo cylinders full of seeds. Everything was made by hand from the jungle. I did, however, find a crude spoon pounded into shape from a piece of aluminum, which could have come from a napalm canister or a crashed H-1.

After seeing enemy encampments over and over, the *montagnard* hamlets were far different. There were no bunkers, the huts had been there for many years, and the inside of the huts were glazed with the smoke and animal fat from hundreds of cooking fires. *montagnard* lived like American Indians did 150 years ago. Reclusive people that they were, they simply wanted to be left alone.

Almost always the huts were burned because we were told that they may be supporting the enemy! I personally disagreed with this philosophy. We were kicking Charlie's ass so bad that even if the *montagnard* did help the NVA, they were so few and far between in this area it could not have made any difference.

These people did not like or trust anyone, north or south, east or west. They had no idea who Americans were until we burned their house down. Don't get me wrong, for the major population of South Vietnam we truly were heroes, and the country was booming in prosperity the longer we stayed.

The trails that we were following were more heavily used than what a few nomads could have done, and it didn't take long for the NVA to begin stalking us again. They seemed to prefer setting up an ambush early in the morning when we were just leaving an NDP. Sometimes it could be as little as one enemy soldier emptying his weapon toward the point man and fleeing into protective cover.

But that starts it. One round from an AK-47, and, by the second heartbeat, a platoon of M-16's are pouring lead from 360° of the perimeter. The noise can be so intense and your nerves wound up so tight, that you cannot tell if your weapon is operating or not.

Only when the chaos has ended and you check your clip, do you know if you assisted in the recon by firing.

Some of this harassment, I believe, was like the killdeer bird that lays its eggs in open fields back home. If you get near the nest, the bird allows you to get very close to it, bending one wing to the ground and acting like it is injured but always leading you away from the nest.

I was becoming accustomed to reading the vegetation. A certain type of fern with about eight to ten flat leaves was used almost exclusively as thatch for a roof and sides on a jungle hooch. I noticed a hand tool mark on a tree or attempts to camouflage the start of a branch trail. We followed the main trails and branch trails, and if we happened to observe an area back in the jungle where the ferns had been harvested, there was an enemy complex somewhere close. This happened one day when a recon became profitable.

We cautiously eased down into a small draw in the ridge where the hoochs and bunkers were very well camouflaged. We could actually smell the presence of people having been there. Adrenalin creeps into your system at times like this, and you notice you are controlling your breathing, your hands are trembling, you cannot feel one ounce of the load you are bearing on your back, every sensory element that a human has is on full alert—BANG!—comes the irrefutable crack of an AK-47, slightly high, at 9 o'clock.

I had already emptied half of my clip as I was diving for mother earth. As I closed the gap between myself and the dirt, I caught the eye of Al Kontrabecki, from Niagara Falls, NY. He appeared to me to be in slow motion, doing the same thing that I was doing and with a look of horror embedded in his face. Elbows and knees dig at the earth, in seconds you are in the weeds, hoping to be concealed. Time passes as your heart pounds. But the sniper was unsuccessful with his first shot and apparently decided the hail of bullets that came at him was not worth another try.

There were only five or six bunkers, and we cleared and searched all of them, reconned the surrounding area and found a nice cache of fifteen or twenty rifles. The weapons, once again, were divided up into the platoon, and the hunt continued.

We NDP for the night with thoughts of a rendezvous with the company the next day, finding an LZ, sending our enemy cache back to the rear and receiving LOG. It was a quiet night, but guard duty is always pure hell. When the human body is subjected to this kind of continuous mental and physical trauma, it needs sleep, lots of it.

Too bad, because we were up once or twice each night for an hour or two each time, to maintain a continuous vigil. Falling asleep on your watch can cost you and the unit everything.

When the morning came, the platoon made ready to move. It was not a good time to heat anything up, so it was cold C's. Only a faint rustle came from within the camp, with voices in very low tones as poncho hoochs are rolled up and sand bags emptied for reuse the next night. The point squad made ready and started its near silent trek out of our temporary perimeter. I positioned my towel around my neck and down my chest and grabbed the shoulder straps in the cross arm rucksack dead lift. I complete the swing and the ruck landed squarely on my back, left arm through one strap and right arm through the other strap. I was preparing to adjust the slide buckles down to give the ruck a high and tight fit, when—RAT–A–TAT–RAT–A–TAT–RAT–A–TAT!!!

I was still in the motion of mounting my ruck as the green trailers came zinging through the NDP The gooks were waiting in ambush and opened up on the point platoon before they could get 50 feet out of the perimeter.

My M-16 was propped against a tree. I dove toward it, and as I hit the ground, the loose straps on my ruck allowed it to roll out over my head, pinning me to the ground with my arm almost straight out. Needless to say, at least three clips of ammo were shot up by each man. The barrels of the M-60's were smoking hot, and ten to fifteen M-79 grenades were shot off and exploded in the jungle. I was flip-flopping like a contortionist, trying to free myself from the ruck, when the shooting stopped.

The air was filled with white smoke and the smell of spent gun powder. I was finally free, on my hands and knees, crawling over enemy weapons, thinking, "Oh my God, we've been overrun by the NVA—Oh wait, those are the weapons we confiscated yesterday (sigh of relief)!"

No one is hurt, thank God. We move out again, successfully this time and begin the hunt for a good LZ site. As we are working our way up this ridge with a continuous pattern of humps, we enter an open area, obviously man-made. Someone spent weeks hacking down the larger limbs from big trees with no more than machetes. They cleared the land between the huge barren tree trunks and were cultivating a plant very similar to a Jerusalem artichoke. The tubers were extremely starchy, and after sampling one, I realized it was used as an ingredient in the big rice bowl we found in the big NVA camp back in December.

The clearing gave a view of a small valley that led to the A Shau, but the infamous place was not quite in sight. There were two of these clearings. As the recons took us slowly up the ridge at the high side of the second clearing, I sat down at the flank in a sunny spot, and after a few minutes, I realized I was on top of a rather large sprawling ants nest. Tiny trails led into the jungle from a central spot a few feet away from me. A great deal of activity was going on with this colony of black ants that resembled carpenter ants in North America. I became distracted by them when a small team carried a large beetle to the main opening, struggled to fit it down the hole, but it just would not fit. They abandoned it, and some headed down the hole while others went back out on the trails.

Several minutes passed when two noticeably different ants emerged from the entrance and approached the slow moving beetle. They had enormous heads and pinchers relative to the other ants and began to swagger around the beetle, which was ten times their size. About the third time around, one dove in, grabbed a leg at the hilt, twisted vigorously and tore off the limb. A regular worker ant immediately picked up the leg and headed down the hole with it. The two Sumo ants completely dismembered the entire bug in a matter of minutes, then disappeared down the hole.

Thus I managed a little entertainment during the seemingly long wait between recons.

The "Move out" signal came again, and we reached the summit in late day, but the humps continued along this high razor back ridge. We found one with smaller trees and dug in for the night.

The next morning, shortly after day break, an H-1 was brought in, hovering over the trees above us. The crew used a penetrator to lower down two chain saws, bar oil and a fuel can, along with several felling axes. It's time to cut another LZ.

"Snake, Doc, you boys know how to handle one of these right?"

"Yes sir,"

"Okay then, where do we start?"

Dan and I quickly agree that we must start twenty yards over the side and fell the trees, all the way around the LZ, then move up, take down the next row and so on, until we reach that center, which gives each subsequent row an open place to fall. Several men were assigned an ax or a saw, moved down with a guard at their side, and each team rotated positions to avoid fatigue. Dan and I traded positions after each tree went down. On the fifth or sixth tree Dan was notching a fairly big one, as I noticed a guy up above us hacking away at a six inch tree with a machete.

Dan moved around to begin the final cut. When I looked uphill again to see how machete man was doing, his tree was toppling down directly towards us. With the roar of the chainsaw, Dan could not here me yelling. So I grabbed his shirt at the shoulder and jerked him away from the fall zone.

Well, no good deed goes unpunished. The top of the tree hit squarely on Dan's spot and would have slapped the crap out of him. However, in the excitement of pulling him out of danger, I must have swung my arm over the spinning chain and took two good alternating cuts across my right arm just above the wrist.

It begun oozing blood immediately but was not squirting. I grabbed the wound with my left hand and applied as much pressure as possible while heading straight to my ruck. While holding my arm in this way, I opened the aid bag, retrieved the appropriate bandages and compressed the wound and checked my fingers. Dexterity was good, no cut tendons, I knew that my platoon leader and the CO would be unhappy about this, but I found them, explained what happened and that it would definitely require stitches. Yup, they were pissed!

I went back to work until the LZ was finished. Then when the first LOG bird came in and dropped the load, I hopped on and went back to Sally. I wasted no time in getting to the aid station, received about ten quick stitches along with a thorough disinfectant cleaning, a good dressing and hopped another LOG flight back to the company.

The following morning the company began taking paths that led downhill. We moved very slowly over the next few days, closer and closer to the edge of the A Shau. We were on the last small foot hill approaching a spur valley leading directly to the main floor.

We woke up the next morning to very dense fog, so dense we stayed put the entire day, then the next. It had been five days since LOG, so the food supply was getting low. The sixth day passed with no let up in the fog, with the exception of small breaks that allowed us to come out of the dense area into the edge of the valley. There we found a small patch of cultivated corn. It was too young to harvest, but we stripped out the tiny undeveloped ears and ate them anyway. Dan and I found this huge root that wound through part of the cultivated area and sprouted out like a rhubarb plant at the end.

"Hey Dan, do you think this was planted here?"

"Kind of looks like it," Dan said, as he hacked at the three inch root with his bayonet.

"Hum, smells like bananas, I'll try it if you do."

We both popped a chunk in our mouths and started chewing.

"Oh my God!"

We started spitting at the same time, grabbed our canteens and began gargling.

"Oh my God!"

Our mouths were on fire, taking our breath away. My tooth paste was in my left breast pocket. I pulled it out, squirted a bunch in my mouth and handed it to Dan. We gargled, swooshed the foam back and forth until we looked rabid. We spit, used more toothpaste, more water, until we were relieved enough to carry on. I learned something that day—don't put anything in your mouth if you don't know what it is. Being really hungry can make you forget that rule, but we could feel that horrible sensation in our throats for another three days.

Unlike with the typhoon, we could roam around in the perimeter if we were careful, shoot the bull with other men, read and, oh yes, sleep. We all took turns napping as much as possible. I thought about the terrain we had just come through. At one point we worked our way down beside a stream that was continuously falling from rock to rock and tree root to tree root. It came to an abrupt drop of 60 to 80 feet, where it turned into a beautiful, almost completely concealed waterfall that turned the clear mountain water into mist.

My father took our family to a great many places in Michigan and beyond. Many were beautiful places, but none could compare to the tropical beauty of these desolate mountains areas.

There was one benefit to our war effort here in the highlands. These tumbling mountain streams were a source of good fresh water that did not need Halizone and did not cause ill health effects.

The seventh day came, and every man had scrounged every possible edible thing from his ruck. I found a C-rat fruit cake deep in mine. I dislike fruit cake, and there is nothing worse than military fruit cake, so I tried to think of it as "breakfast" food, opened the can, cut off a chunk and chewed on it for a while. But as hungry as I was, that's all I could eat of it. I offered it to all the other guys around me, but got no takers.

I dug all through my medical bag, looking for throat lozenges, cough drops, anything to satisfy the feeling of hunger. Deep in one of the storage pocket I pulled out a plastic vial of capsules, with the label nearly worn away. Diet pills. Huh! Doc Summers gave those to me six months ago. I wonder if they shrink your stomach?

Radios worked just fine despite the fog, and Captain Graney was receiving information that the fog was not going away for several more days. He then set to work with the platoon leaders to plot a way out. There was a creek nearby that followed a crevasse back up through the mountains and eventually came to the base of the mountain supporting the new Firebase, Whip.

"Pack your shit and ruck up, we're going to march to a Firebase called Whip. If we leave ASAP we can make the summit before dark."

Lt. Pue went from man to man in the third platoon, making

sure they knew what the mission was. Pue got to me, went through the drill and ended the conversation with, "Hey Doc, you have any extra chow?"

"No, but there is part of a fruit cake in the bushes over there," I said.

He understandably declined and was ready to go to the next man when I said, "Lt. Pue, I have a vial of diet pills, they shrink your stomach right?"

Well, Lt. Pue being a little older than me and a little more street-wise about certain chemicals, said, "Give me one, no, two, no three and give one to every man in the third platoon."

I followed his order, took one capsule myself and gave one to every man, telling them my theory that it would shrink your stomach and override the hunger.

First platoon took the lead, scouting in the fog to find the stream, followed by second platoon, and finally third platoon brought up the rear. We knew that "Charlie" could not see shit either, and we proceeded with very light recons to connection with the flowing landmark. First platoon found the creek, made a turn north and began following the water up the hill.

After about an hour, I became very anxious about the lack of progress that was being made, all the guys in third platoon seemed to agree and began passing the guys in second platoon saying, "Come on you slackers, let's go. We can sleep on a Firebase tonight if we kick some ass!"

That was one hell of an upward climb, fog so thick you could barely see the man in front of you. We were soaking wet up to the crotch from wading up the mountain stream. We began to pass men in the first platoon four hours into the march, and by the fifth hour, we are at point, pushing our way up.

After about six hours of hard humping, only stopping for short recons, we reached a point that Sgt. Duke recognized as an area we were in weeks earlier. He felt we should turn east, leave the stream and head straight up the mountain. He called in an artillery air burst to confirm our location, and the march began again. The short respite gave first and second platoon time to catch up to us before making the final push to the top.

The effect of the diet pill was beginning to wear off. I began to understand how this particular variety of diet pill worked, a fairly strong stimulant taken on very emptied stomachs.

Another solid hour passed before we reached the lower edge of Firebase Whip's perimeter, an absolute tangle of downed trees and jungle brush pushed in by a bulldozer.

The engineers apparently cut down enough trees to have a D-5 Cat 'dozer airlifted onto the top of the mountain, then used the 'dozer to level off three separate areas each the size of a football field. All the tree trunks, roots, limbs and ferns were pushed down the slope and banked up against the standing forest. Then, on top of this they pushed all the extra subsoil, making the three levels somewhat flat.

We were searching for a breach in the massive tangle, when we were notified to stay put below the perimeter until the 'dozer could be air-lifted back out. So we all pulled off our gear, found places to get comfortable and lit up smokes.

The mountain top was peeking out above the fog bank, so the sun was out, and it felt very good at around 1700 hours in the afternoon. About an hour passed when we begun to hear the rumble of a flying crane called a "Hurricane" approaching to the LZ The engineers had split the 'dozer tracks at the top center, and laid them out fore and aft of the machine. They also removed the blade, all in an effort to reduce the weight of the machine.

The helicopter arrived and maneuvered over the 'dozer, as one of the engineers ran out through the steady increasing dust storm, climbed up on the 'dozer and supported a very heavy hook that was attached to nylon straps cradling the 'dozer. The crane lowered so that the engineer could make the final connection. Then he promptly jumped down and ran for cover.

Now I have seen these flying cranes off in the distance in flight, but up close, you just can't believe how big they are. It would easily require a space the size of a football field to legitimately land one of those suckers. It looked like it took three people to operate the flying muscle machine, pilot, co-pilot and loadmaster, who had a large window facing the rear under belly of the craft. We could see the load master directing the pilot into position, lowering the cable hoist, making the connection and giving the subsequent signal to lift.

We were all fighting off one heck of a rotor wash as it was, then we could hear the engines begin to rev-up. The crane maintained position for some time as the rotors spun faster and faster. I was thinking that maybe they could not make the lift. But the crew must have been waiting for enough blade velocity and centrifugal force to build, because about then the pilot apparently pulled back on the collective, changing the pitch of the rotors, and all hell broke loose.

The 'dozer had to weigh eight to ten tons, and it was beginning to lift off. The entire event was awesome and extremely interesting to me. I did everything I could to watch every move, but we were being sand blasted and poked by flying debris to the point of danger. The pilot must have kicked in the after burners as a new high pitch roar came from the giant craft. It rose higher, began making a gentle turn and eased away into the sky with the D-5 hanging under its belly. Soon it was only a speck in the sky.

Later a Chinook flew in, also a big cargo helicopter, and hooked up to the 'dozer tracks and blade in the same way. That alone would have been impressive, but it paled in comparison to the flying crane.

We were finally able to move up onto the FB plateau and try to make quarters before dark. As I was rucking up, I realized that my glasses were gone. What the heck! They must have been blown off during the lift!

I hunted for those black, horn-rim glasses in the tangle of the roots and tree trunks, but gave up and headed onto the plateau for some rest. The effects of the stimulant that everyone in the third platoon had taken may have put most of us at the top of the hill first, but now we felt like our butts were really kicked.

15.
WHIP

The entire company filed through a breach in the tangle and onto the freshly made plateau and began picking out positions around the perimeter of the lower and larger area. It was all freshly exposed dirt, no bunkers for us, no toilets and no showers. We were like ducks out of the water trying to set up our two man hoochs without the assistance of the jungle plants. That first night we dug foxholes like any other NDP in the jungle, and just spread our ponchos out on the ground, inflated our mattresses (if you had one) placed it on half the poncho, rolled up in our liner and pulled the remaining poncho over the top.

The next morning we awoke to very dense fog that made for a lazy start to the day. We needed a rest from the equivalent of a double marathon effort of the previous day, anyway. Everyone was trying to sort and clean his gear, but the environment was not the best for it, with so much fresh dirt everywhere and no piss tubes or outhouses. There was, however, plenty of drinking water and cases of C-rats, which we raided quickly and tried to fill the void of our three days without food.

I took care of whatever chores that were necessary, then went off to explore the FB and hopefully find a better place for a hooch.

The two lower sections were divided by a crevasse that resembled a giant hog trough full of broken trees and debris pushed by the 'dozer. It gradually increased in width and depth as it went out through the perimeter, 60 yards from its start. To get around it and to the opposite side of the lower half, you needed to walk nearly to the center of the FB.

Just beyond the beginning of the crevasse and the start of the next level, I climbed the steep bank, fifty or sixty feet to the smaller top where a battery of howitzers sat. Fresh bunkers were built all around the big guns. One bunker was quite large, with several large antennas sticking out. It must have been for communication.

A company of ARVN troops also occupied this high ground, and their bunkers were built like terraces, all over the side of the hill facing the lower levels. I looked them over closely. They did not use many sand bags, but instead, used logs, woven sticks and rocks to construct half-cave, half-bunker fortresses. Each one had a integral parapet wall that came out from the face of the bunker and turned to cover the entrance. It was skillful and rugged work with simple materials accomplished by these Vietnamese troops. On my way back down I could here a faint "whop-whop-whop" somewhere in the distance—the ever familiar sound of a helicopter.

As I descended from the upper plateau, the noise became louder and I thought, could the helicopter be above the fog?

As I reached the lower level, I could see other men standing up and paying attention to the noise. It was getting closer and closer, maybe even below our level on the mountain top?

Men stood motionless as the sound moved left, then right, left, then right, closer and closer. The crew must be lost in the fog!

"Holy crap, there it is!"

Just barely clearing the trees was a cobra gunship still carrying ordinance! It hovered, pointing the nose of the bird left and right, obviously looking for a place to land. As this was taking place, the men at the point of the bird's entrance, were scattering for cover, as the rotor wash sent ponchos, air mattresses, poncho liners and anything else loose, hurtling into the air like a Texas tornado.

It only took a couple of seconds for a poncho or liner to snag the rear (steering) propeller, rendering it useless.okay, now it got serious. The craft began pinwheeling in circles, the primary rotor holding approximate center as the entire fuselage went round and round. There were two 1,000-gallon rubber blivots lying on the ground beside the mouth of the draw. One was labeled "potable water" the other "gasoline."

The pilot must have seen he was somewhere near the draw. He killed the throttle and fell toward the ground, still in a spin. In a split second, the bird made a direct hit on top of the fuel blivot, the landing skids straddling each side. The bird bounced once or twice, as if on a trampoline, and finally came to rest.

Downed Cobra on Firebase Whip with Charles Hyatt and Clyde Crossguns. Note fuel blivots under the front half of the chopper, between the skid rails.

I was only about 75 feet away when this happened. I did an about face and must have looked like the road runner heading back up the hill. I stopped and looked back to see if it was going to blow and could see the pilot and co-pilot struggling to get out of the cockpit as fast as they could. Now I ran back down the hill and straight to the downed bird to help get the guys out. I thought I would pee my pants in fear, being so close to the fuel blivot and a steaming hot engine just a few feet away.

What could have been an unbelievably horrible accident, turned out well, and the Cobra sat perched on top of the fuel blivot for several more days before being picked up by a Chinook. I later learned that the A Shau was also notorious for sudden fog cover.

I teamed up with one of the guys and went in search of a little real estate to build a new home. We found a nice level spot near the draw where we dug a rectangular hole about five feet by six feet and a foot deep. We filled sandbags as we went and stacked two rows around three sides of the hole. We then stretched a poncho over the bags, tied the four corners tight, and added a ridge pole from a bent limb. It was sleeping room only, but fairly well protected from the elements and any incoming mortar rounds.

The fog burned off on day two, and the weather remained nice and sunny the remainder of our stay. It was mid-March, and the monsoons were dwindling somewhat.

Activity rapidly increased when the air travel resumed. No doubt the brass wanted this base up and running quickly. Many of the guys were conscripted during the day to fill sandbags and perform grunt labor for the engineers, and, in three days, the character of the FB changed considerably. A rectangular building made of sand bags, heavy central roof support posts and a PSP steel roof had been completed at the base of the hill. It was quite large for a bunker, possibly 16 feet deep and 24 feet wide on the inside. There were two entrance doors at the extreme ends of the front, facing the flat lower level.

There were no parapet walls in front of the doors, instead, a heavy canvas curtain was hanging from the inside of the openings.

Bunker construction, 1969. Edwin Dotter (KIA) nearest camera. "Moose" McCoun top center.

I know curiosity killed the cat, but I needed to inspect this structure and find out what it was. So I parted the drape and walked inside to have a look. I saw a nice flat neat floor, although it was quite dark inside with the drape closed. There were at least thirty folding military cots placed neatly throughout the inside. It's a barracks, I thought. Then a GI with a clipboard in his hand walked in the opposite door, preparing to take a few notes. He noticed me, smiled and proceeded with his business.

After a moment, I asked, "Who is the barracks for?"

He looked back at me, no smile this time, and said simply, "It's a morgue."

I made my exit promptly. His words were a bit of a shock to say the least. I had never seen anything like this on a intermediate

Firebase, not even on Sally in the early days, and sure as hell, not ever on a forward (not having road access) Firebase.

A morgue on a forward Firebase had to be calculated anticipation of something, even a dim witted grunt could see that, but anticipation of what?

We grunts had important jobs to do, in fact about 90 percent of the entire military machine was designed to keep the foot soldier doing what he does best. But grunts are rarely if ever included in the grander scheme of things. Heck, most of the time, we barely knew where we were.

However, even if the brass made deliberate efforts to keep blinders on the grunts, and even if most of us entered the military service at the lowest possible levels, there were amazingly intelligent people mixed into the ranks, and the plans could be deciphered. Information came to highly isolated troops like us from letters, chopper pilots and crew, new recruits or guys coming back to the field from R&R. One day, the puzzle pieces began to fit.

Information of another kind was slowly creeping in, as well, like tiny pieces of a puzzle floating around in your head without a picture to guide the assembly. The armed forces provided a great deal of information and news for keeping a soldier in good spirits, but they definitely did some whitewashing in regards to the sentiments being placed into the minds of the college students back in the "world." (The USA simply meant the entire world to us, and we all referred to America as the "world.")

Please allow me to take a diversion for a moment.

There were some obvious and hideous conditions during the Vietnam War. If your family was affluent and you were sent to college after high school, you could be a complete idiot and still avoid the draft. On the other hand, if your family was poor or middle class, especially if you were from rural areas or suburbs, and could not afford tuition, you were usually drafted straight into the military meat grinder.

As I continue to take part in our B-Company reunions, the success of so many of my comrades is the proof of the ambition, fortitude and intellect of so many men that bore the burden for those who hid behind the pathetic laws of the time. Even I can say that I have, in the long run, bested the majority of the "drug-sucking slackers" who hid in the shadows of their college deferments.

We veterans seem to have attributes they do not, such as: nerve, guts, a knowledge of the world, a driven will to live life, not only for ourselves but also for our fallen comrades—and a never quit, never stop, never give up attitude.

I could see clearly in later years, that it was primarily the gutless group that made up the pot smoking hippies who protested the war and eventually aided in the forfeit of a war that had already been won.

Eventually we realized that many of the kids we went to high school with were actually turning against us. It was bad enough that there were protests against the war, with organizers that were interested in the demise of our country and others trying to perch themselves on top of what they thought was a growing political issue, even throwing their medals over the White House wall and surrounding themselves with "silly" people. But now they were beginning to protest the soldiers themselves and, in some cases, even their families.

We saw that in dramatic form in the early stages of the Iraq and Afghanistan Wars. People had enough hideous gall to disrupt the funeral of a fallen soldier.

It was the Vietnam veteran that rose up, formed hard and fast decisive ranks and put a stop to that practice. The Patriot Guard was established, almost entirely of Vietnam veterans, and I salute them and their cause.

Somehow, the WWII veterans had notions that soldiers

fighting in the Vietnam War, in some strange way, were not really veterans or somehow not worthy of the title. A little of that happened to Korean War vets as well. The stance was more like passive aggression. Many simply stayed silent without defending us.

That has all changed over the years, and the "Greatest Generation" has now given us full respect.

My point in all of this diversion is this, we were miserable in about every way possible. We were at a point where you could find comfort by simply lying down on a pile of soggy dirt, eating a can of cold rats, then taking a nap, and no one thought it was odd. Your next mission was about to start, you knew it was very likely to get worse out there, you were sick with fear, enough so that it was hard to hold down your last can of food. You were ready to board a Dirty Slick (a helicopter with unnecessary equipment stripped away, but had two door gunners) that will deliver you to the "Bad Place," and thoughts were rattling around in your mind about how people back in your "world" were acting and the things they were saying about you that were not true.

Yes, you are correct in thinking that their actions added yet another level of misery to our job.

One last note. I have put the hippies, college students and academia in one basic lump, as if all of them were against the soldier. I know that's not true, but the Vietnam veterans were certainly put into one group, all bad. Back at ya.

The real killers of the country are the bosses of the media.

Back to the story.

There were ways of collecting intelligence, even for the ground pounders. We knew our missions were a constant probing of the mountains on either side of the infamous A Shau, and we knew the subsequent missions took us further and further north. The rumor mill was grinding out stories of heavy fighting and heavy losses. Something was culminating in the north end of valley, and we grunts were putting the pieces together. Reports were coming in of other units involved in the Massachusetts Striker offensive. The 2/327th 101st Airborne fought its way into NVA base camps near the Laotian border and found a newly constructed road with bulldozers and trucks.

On April 16th, the 1/502nd 101st Abn. found a cache of radio communication equipment, medical supplies, food, 600 new SKS AK-47 and 14 trucks. It was estimated to be over 100 tons of supplies denied to the enemy and possibly the single largest cache ever found during the war.

By now the majority of the men in B-Company had been together for a long time and subjected to misery, death and intense fear many times. While on Whip, it was good to be out of the jungle, away from humping, endless recons, night ambushs and silence, silence, silence. Oh yeah, we smiled and joked, but the hollowed eyes and thousand-yard stares gave away what was inside.

The idea of getting away was strong and Sgt. Jim Duke, 1st Plt. Squad leader, got his wish on Whip with notification of R&R. Duke had proven his worth to Lt. Driver by then and, as soon as the fog had lifted, Driver pulled out all stops to get him on the first flight out. New recruits can come at any time, as I did, but like care packages, it's best if they come while on a base, no matter how remote. We received two new men while on Whip, a medic, Mike Edwards from Kansas, and a new grunt, Garry Nieman from York, Pennsylvania. I introduced myself to the new grunt, so out of place in this place but needing a connection to someone. Gary was attached to second or third platoon, and we crossed paths from time to time over the next few weeks.

Doc Edwards started his tour similar to mine. He was with a field unit for three months prior to being assigned to B-Company, and contact with the enemy had been light. He was a permanent replacement for one of our other medics, but I no longer remember which one.

The Firebase was shaping up with preparations for more gun batteries on one side of the lower level and helicopter pads on the opposite. About the fourth day, the first PSP pad was sand bagged in so that when choppers landed the dust clouds were reduced considerably. More GI's and more equipment continued to arrive. Possibly on the fourth day, the engineers set up a couple of shower tripods, hooked hoses to the water blivots and turned on the water. The rule was; get wet, turn the water off, use soap, rinse the soap off, cut the water off again and move out. After three weeks without, even a hasty shower felt very good.

Possibly on the fifth day, some "Brass" arrived at the new LZ. A short while later about a dozen folding chairs were set-up nice and straight in an open space about ten feet back from two portable military tables. Two officers took up residence behind the desks, and every so often a group of men would be seated for 15 to 20 minutes, leave and be replaced by another group.

"Flory front and center," this was formal. I reported to the captain and addressed him with a salute. (The practice of saluting, for obvious reasons, is rarely practiced in the field or even on most Firebases.)

"Trooper, we have a promotion board here, get in line with the next group and, well, good luck!"

"Thank You Sir," ended with another salute, and I joined the ranks.

Now this was a real surprise, a promotion board being held out here on this piece of remote dirt, but I had no arguments.

In short order, we ended up seated in front of a one man panel and a clerk. We were all looking dapper in what I will call our severely pre-washed outfits, where not one name tag matched the man wearing the uniform or anyone in our unit for that matter. With the black leather on our jungle boots worn down to the point of tan dirt suede and coarsely cut hair, but dang, we had a shower yesterday, so we were standing tall!

The officer began firing questions as the clerk would shout a name responsible for answering. They kept this up in rapid fire for about twenty minutes, and we all had the opportunity to answer many military oriented questions.

This was one time that the military conducted a program that truly matched the condition that we were in. The officer in charge of the promotion board must surely have done time with the ground pounders. He must have gone back to the rear that day with a good feeling, because there were near zero incorrect answers. We were hardened field troops. His questions were geared for infantry, and we knew the answers. I personally moved from specialist third class (SP-3) to specialist fourth class (SP-4) that day.

I was proud of my accomplishment and how the military conducted the review. It meant I would be receiving nearly $100 additional pay per month, yes, I said *per month*. That, of course, was in addition to the $100 per month "Hazardous Duty Pay." Add that to the $160 per month regular SP-3 pay and ou-wee, I was rolling in the dough, a whopping $360 per month—*Ha ha!*

At this point in the game, I had been in the field for about seven months. I had nearly no opportunities to spend any money. Most of my pay went home to a bank account. I kept a small amount each month in my wallet, calculating about how much money I might need to take on R&R (some day).

Most of the men were given opportunity to travel on an R&R at the point they accumulated six months in-country. I continued to ask permission to go after my sixth month was complete, but the CO would say, "Not until we have a replacement for you."

My carry-along savings account continued to grow, so I made a habit of trading for larger denominations of *Dong* (military currency used in RVN) to keep my wallet thinner.

We must have stayed on Whip for seven days total. About the sixth day my hooch mate and I were told to move our things to a new place because the engineers were starting construction on another gun battery area on the spot we built our hooch.

Fast forward forty years. I get an e-mail from David Reinheimer (B-2-501 reunion president) that says one of our old M-60-gunners, Patrick O'Leary, has his mug shot on a new book by James Durney, an Irish national, who entitled his book, *Vietnam, the Irish Experience*. I ordered a copy in November 2008, just because it had Pat's picture on the cover.

A month passed, and then I had a business trip to Saint Paul, Minnesota, (Home of Dan "Snake" Wakefield), and I decided to read the new book on the trip.

I consumed about a third of it (good book) on the flight there and was working on the next third that night in the hotel, when I discovered a group of photos of some of the men in the stories. They included Lt. John Driver, also from Ireland, and one additional photo of Pat O'Leary. Well, I took my time, looking the photo over closely. There are two men up close in the photo, Pat, sitting up for the camera, another man lying down, his face and legs, from the knees down, out of the range of the camera. As I studied the large flat dirt area behind them with a hill projecting up in the background, I thought to myself, this looks like it was taken on Whip! I scanned the photo a little more and saw a small two-man hooch with about two rows of sand bags around it and a poncho stretched tightly over. A guy sitting on a block of wood in front of it had a nicely shaped boonie hat with a cut down rim on his head.

Kiss my rear, there I was, in the background of the photo, sitting in front of my six-day home. I e-mailed Pat as soon as I arrived back home and asked him if the photo was taken on Whip. His answer was yes and the man lying down beside him was a good friend and co-medic, Paul Pawlak.

Who would have thought you would find yourself in a photo taken at an extremely obscure place, 40 years ago, in a book written and produced in Ireland!

Pat O'Leary at Firebase Whip (the author above Pat's hat).

Orders came that we would be going back to work the next day and to prepare to make the assault directly from Whip. It was progressively warmer again, and the sun was out thatday. We were going through our gear, making ready for another undetermined period of time in the field.

As we were making our preparations, a very large black bird flew over the LZ. It looked like a common crow from back in the States but somewhat larger. It floated gently across a 300 yard gap between us and the next ridge, where it landed on a high branch of a dead tree.

Firebase Whip, Paul Pawlak (Pat O'Leary's ruck to the left).

Lt. Pue looked at the bird when it took up residence on the branch and said, "What will you bet me, if I can shoot that bird out of that tree?" It was probably Lt. Driver that took up a wager with him. Pue stood, no shirt on, racked a around into his M-16, took an off hand stance and as we heard the report of the M-16, the bird simultaneously fell from the tree. Speaking for the group, I thought, "Well I'll be dammed, he hit it."

Lt. Pue jumped up and down, shaking his fist and saying, "Yes-yes," and collected his wager.

I have already explained clothing, so lets talk about the gear just a little. No one could substitute anything for the rucksack we used. We simply had to have them. Most men developed their own style of harnessing things to the frame, to suit their own comfort and carrying capacity.

Me and some of the others started with a pistol belt equipped with suspenders, the shoulder straps having good padding and attachment holes down the breast straps the same as the belt. I carried two, two-quart canteens, one on the left and one on right, as far back on the pistol belt as possible, without interfering with the ruck frame, and two one-quart canteens riding just in front of the two quarts. I started every mission with a full one-and-a-half gallons (12lbs.) and tried to maintain that amount of water at all times during missions.

The breast straps of the suspenders held four smoke grenades for hailing a Medevac and two hand grenades, which added another six pounds or so. I really liked the suspenders/pistol belt combination because you could carry the extra weight comfortably. I could leave the belt unhooked, which made it easy to move and quickly get in or out of.

The military issue ruck consisted of an aluminum frame, well padded shoulder straps with easily operated adjustments, and a wide cloth band across the bottom that rode across the high side of your hips, like a large shock absorber, and it supported part of the load. The rucksack itself was nylon and had one large pouch at the rear and a medium sized pouch on each side with heavy flaps to keep the rain out. The main pouch opened up as big as a bushel basket and just as deep. It had draw bands around each side coming out at the center of the back and a device that locked the two cords in place when you pulled the opening closed.

Most of us packed 15 boxes of C-rats at the start of a mission (3-C's per day x 5-days = 15). One C-ration per day is enough to sustain a moderately healthy life, but I had no trouble consuming three C's per day. You basically dumped out the ration boxes, threw all the cans of food into the main pouch, sorted out the toilet paper, cigarettes, lifer bars, plastic spoons, coffee or cocoa and matches into all the other pouches or pockets. I folded my poncho liner (light weight nylon blanket) up and stuffed it over the loose cans, then pulled the draw strings very taut.

I folded my air mattress small enough to fit under the flap

that sealed off the opening of the main ruck. Two straps on the flap were then cinched down tight. My poncho was folded, then rolled and strapped down across the top of the aid bag, and it doubled as a helmet head rest. A machete or entrenching tool could be slid down between the bags and the frame and rode well without being tied off. Extra M-60 ammo, "laws" rocket, det cord, repelling rope, C-4 explosive or recovered enemy supplies were tied on or strapped down, however you could do it best.

Letters received from home were burnt, save one or two. In the end, our pack and suspenders probably scaled out on an average of 80lbs. Gear harnessed high and tight, weapons cleaned and oiled, and we were ready for the next assault and mission.

The last day we were on Whip, a Chinook helicopter approached the base with something hanging under it. I watched as it came close enough to see what it was. It was a very large rope sack, seven or eight feet in diameter and drawn tight at the top. It looked like the rope net you see in the movies, used to load something onto a ship.

Chinooks are large and can carry around thirty troops with field gear or three jeeps. The twin rotor bird, made its final approach above the LZ and began descending. All sorts of cargo came in all week, but I could not yet identify this load. As the big sack neared the PSP, the helicopter made a sudden drop, and the cargo bounced once on the landing pad before coming to a rest.

Chinooks create a large rotor wash, and I stayed back a reasonable distance while someone unhooked the cable, and the craft quickly left. I moved in just a little closer to see black rubber sacks with heavy zippers.

"Oh God….. body bags…..with men inside of them."

We were at the pad closest to the morgue, and a crew of four men raced out with litters to remove them from the rope net and get them out of sight.

I was born with a tough gut, and I had seen a fair amount of gore over the last eight months, but there was something demeaning and morbid about the bodies bouncing on that steel pad. I was near the draw, headed there and quickly emptied the contents of my stomach.

I didn't think many of our men had seen it or knew what was going on. We were hours away from our next mission, everyone knew the stakes were going higher yet, and the shit was obviously hitting the fan out there somewhere. I did not tell the guys about the morgue or the men that were just put in it. Better it was left unsaid, at least until now.

Please think about what goes through the minds of the pilots when they are required to make deliveries like this. And who were the men that operated the morgue? It is heroic what they did, even if it was their job. I thank them and salute them for what they had to do.

Our flying taxies to hell were approaching the helicopter pads. It was time for us to go back to work. Little did we know then that it would be more than six weeks in the jungle and many more firefights before we would have the respite of a Firebase (I never found my glasses).

16.
Hard Times

It was mid afternoon when we made the assault on another hillside LZ We met no resistance on what looked like an abandoned artichoke patch which revealed the presence of *montagnards*.

We were taken a considerable distance north through the string of mountains that skirt the A Shau, always avoiding the valley itself. It was like the battalion was playing a game of hop scotch with the companies, going from one side to another, slowly working our way toward the north end. That first day, the company only reconned enough to find a good spot for NDP and dug in. It was obvious from the get-go that we were in one of Charlie's sweet spots. There was evidence of *montagnards* but much more evidence of heavy traffic on the trails. We were all uneasy and on very high alert.

Recons were slow and tedious as we moved along a continuous ridge. We could see that the *montagnard* people, also primitive hunters, built long sections of fence that meandered through the jungle, all carefully hand-crafted of jungle materials. Every one or two hundred yards, there was a small gap in the fence for allowing animals to pass through. Each opening was equipped with a spring-loaded spear and trip mechanism, all built from wood, vines or bamboo. They were apparently trying to corral a small Asian deer into these traps. I never saw the deer but found tracks once in a while.

The second or third day we discovered a *montagnard* hamlet. The people were long gone, hiding in the jungle somewhere, but some of their livestock were still running around loose. As usual, we formed a perimeter around the area and conducted searches.

In mid-afternoon, several of us observed a chicken struggling to retrieve a worm from the ground, big deal right? Well, like all the other bugs in this country, there is a variety of night crawler that is 16 to 20 inches long and as big around as an "Old Dutchman" cigar. The chicken had a good grip on the worm and the worm likewise with the earth. The two played tug of war for at least 30 minutes, when our Vietnamese interpreter, Tie, decided to help the chicken. He extracted another foot of worm from the hole leaving the chicken in a perilous state, with one foot of worm in his gullet and one foot hanging out, and trying to swallow the remainder. Talk about the chicken dance. That bird was making contortions that Michael Jackson couldn't follow! (My condolences to the Jackson family. I wrote this chapter about a month before he died).

When that multicolored rooster finally consumed the remainder of the worm, he seemed quite content, apparently having eaten them before, and was happy to stay close to Tie. Later when we moved out, Tie put the bird on his ruck sack, where it rode along for the day. The remainder of us who watched the show, were suffering from aching guts and watering eyes, having laughed so hard, without making a sound.

This time the hooches were not torched. We just moved out quietly and continued the hunt. We NDP'd that night as a full company, which we were doing on a more regular basis, with "strength in numbers." The next morning as the dim light began peeking into the jungle, the chicken let loose with rather a long and loud reveille, waking anyone still sleeping and marking our position for any bad guys that might want to know where we were.

Tie quickly silenced the chicken before it could report again. He was ticked at the bird for what it did "naturally," but mostly because he had visions of cooking the bird at a later time, if the right opportunity arose.

Tie was a South Vietnamese soldier who volunteered as a scout and interpreter. He was with us for quite some time, and was very good to have along. He was outgoing and funny, pulling pranks or jokes on us from time to time. Everyone liked and trusted him. His English was badly broken but was good enough to carry on decent conversations. Tie would walk point with anyone and did it often. He wanted his country to be free.

The mission continued for days without incident, nearly enough to relax a bit and let your guard down. We were working our way along a ridge that kept bearing left as it gained altitude. When we stopped for a typical recon, I moved a small distance to the left and could see fairly well down through this bowl-like valley. Several minutes passed, and I spotted what looked like a North Vietnamese Regular, some 100 or 150 yards down the slope. He was facing away from me in a *kimuchi* squat and leaning against the base of a big tree. It looked like most of his left side was exposed, his head turned to the left, looking up toward the trail we were on.

I rubbed my eyes. Was I seeing something or not? I watched carefully for movement, but he didn't budge. I called over two more guys and carefully described what I was seeing, but they just couldn't see him. I propped my M-16 across a fallen log, took careful aim and, holding the weapon as firmly as possible, leaned away far enough to allow one of the guys to look through the sights. But he just could not see what I was seeing, a man with black bushy hair and khaki clothing. We were signaled to move out, and I did, reluctantly, not knowing if it was a gook or not.

I had an experience while hunting deer once, when I spotted what appeared to be a doe, nibbling something on the ground. I watched the doe for a long time as it would raise its head, wiggle it ears and go back to grazing. In deer hunting, I simply will not shoot unless I believe I can make a clean kill, and this doe held her position at a disadvantage to me. I made small noises and a slight whistle, and she stayed right there. I finally crept from my position, keeping an eye on the deer and moved in closer. As I did, the deer simply vanished. I made my way back to my blind wondering how I lost sight of it so quickly. I sat back down, eventually looking back at the spot.

"What the Heck," there she was again.

She turned out to be a mirage made up of leaves, forming ears, eyes and snout, slowly moving in coordination with the breeze. Possibly this same thing was happening again?

As evening was coming, we stopped again for recon, looking for a place to NDP on the summit. The third platoon was pulling up slack, and we disappeared into the edges of a small clearing to wait. About 15 minutes passed. I was at the three o'clock position in the clearing, maybe thirty feet from where the trail led in.

"Gooks! Gooks!" someone screamed from near the opening.

I spun around to look and saw a figure who had inadvertently walked into our perimeter, then spun around and made long jumps in retreat. I saw a khaki uniform and long black bushy hair, as he hauled ass out of sight.

Lt. Pue was already in hot pursuit. Stopping at the limit of our perimeter, he hurled a grenade out into the jungle as far as he could. When the blast went off, Pue and two others charged down the trail, but came back ten minutes later, empty handed.

Everyone agreed that the gook didn't have a weapon. He was just walking along with his head down, following our trail. I knew one thing for sure. I did, in fact, spot him down in that valley. We all knew we were being stalked and that the enemy knew the size of our force.

We made NDP and dug in again, but with a refreshed sense of alertness that remained with everyone in the following days.

On a LOG day, about the second week of March, B-Co. and third platoon said good-bye to Lt. Pue, as his required field time was finished and his replacement, Lt. Bohdan Kopystianskyj, had just arrived and was ready to take over the platoon. Art Pue was a good and brave leader, "Airborne All The Way," and our new Lieutenant would also prove to be a great leader as well.

Days passed without incident. It was time to receive log again, but there were no LZ sites to be found. On many occasions, this time included, we marked our location with smoke and talked the supply helicopters in with the radio. The helicopter hovered overhead as everyone moved away from the DZ (drop zone). Then someone on the chopper shoved the boxes and bags out of the cargo hold and down through the jungle canopy. I learned at our 2007 reunion in Oregon that James Motika was one of the supply guys who usually had the job of accompanying the LOG freight out to the jungle when the helicopters couldn't land. He said how he was always afraid that a box or bag would drop onto one of us.

We had not used any ordinance as yet on this mission, so most of the supplies were boxes of C's along with mail and a few medical supplies, including malaria pills. The mail was quite light and might become lodged in a tree branch. So it was stuffed in with what we will call a treat—soda pop and beer—two cans each for each man.

To a man, we were jonezin' for a beer. It had been six or eight weeks since the last one, but you have to think about this for a minute. The canned beer was dumped from case boxes into duffel bags, hauled on a mule to a PSP helicopter landing pad, thrown off into a pile along with boxes of C's, then sat there in the hot sun for six or eight hours. Now, it's piled onto a helicopter and flown 40 miles at high altitude in a vehicle that has a very rhythmic bounce. The cargo is then thrown 100 feet or more down to the jungle floor and handed out to a bunch of troops who haven't had a taste of the "world" for nearly two months.

Soooo, we get our ration of steaming hot beer that just went through the equivalent of an industrial paint shaker. What do you do? You open it! We could have used the explosive effect against the enemy, and 90 percent of the liquid in the cans ended up in the canopy of the jungle. So, you save the second can, set it just out from your hooch that night and drink it the next morning when it has cooled down to 80 degrees.

As I said, pop came down in the bags also. The next night Irvin "Moose" McCoun said quietly, "Hey Doc, you want a Jack and Coke?"

I said, "What?"

He revealed a fifth of unopened Jack Daniels whisky!

"Moose, how long have you been humping that fifth?"

"Since the last time we got care packages."

That was about two months ago. He told me that he had already drunk the other three bottles. Moose was just one tough old boy who deserved his nickname. We had mixers that evening, and my good friend Moose did something medicinal for the doc.

One afternoon when the Company was temporarily split up, the first platoon managed to find Charlie on one of the branch trails, and a sustained battle ensued. The NVA had a small tactical advantage behind a knoll. They could pop up, launch RPG's into the platoon's area and lay low again.

As sporadic fire continued from both sides, we began to maneuver to cut off an enemy exit and flank their position. Several men were wounded in the initial action and were being moved to an area that was open enough to use a penetrator to extract them. The Medevac arrived, but the crew could tell by the radio traffic that the fight was still on and did not want to risk making multiple extractions.

They radioed that they were leaving the area. Chaplain Cherry grabbed the radio, and since he out ranked the warrant officer pilot, ordered him to extract the wounded men—NOW!

This was the only time during my tour that a chopper pilot hesitated to extract the wounded. But in the end, they did the job anyway, just as they always had.

Two men took hard hits from the RPG's. One was Tim Gould of Dothan, Georgia, with frag splattering him from head to toe, the majority of which was in his lower extremities. To this day, Tim has bits of junk and frag working out of his skin and causing infections.

At my first reunion in 2003, I met Doug Grier from New York, who had a nearly identical experience in 1970. But he caught it in the upper extremities and was blinded for life. A medic named John "Doc" Marks from Indiana did what he could for him before putting him on the Dustoff. These men survived the war, and we have had good times together in recent years.

Doug Grier, 1969.

The platoons were hanging together fairly close as we poked and prodded our way from one ridge to another, day after day, week after week, firefight after firefight, LZ's, Medevacs and LOGs. We finally settled on an extended hilltop, where we stayed for about three days. It was unusual for us to be in any one place for more than 24 hours. Was this a new tactic by the captain? It did have a good spot for a LZ, which we would need soon for LOG.

Each platoon covered an area of the hill for NDP's then went out on hunting parties by day. Every night, ambush squads or O.P. (outpost) were sent out to cover any trails leading to the main body of the company.

On the morning of April 17th first platoon's O.P., including Specialists James Ervin, Charles Hyatt and Donnie Vaile, were extremely fortunate in spotting NVA troops sneaking up on their position. They blew their claymore mine and begun spraying the area with M-16 fire. Lt. Driver was the first one on his feet and headed down toward the O.P., as return fire from multiple AK-47 could be heard at that point, and an intense firefight was on. Driver's RTO, Clyde Crossguns, took a few extra seconds to detach his radio from the main ruck and was quickly on Driver's heels and running hard down the steep trail toward the firefight. Rifleman Patrick O'Leary was next, following by William (Tiny) Kaufmann, the platoon's artillery forward observer.

The platoon was quickly forming an attack squad, as Driver and the small group joined the action. Their sudden presence redirected the enemy fire from O.P. toward them. Kaufmann and O'Leary jammed in behind a large tree as the bark splinters were being shot off right beside them. Driver and Crossguns were another twenty feet ahead. Crossguns dove for the base of a small tree, unable to move from the barrage of bullets tearing up the ground around him. Lt. Driver, who had continued the open charge, was lying on the ground several feet away, mortally wounded.

With Crossguns pinned down and Kaufmann and O'Leary getting split second opportunities to fire around the tree, the larger group made it down the hill and charged the site, finally driving off the attackers. Crossguns got to his leader first, and saw that the bullet had entered through Driver's right eye. He kicked in the final throes of death. Wounded badly were Hyatt and Vale (Vale also being a Native-American and good friends with Crossguns). Doc Michael Edwards, 1st platoon medic, came down with the attack group. He couldn't do a thing for Driver, but he patched up the other wounded men. Edwards had been in-country for many months, but this was the worst incident he'd dealt with up to that time, and he was very upset about loosing his platoon leader.

When the Claymores detonated, the third platoon was headed out of the perimeter to recon another area of the hill, but close enough to hear the blow by blow of the firefight. It wasn't long before the radio traffic told of the tragic loss of Lt. Driver. We returned to the DP as 1st platoon carried the dead and wounded to the LZ. Medevacs were on the way.

You can read about the details of this event and an excellent tribute to John Cecil Driver in James Durney's book, *Vietnam: The Irish Experience*.

The enemy encountered that day was different. It was not one or two gooks doing a harassment run, it was eight to ten well-trained men, out with the intent of making contact and sustaining a battle. One of the enemy died quickly from the claymore blast, and blood trails were found, but no other bodies.

In my experience, especially during the last five months I served on the line, we had amazingly good leadership. From platoon leaders, sergeants, officers, company commanders and even our battalion commander, Colonel Bob German, who traveled in the field any time there was more than one company traveling together. His code name just happened to be "Driver." They were just good, damn good. They were all Airborne hard chargers who stuck to the task. They all had to do the difficult work of putting men in mortal danger but trying to do it with caution. John Cecil Driver was simply a different type of man – 100 percent soldier. He had no obligation to be in Vietnam, he just wanted to be. He was an Irish national who had already completed his first tour with the 1st Calvary. Then he completed OCS and airborne jump school between tours and came straight back to the war.

 Lt. Driver didn't just come back to the country, he came straight to the worst of the worst. He was older, had ten-plus years on all of us. He had amazing "Soldier of Fortune" stories mixed with a great quiet sense of humor. It was always obvious that Lt. Driver fully respected every man, no matter his job or rank. He was a soldier's soldier who earned respect from all of us. It showed when he charged down that hill to defend the men in his OP. He charged the enemy, and every man followed him.

John Driver.

Putting his body on a helicopter that day struck a blow to every man. We had not only lost a great military leader, we lost a respected friend. It also added one more notch to our level of misery. No one could help but think, "If this could happen to Driver, it can surely happen to me."

Before the day was over, Lt. John Walsh, XO at Sally, arrived at the LZ to fill the space left by Driver until a new replacement could be found. Lt. Walsh was already a wellexperienced platoon leader and was respected by the men as well.

The next morning when I woke up, there was a large ball of coagulated blood dripping from my left forearm. A damn land leech had got me at night. I hate leeches, we all did. They were the Vietnam version of a wood tick, and the ending of the monsoons must have signaled a new hatch.

Land leeches are about half the length of a wooden match and slightly smaller in girth. They get from one place to another like an inch worm, but need foliage or leaves to move on. Everyone tried to make a small trench around their hooch every night, as they could not cross over open dirt. But if you laid your arm across the gap at night you might wake up with a slimy, bloody surprise.

The leeches were tough, unbelievably tough. Moose may have been the only man among us that could pull one of them in two. They definitely added misery to our day-to-day lives, because they were almost everywhere, especially in the hills and mountains. However, we did get relief from them on some of the highest mountain peaks.

Leeches also made for entertainment. If we were required to sit for extended periods during recon, we could take advantage of the convenient flaws in their design. You could spot them coming and block their path or play tricks on them, like bending a branch down and providing a leaf to walk on, then letting go of the branch.

They had great difficulty surviving even a few grains of salt, but the two most effective weapons were the hot tip of a cigarette or, better yet, the iodine vial. Give it a tiny drop of iodine, and a leech will do a great little (brief) dance for you.

On many occasions I rolled one up in a ball between the side of my first finger and thumb, slowly adding pressure until it was a small hard ball. Believe it or not, in five minutes they could assume their original shape and inch back towards you again.

I believe that we stayed in this area or near the LZ for several days. It may have been the next day on a long sweep that we linked up with a sister company. I met First Sgt. George Shorr that day. George was from Chalmette, Louisiana, near New Orleans. He lost his home in 2005 to the *Katrina* hurricane—got out just in the nick of time.

He was a career soldier, a damn good one, tough as nails, and he spoke his own version of Southern Creole. The next morning as we were rucked up and ready to head out, George, Dan Wakefield and I were talking when we heard an unfamiliar "thump" in the distance. What the heck?

Several seconds passed, then "Whistle-BLAM," a mortar round hit, just down the hill from us!

Dan dove behind a rotting log, George and I both jumped into a hole in the ground and waited for round two. Only seconds passed when we heard, "Medic! Medic!"

I got up, mumbling obscenities, as First Sgt. Shorr pulled at my pant leg, and hollered, "Hey Doc! Yo bleedin'" and pointed at my neck.

I couldn't see it, but I touched the area as I grabbed the catastrophe bag and high-tailed it down to the location of the calls. Sure enough, there was blood on my fingers.

Chaplain Cherry was nearby and arrived just before me. Together we worked on two wounded men, their legs peppered with shrapnel from the knees down. We quickly cut the trousers away, but there was little we could do other than stop the bleeding and cover the wounds. Most of the flack passing through the trousers took some of the cloth with it, and some threads were imbedded into their flesh but hung onto the trouser as it was removed. Drops of blood occasionally fell from my neck onto our work, but there was no time to worry about that then. These men were very fortunate and would probably end up back in the rear or back in the "world." They were ambulatory, and we were getting them around to hump back to the LZ, when Sgt. Major Shorr arrived with a note pad, writing down the names of the men for Purple Heart medals.

He, of course, knew I was also hit by a piece of the ordinance and said I would be receiving a Purple Heart medal as well.

I (foolishly or pridefully) declined, saying, "Not for this wound."

It didn't hurt much, and these two men, would be picking festering junk out of their legs for years to come.

I thought that the flack must have bounced off. It hit directly on my collar bone, about one inch from my throat. I tended the wound for about two weeks as it disappeared to a small scar.

Fast forward again another 30 years. I have a routine physical that includes a chest x-ray. The technician developed the film and applied it to a backlit viewer. As the technician began reviewing the image, I couldn't help noticing a very bright spot at the end of my right collar bone. I asked the technician what it was, as I pointed to the spot in the photo.

The technician looks at the spot, thought a bit, and said, "Well, there is nothing wrong with the film."

He turned around, put his finger directly on the spot where the shrapnel hit and said, "Something's in there."

"Well I'll be damned!"

I carried that piece of flack all these years and did not know it was there! I had all but forgotten that day, but in an instant it all rushed back. If I had known at the time that a small fragment from that exploding mortar round had driven itself deep into my neck, I may have accepted the Purple Heart medal that day!

In 2003, I proceeded to correct my military records so as to reflect the Purple Heart medal. I may have to write another book about what it takes for a layman veteran to navigate the black hole called the Military Records and Reserve Board, located in St. Louis, Missouri. Let's just say I have provided solid proof and testimony for my case. It's now 2010 and—even with the help of my congressman—we are still on a dead end road.

On April 20th, the entire company was to move out into new territory. It was very quiet among all of us, as we all still had a sour ball in our gut from losing Driver. 1st platoon took point for the company, but needed to pass through the third and the second to clear the perimeter and begin its recon. Third platooners were falling in behind the slack man in the first platoon, and squad by squad the perimeter guards were leaving their posts to fall into the ranks.

It is customary and tactically important for each man to maintain a space of 10 to 20 feet between each other, because it just makes it harder for the enemy to take out more than one or two men at a time. However, like any other traffic situation, when the light turns green, you are bumper to bumper for a while before the line spreads out (a cluster). Besides, most of us were still in the "presumed safety" of our perimeter.

The 1st platoon point had pushed out of the perimeter 60 to 80 yards, and the clusterf**k (men too close to one another) was still in effect, when the point man spotted movement and fired first. But all it did was to trigger the start of another ambush. I had never heard that many AK's firing at the same time. I didn't hit the dirt, nor did anyone else. It looked like the gooks were over the edge of the ridge far enough, so that the tracers could be seen on an upward trajectory over our heads. 3rd platoon CP were pretty much together, Lt. Kopystianskyj, his RTO, myself and possibly the red leg. We had just shouldered our packs as the radio began to bark a message from Lt. Walsh, "Get a gun up here—NOW! I am all full of holes."

We went in full charge toward the action.

No one in our group could return fire yet, because we were unsure where all of our guys were. In seconds we closed the gap to 30 or 40 feet, but the NVA must have been moving in closer at the same time. Moose McCoun who was well ahead and to the left of me, was suddenly hit by a barrage of gunfire coming from the foliage. The tracers could be seen coming out through his pack and gear as he tightened up his body and seemed to tiptoe in a circle before returning fire.

The green tracers were coming in at a critical level now. I realized I was dancing through the bullets that popped as they went by at lightning speed. It was time for Doc to hit the dirt. I knew about where Lt. Walsh would have been and started a fast low crawl toward that spot.

Some of our group hit the ground while others charged the location of the enemy. There was a lot of lead in the air, when I spotted the lieutenant and made my way to him. Doc. Edwards was already there and appeared to have just stopped CPR.

Mike was crouched down low on his knees, holding his own face with his hands, sobbing and shaking. The trauma of losing another platoon leader in just three days was taking its toll on him. The Lieutenant was laying face up, his rucksack under him, propping up his torso, his head tipped back, helmet on the ground.

I grabbed Mike, shook him hard and instructed him to get the ruck straps off Walsh on his side, while ripping them off my side at the same time. Mike was recovering as we stripped the gear away. Not being able to see the wound, we needed to cut off his fatigue jacket. Lt. Walsh was making ragged breaths as the work progressed, but he was not responding to vocal prompts. The firefight was slowing down. It could have been as much as two or three minutes by now, as we uncovered two bullets holes just below his right arm pit. We cut more clothing away and rolled him to his left side to look for an exit wound. We saw it, and it was not good. We compressed the entrance wound, held it in place with his arm, rolled him to the right side, compressed the exit wounds in the center of his back and laid him back down on the compresses. We tried a regimen CPR again, but he was no longer taking breaths. His color was gone along with his pulse.

Five minutes could not have passed yet. We tried CPR again with no gain at all. The bullets that went through Lt. Walsh, no doubt caused internal damage beyond our ability to help.

I had the "What-if-we-had-done-so-and-so..." dreams for many years after we were forced to give up on Lt. Walsh.

I must now fast forward to September 20, 2010. I received an e-mail from Mike Edwards, stating that he had just received an e-mail from the widow of Lt. Walsh. She had stumbled onto our B-Co. web site, went to the memorial page, and found a note that Mike had written there. Mike knew that I would have great interest in her letter too. I have also corresponded with her now, and it's so wonderful to correspond with her, but very hard to believe.

Please fast forward again to our B-Co. reunion in Branson, Missouri. Mrs. Denise (Walsh) Weldon and her husband, Art elected to join the reunion.

Her presence and address to the group during the primary event, gave proof to the amazing woman that she is. Her husband Art is also an understanding and amazing man.

Denise told us that the government has not explained anything about the circumstances of John's death, and that it remained a mystery until now. Denise was able to meet with many men that were witness to the events of that day, and she heard what a respected leader he was. My personal reunion with Denise was filled with tears, but I was able to hold her for a while, and everything was alright.

New calls for "medic" could be heard. Mike and I both bowed our heads and made quick prayers before hunting for the other wounded. There were several more, but by now all three medics were on the scene. The NVA had fled, and recons were sweeping the area. Blood trails were found but no enemy bodies.

One of our men, shot through both of his shoulders, was carried to the LZ in a poncho and laid on the ground. The Dust-off was called but had not arrived yet. I was checking on some of the men, when I heard a faint voice come from the man with the shoulder wounds. It was fortunate that I heard him, as his voice was faint, and my ears were ringing bad from noise of the gun fight.

The wounded trooper was a tall, wiry built black man. I knew his name well then, but simply cannot remember it now. I knelt down beside him, and he whispered, "Doc, I think I am still bleeding."

His dressing looked good from the top and I told him it did.

He said, "Check the back."

I could not move him without hurting him, but it needed to be done. He groaned as I lifted one side, and sure enough, his compresses had pulled away while he was being carried in the poncho.

I went to work on him immediately. A one point I needed help to hold him in a near sitting position, as I all but mummified him in compress and ace wrap. It helped in the end because the process immobilized his arms, and he was more comfortable.

There was a great deal of blood in the poncho, and he was acting quite foggy, saying he was cold. He needed blood fast, but we only carried a blood multiplier called Albumin. I quickly prepared a vial. The veins in his arms were totally collapsed. With his feet propped up on a ruck, I removed a boot to find a vein in his ankle, but they were collapsed also. I did not know how bad

I was hurting him, but I tried in vain on both feet to make the IV work. The only place remaining was his neck, and that was taboo out there in the field. I could have put his life at risk more than it was already.

I could hear the WOP–WOP–WOP of the Medevac on its way. We quickly put him and other less wounded men on the chopper as soon as it landed. As we finished loading them up, I got face to face with the flight medic and told him of the man's critical condition.

The helicopter headed out for the field hospital and to this day, I do not know the man's fate. I pray that someone will read this one day, identify with the incident, tell me who he was and if he lived. If I knew his name, I could at least look for it on the Wall.

Officers, left to right: 1st Lt. Graney (CO), 1st Lt. Pue (3rd Plt.), 1st Lt. Walsh (2nd Plt. – KIA) and 1st Lt. Julien.

While enquiring about him at our 2009 reunion, Lt. Jim Julien told me that he talked to the man just after he was moved to the LZ, and that he was in a good mood despite having bullet holes through both shoulders. Jim couldn't remember the man's name, but chuckled as he repeated the man's question, "How in the hell am I going to be able to take a piss?"

Let's not forget Moose McCoun. When the firefight ended, Moose was still standing. Most of his ammunition was shot up, and his trousers were soaked with the water from his canteens. Every can suffered from bullet holes, and his back pack was riddled. Most of his C's were shot to pieces, and the smell of Jack Daniels mixed with gun powder dripped from his pack—but believe it or not, the big man did not have one single scratch on his body!

He got new canteens and food from left over back packs of wounded men, but the big guy really got pissed when he discovered his air mattress had been shot up too.

You would need to talk to Moose, if you want to know how he treated the enemy after that.

Later that day, I noticed a ragged but round hole through the fiberglass forestock of my M-16. It was about the size of a 7.62 mm projectile. Maybe not all of the enemy fire was above our heads as I thought it was, and maybe I should have hit the dirt a little sooner.

Something else was becoming more evident. I noticed it in myself and most of the others, but it did not really sink in until years later. When we were subjected to extreme adversity for long periods of time, the intense drama of firefights and booby traps, and witnessed over and over the destruction that our modern military machine could produce, we simply became part of it. I will attempt to explain this condition in a later chapter of this story, but let me say now that the condition would cause us to do things we would never normally do.

By noon we are ready to move out again.

Now, put yourself in a platoon leader's position and make a choice, from your three options, as to who will be the point group today. 1st, 2nd or 3rd squad? Then the squad leader decides who walks point. A choice must be made—and at times like that you may see the chosen man vomit out his breakfast, collect himself, move out and do his job.

For the remainder of us, our fear of what can happen to the point man is parallel with our trust in his ability.

It turned out to be a three-day, two-night sweep that eventually brought us back to the same hilltop with the LZ. But on the second or third day, while working slowly along a ridge, someone heard noises in the jungle ahead. Recons moved forward with extreme caution as the column of men disappeared into the flanks. We held the position for about thirty minutes, when a violent crashing in the tree came from beyond the point area. All heads must have spun in the direction of the noise as well as the gun barrels.

"CRASH!"—then "CRASH!" again!

Suddenly a figure swung violently down through the upper canopy, hurtling itself from limb to limb.

An orangutan—and it looked really mad!

It was throwing itself 15 to 20 feet with one hand, catching another limb with the other, howling and catapulting to the next limb.

Long, reddish-brown hair streaming back as he swung in scalloped arches from limb to limb. In seconds he came within a few feet of the ground, between the flanks, then disappeared back into the upper foliage. He kept going like that until the noise slowly faded in the distance. It was a truly amazing sight. I will never forget it. But we really did not need it then. We could hear monkeys quite often but just never had seen them. Late in the third day, we returned to the LZ area. We came in on a trail the other platoons used, but we had not been on yet. It was a steep-banked ravine, and we worked our way down, crossed a rocky, tumbling stream, and climbed up a very steep forty-yard hill to the plateau that we were familiar with—and had bad memories of. I took advantage of a small pause while crossing the stream and topped off my canteens before climbing to the old NDP site.

The evening was a little easier on the men as foxholes were already dug around the perimeter. We just filled a few sand bags, put the claymores out, pitched a hooch, and there was still time to eat.

"Hold your fire" by Rebecca (Flory) Hoekman.

These were somber times, however. We suffered great losses during the last week, and we were still in the same area as a constant reminder. We remained on high alert. Word was filtering down about the next mission. We would be moving out and could plan on humping a long distance the next day.

It was barely breaking daylight the next morning, when it

became official. The hike would be long, and platoon leaders were advised to fill all the canteens because water might be hard to get.

Eight or ten men who volunteered from the CP and platoons were formed up as a watering party. Each man carried six or eight canteens to be filled. They headed out of the perimeter and down the forty-yard bank to the creek at the same spot I filled my canteens the day before. When they reached the creek, several men were dispatched up the trail and up the banks on each side to act as guards. The remaining men begun filling the jugs as fast as they could.

I was making final adjustments on my gear in preparation for the day's hump, when the distinctive sound of two AK-47's on full automatic came from the direction of the creek. I dropped to my knees as men dove toward their defensive positions. A split second passed before the M-16 fire answered, but in between, I could hear the screams of men echoing up the canyon through the gunfire.

Back on my feet, I grabbed the top rail of my ruck and ran for the slopes as hard as I could, leaving my M-16 and catastrophe bag behind. I used the ruck like a cane to help stabilize my rapid decent down the hill. Within seconds I was nearing the bottom, with gunfire seemingly in all directions and screams beginning to reveal the direction of wounded men. As I broke into the clear area caused by the stream, I could see the water was flowing bright red. To my left, several steps up the stream, I saw the figure of a GI on his knees, face down in the water. I leaped to him, grabbed his collar and jerked his head out of the water. It was the new guy, Gary Nieman. His wound was fatal. I hesitated for a second, and because it seemed best, that the water was washing away the sin, I laid him back into the stream.

One man seemed to be hollering more than the others, over on the opposite bank. Spinning in that direction, my eyes caught another figure sitting on a rock, looking straight up at a gap in the canopy that was letting light stream in.

It was David Krautscheid, his right arm hung down at his side with a very large hole through it, just above the elbow, and another into his ribs where the bullet had continued its path. His mouth was open as he looked up, motionless, not making a sound, his blood oozing into the stream.

I threw my back pack down near David, opened it and grabbed a tourniquet, but first I headed to the man doing the hollering. It was Bill "Tiny" Kaufmann. He was just up the creek bank and shot through the left thigh, blood squirting out whenever he moved his hand away. I stretched the tourniquet into place, tied it off and instructed Bill to release the pressure a little every minute. About that time, other men who had been on the watering party joined the work, I supplied them with what they needed to deal with Bill, and went back for Krautscheid. Dave had what would be my first sucking chest wound. I opened a petroleum covered patch that is made just for that purpose and slapped it on the hole in his chest.

David Reinheimer.

It's designed to work like a patch on an inner tube, to keep air from getting into the chest cavity and collapsing a lung. Dave was a good sized guy, who happened to be wearing an OD t-shirt that came off easily, and I dove into working on him.

The gunfire had stopped and men were coming up the stream, some wounded. Many men had charged down the hill to defend the watering party and now were taking guard positions and helping the wounded.

Frantically I worked on Dave. It took time to wrap the ace bandage around his chest. Another man held a large compress around his arm as I worked. The remainder of the wounded men were ambulatory, and, as they came to my location, I made quick assessments and gave the appropriate materials to anyone available, with directions for application. I ended up ace bandaging Dave's arm directly to his chest. As soon as I finished, I pulled him up, hooked his left arm over my shoulder and headed up the hill with him on my back, while his legs dangled off each side.

He began to come out of his daze, and gave an occasional push to aid in our climb back up. About 20 feet from the top, the squad leader, Sgt. Walt Bouman, was headed down. I stopped him and asked him to take Dave to the top, which he did. I returned to the creek to see if there were any remaining wounded and to retrieve my ruck. All the other men had made short work of assisting the other wounded: David Reinheimer with a bullet through his right thigh and a deep crease from a bullet in his helmet; William Christensen and Vernon Withers, both with multiple wounds; and last was Steven Johnson from Indianapolis, Indiana, shot through the right forearm. The arm hung down with bones protruding. He got himself to the top of the hill..

The men also packed out their gear and a pile of empty canteens. Anyone who had seen the creek, that was still running bright pink, had no interest in filling them. I made my way back to the top of the hill and to the remainder of my gear, then on to the LZ to assist in getting the wounded on Medevacs.

Dave Krautscheid had already been air lifted from the LZ in a Loach. I did not know that until 2003. At my first B-Co. reunion in Kansas City, Missouri, I was in the reception room registering at the sign-in table, when another first-timer walked up to the desk and asked if this was the 101st reunion. Here was a big man, six feet tall, in a short-sleeve Hawaiian shirt. I couldn't help but notice the large scar just above his right elbow.

"My God, I know you," I said, "You're David. You were gone when I came back to the LZ, and I never knew what happened to you."

David explained that some high brass was in the area, and there was one open seat remaining on that Loach. Dave, the first wounded man on the LZ, was strapped into the small chopper and taken directly to Camp Eagle Field Hospital. Dave and I hugged one another, and the tears did flow.

In 2009, Ann and I hosted the B-Co. reunion in Kalamazoo. Dave and his wife Pam arrived several days early and stayed at our home, as we did at their sponsorship in Portland in 2007. The bond remains.

We held ground near the LZ for another day or so. On the morning of April 24th, a helicopter landed at the LZ and several men jumped off. One was a very big man, all of six-foot-two, 220 pounds, and a captain at that. Captain Grainey mustered a few men around the CP and quickly performed a military ritual, giving command of B-Co. to the new captain. Graney had already passed his required field time and was past due for R&R. This was a sudden and uneasy change for us, but the new line backer-looking, Captain Franzinger, seemed to have some of that "been there, done that" air about him, and that helped in the transition.

I missed Captain Graney. He was a very good leader, although some didn't think so, because he was also one of those "Airborne All The Way" guys who took his infantry job serious. He would often volunteer us to stay in the field for extended periods of time if he thought we could corral the enemy. Well, that was our job!

Please fast forward once again to spring 2010.

I was sitting in the Canteen at our VFW with a good friend, John Depierre. I happened to mention Captain Graney in a story about my VN tour, when John said, "Graney?"

I replied "Yes."

"Pierce T. Graney?"

"Yes, how in the heck do you know that name?"

"He was one of my base commanders when I was stationed in Germany about 20 years ago."

He then dug down into his briefcase and pulled out a citation of merit given to him by Colonel Graney. I had called Tom Graney for information while writing this book, and called him back again in regards to John. Tom remembered him from his command in Germany, but of course, John is one of those guys not easily forgotten. Sorry John!

A sister company also took advantage of LZ LOG, and while they were there, Chaplain Cherry packed out with them. Some days later, they became involved in one hell of a firefight and the chaplain charged straight into the battle to help the wounded. He was carrying a man to a safer place and stepped on an anti-personnel mine that blew off his left foot. That brought his field service to a sudden halt.

Our amazing chaplain survived the war and has spent the last 40 years involved in veterans support programs. He retired from San Francisco VA Medical Center, as Chief Chaplain. He uses golf tournaments across the nation as fund raisers and awareness events.

Jim Duke made his way back to the company on one of

the LOG birds. He had arrived at Sally's gate on a deuce-and-a-half the day before with several new recruits whom he directed to headquarters. One of the new recruits, Phil Hazen from Oregon, had orders for B-Co. Duke accompanied Phil on his first H-1 ride out to the bush and, upon arrival, had to face the fact that there were only three men remaining of his original squad. All the rest were new replacements. And, he had to swallow the news that two of his platoon leaders had been KIA during his absence.

We all knew something big was going on, as day and night we could hear air strikes and artillery bombing in the near distance. For us ground pounders, there was, as yet, no knowledge of Hill 937, even through the work we and other units had been doing for months, was slowly pointing toward that particular hot spot. Later we learned the hill was the source of the bombing we had been hearing. More importantly, there is little doubt in my mind now, that the emphasis in packing for a long hike and extended stay could have put us at the base of that hill. However, with the loss of Driver and Walsh, the watering party incident and a change of the company command, we didn't go.

17.
Back to Pohl Bridge

It was probably April 28th when we were extracted from that ugly place and flown back to Pohl Bridge. It was so good to be back at the bridge. Temperature and humidity were increasing daily, and the river made for a cool respite, when time allowed. The bunker we had spent so much time rebuilding months earlier was in good condition, clean and even a few improvements. There was something different in our state of being now. We had done our job well in locating the enemy, but the price had been high and very hard on all of us. Field troops subject to constant hardship and horrible things, do get calloused and develop an ability to simply move on or look away. But it remains in your heart and your mind and shows in your eyes.

I went to see Hoah and her family. We had a nice reunion, and I brought them extra sundries as gifts. I figured if they could not use them themselves, they'd be good for barter. The C.B's water purification station was at full capacity, but the old crew was all replaced.

As resilient as young GI's can be, it was simply hard to muster up the ability to have fun. The news was in the wind that a large operation was coming soon, that we would be part of it and were to get prepared. Our new CO, Captain Franzinger, was making sure we were well supplied and even managed to have hot GI chow delivered twice that week. We were advised to write letters home then and to tell our loved ones that they might not be hearing from us for a while. We had never been told that before. We didn't know what the mission was going to be, but that news was certainly setting the stage for growing ulcers.

Pohl Bridge.

    A few days into our stay at the bridge, Hoah ran over to our side, searching for me. She was frantic about an old man who was hurt near her house. I grabbed my catastrophe bag and followed her back across the bridge.

    Near the intersection, just one or two hoochs from Hoah's place, an old man (*papasan*) was propped against a tree by the edge of the road and a local man, some form of constable, had drawn a line in the dirt road in the shape of the man's body, like you see with chalk on TV. He was taking depositions from a produce truck driver, the *papasan* and other witnesses.

Meanwhile, I checked out old *papasan* and discovered he had a broken collar bone and a few minor wounds. Hoah explained that the man had been walking down the road and something hanging from the truck struck him. I hadn't been around the civilian population very much, but it had always seemed clear that we should help the native people if we could. The business with the constable was settled, and Hoah asked if he could be taken to a hospital. The C. B.'s had a jeep and agreed to drive if I wanted to take him. I cleared it with my platoon leader, and we were good to go.

Now, there is very little you can actually do for a broken collar bone with the exception of making a figure eight with an ace bandage around one arm, then across the back to the opposite arm, thereby creating a horizontal eight pattern. Tension on the wrap increases with each of four or five wraps, until the shoulders are forced back somewhat, as if at attention. This pulls the sagging shoulder back into alignment, and the collar bone follows suit.

I gave him two Darvons for pain, constructed the figure eight shoulder harness, put him in the back seat of the jeep and headed south to Camp Eagle. It was a well-used gravel road with plenty of bumps. Even with the rough road, the old man never let out a peep, but you could see the pain he was feeling in his face.

When we reached the field hospital at Camp Eagle, the medics were quite willing to work on him, starting with an x-ray. Hoah was not with us, and communicating with this old guy was quite difficult. When we showed him the x-ray he seemed to understand and allowed the work to be done. My ace harness was removed, and another more substantial figure eight harness was placed on him. He also received one morphine syrette. A few polite bows between the *papasan* and the medics, and we were on our way back.

It didn't take long for the morphine to kick in. Like the ride in, he never let out a peep, but when I occasionally looked back at him, he was bobbing around with a big smile on his face.

We dropped him off near Hoah's house, and after she helped me explain for him to leave the harness on at least six weeks, he went on his way.

The next day, I was summoned by one of our guys at a perimeter bunker near the bank of the river, where a family in a large old sampan had pulled on shore and was looking for medical help. Again, I took my "cat" bag and found my way through a gap in the concertina wire and down to the river's edge where the family was temporarily moored.

A young woman with a baby wrapped in a light blanket stepped from the boat onto shore to greet me. Again the language barrier was a serious problem, but when she unveiled the baby to show its head, the language barrier didn't matter for the moment. The baby had what looked like the worst case of cradle cap one could ever expect to see. But the bag I was carrying had nothing in it that would be of any help in this case. I signaled for them to stay put the best I could, and they did. I went back to the bunker and returned with my full rucksack containing better supplies.

I examined the child and found him to be in fairly decent health, but in place of what should have been hair on his scalp was nothing but heavy scabs. I beckoned the women to allow me to hold the child, and I knelt down by the river edge and began washing the babies head using Phisohex and gauze patches.

I sent one of the men to find Hoah in hopes of being able to communicate with the family and explain to them that the condition of their baby was beyond my training, but Hoah was nowhere to be found. I spent over an hour using the soap, swabs, and nearly all the fresh water from my canteens. The work, however, seemed to have paid off, as I had slowly removed nearly all the scabs. The work had finally gotten to the point that the child would be harmed if I tried to remove the most deeply rutted scabs near the middle of its head. So I gave him a final rinse, patted his head dry and then rubbed in a good coat of antibiotic ointment.

The next trick was to attempt to explain to the family that I would like them to do this every day until the bottle of Phisohex soap and ointment ran out. I used every means of physical and vocal communication to transfer the information. Whether I was successful or not, I will never know. But they looked like they were happier as they shoved away from shore and continued their journey.

Years later, after having used Phisohex soap on all of my own children, the stuff was found to be unsafe for infants and taken off the market. My thoughts found their way back to that poor Vietnamese family, and I wonder, yet today, if I did the right thing.

There is something else that happens at times like this that I have never talked about until now, but I suspect it has always happened and always will. I also suspect that it may happen more often to people who have been exposed to certain stark realities.

The men of B-Company were exposed to the reality of jungle warfare, and, as gridiron-tough as these men were, their minds could not help thinking about how truly miserable they may be on the next mission. Nor can they help thinking how fortunate they have been this far, still in one piece. But they know by trial just how quickly that can change.

With the thought of a very serious mission looming in the near future, some men came to me in private, expressing fears that they would not survive it, and asking if there was a way (as a medic) to send them to the rear.

The first time it happened I was taken by surprise and wished that my medical training had prepared me for it. My own thoughts would drift in that direction at times, but I was in outstanding physical condition, like all our men, and I knew there was not a snowball's chance in hell of getting myself sent to the rear.

I quickly developed a stance on the matter, "If I can't go, there is no way in hell I will send you back."

That did not mean that I didn't try to counsel these individuals, because I did. I am, however, a lousy psychologist, and the above may have been the extent of my bedside manner.

One particular individual had a very bad case of jungle rot on both shins, and despite the work I did on him, the infected area seemed to slowly grow larger. He came to me at the bridge, expressing his nightmares about dying in the jungle, and asked if I would send him back to Sally because of the infection. His timing was bad. I turned him down because I had learned earlier that day that he had been removing the bandages, damaging the healing process and contaminating the infected area on purpose. Someone in his squad witnessed him doing it at night and reported it to me.

Our dear Lord explains in the Bible, that "We know not the time of the end," and I believe that.

It can make you wonder about the premonitions and actions of this man. My mind returns to him when conditions are right, and I wonder if I did the right thing in his case.

The thought of leaving the field did not escape me either. I explained, once again, to the CO that I was in my ninth month in-country and hadn't gotten an R&R yet. My reason was actually legitimate, but the answer was still "No."

It was also at times like this at the bridge when some of the men endured yet another form of misery. It was delivered right into their hands in the form of the *Dear John Letter*, and could cause a hard-nose Airborne trooper to go straight to his knees. It might also cause him to become a bit unstable for a while—*not good out there!*

We all worked hard to help the men this happened to. But, here again, he was miserable, facing even more misery, danger to his life and limb, 5000 miles away from home, with no way out but doing the hard time. All his dreams included her, and they helped him survive, but back in the "world" some dim-witted, self-serving chickey-poo, decided it was a good time to tell him to take a hike.

Here is an example that truly takes the *Dear John* condition to it's highest level.

One of my friends in the 3rd platoon was married and had one child before entering the Army. He and his wife had made plans over many months to meet in Hawaii on his R&R, and, of course, most of his pay was sent home for their care, and to fund the trip.

The day finally came, and "John" left for his R&R. His wife met him at the airport in Honolulu, but instead of his daughter in hand, she introduced her new boyfriend and handed "John" a set of divorce papers that needed to be signed. She told him they had already been there for a most glorious week and needed to catch their plane home in a few minutes, then were quickly lost in the crowd.

Uncle Sam kept his end of the bargain and supplied him with the hotel room for seven days and nights. But he had less than a hundred dollars in his pocket and found out quickly that his bank accounts were closed out. He needed to wire his parents for money just to eat.

For me, I had envisioned the potential problems of a close relationship when I was drafted and cut them off, face to face, before I left. I never felt this misery myself, but I saw the damage those letters produced for others. These women (girls) simply couldn't conceive of what their boyfriends or husbands were going through, and maybe they deserve forgiveness. But most of those bitches are about 60 years old now and probably ugly as hell. If they ended up with shitty lives after their *Dear John* bomb, it's probably okay with us old GI's.

For the young women who loved their soldier husbands

and supported them in every way, how hard it must have been. How scary—how much they had to worry. This could only be second to the love of a parent with their young son in such a horrible place. I cannot imagine how I would feel if one of my children were in such a condition.

Lt. Pue and David Krautcheid, at our first duty at Pohl Bridge.

With only a day remaining at the bridge, supplies were coming, and it seemed we were packing our gear with more care then ever before, with an extra ammo clip here, an extra grenade there. We had recently been given a new food choice called an L.R.P. (Long Range Patrol), we called them "lurps." They came in a poly/canvas looking vacuum sealed OD (Olive Drab) bag that held the usual sundries and condiments, along with a poly sack full of freeze-dried food. I think there were about six varieties, rice and beans, rice and pork or chicken, beef stew and chili-con-carne. Their advantage was size and weight, being smaller than C's and much lighter.

The down side was that they were all but impossible to eat unless very hot water was poured into the bag and it could set for a while. You just couldn't heat water anytime you wanted while in the bush. From my normal 15 C's, I packed ten and five LRP's, which worked out quite well.

It was May 7th, and we were notified that we would be leaving by truck the next day, and to pack a little extra food, as we would be staying near FB Birmingham until the ninth.

This entire thing was different in approach from other missions. We couldn't pry any information from the CO or any of the brass. Everyone was nerved up, and there probably wasn't much sleep that night either. The next morning there was some hustle, as we all ended up at the south end of the bridge in full pack, waiting for the trucks. I found time to see Hoah and explained that I might never have a chance to return to the bridge, but I really hoped I could one day—and that I missed her already.

It was the last time I saw her.

On the road from Pohl Bridge to Firebase Birmingham.

God has given me the opportunity to raise three daughters of my own. I love them so much and thank our Maker every day that they were born in America.

It was afternoon when the trucks finally arrived. In the full sun, hot and dusty, the ride was only about 45 minutes. We were dropped off at an old, abandoned air strip near the base of Birmingham.

18.
Apache Snow

On mid-afternoon of May 8th, we arrived at what looked like an old air strip for smaller fixed-wing planes. It also served as part of the road passing the base of the hill that Firebase Birmingham sat on.

Let me tell you, what we saw on and around the strip was a shocking sight. There were more helicopters and more field troops than we had ever seen in one place. I believe our entire battalion, along with other battalions from other army units, was there, and others were arriving by chopper and trucks. The entire area was full of activity and, of course, dust from the constant air travel.

Our convoy stopped as it pulled onto the beginning of the old strip, and we merged off to the side in an unoccupied area. We linked up with the sister company's defensive perimeter and were told to hooch up for the night. As we went about the routine business of setting up a temporary home/NDP, there was a GI buzz in the air that all boiled down to one question:

"What in the ——— is going on?"

And by the way, with all these troops out here, who is pulling perimeter guard on all the Firebases and the bridge we just left?

However, it's spooky, to say the least, that you can feel safe in knowing you are part of a huge group of men, battle-hardened and armed to the teeth. Our position was greater than mortar distance away from the surrounding hills, and there was only sand and low scrub out in the distance, so vision was good. This place was actually quite safe at the time, but we had yet to be told what was about to happen.

The author with Frank Hilley.

Tie and Pat O'Leary prior to Operation Apache Snow.

It all made for a restless night. But I did fall asleep in the wee morning hours, laying back against my ruck, almost as if wearing it, helmet still on my head. I remember it well, because I slipped into what I will call a very bad dream in which I felt I was awake inside the dream—like my psyche was awake, but my physical body was not. This seemed to have lasted for a very long time. I could sense activity around me but simply couldn't move a single muscle. I couldn't figure out if I was in a coma, if I had died or what. I finally woke up as the sun found a place to shine directly on my face.

The guys were already chowing down and packing their gear. I couldn't eat anything, as the dream, or condition, left me feeling sick. But, I got on my feet, did my chores and made ready for whatever was to come.

The dream condition returned and haunted me on a totally random basis for about twenty years afterwards. I thank our Lord, from time to time, for relieving me of those nightmares.

Helicopters began coming in again that morning, and at one point, there must have been 60 to 80 birds all on the ground, end to end, down the length of the old gravel runway. It was actually an awesome sight to witness, even if we were all scared shitless.

Late in the morning, the first assaults begun to take off, usually six birds to a group or sortie. Volley after volley left the area, heading north, until all the aircraft were gone. About an hour later, they began reappearing, taking on more troops and departing again. This continued every hour into the afternoon, when it became our turn to make the assault.

Our sortie took us northwest along the east side of the mountains forming the east side of what we knew as the A Shau Valley. We flew to the northern end, banking left between ridges, and for the first time came into full view of the valley on a very clear day.

Now, I am going to try to describe to you just what *the valley* meant to us. I will start with a excerpt from the book of Psalms, "The Valley of the Shadow of Death."

Think back to your childhood and of the thing that frightened you most, The "boogie" man.

This is the home of the boogie man, and we were going straight into the airspace of his back yard. I had heard stories of death in the A Shau from the time I arrived in-country. From our altitude we could see an endless string of large and small bomb craters and the skeletons of old crashed helicopters. It was obviously a fertile valley, but there was no farming going on there now. This place remained the property of the enemy after nearly five years of war.

I had quickly forgotten the bad dream and accompanying sickness, as we ground pounders looked at one another in stark fear. We were about the fourth bird in this lift, and I can well bet that the other guys on the other flights were going through the same thing. We began beckoning the door gunners—

"Why are we out here in plain sight?"

"Where in the hell are we going?"

They ignored us for the most part and concentrated on their jobs, because they also knew they were flying in the "bad place."

From my position on the craft, I could see forward, and it wasn't long before I saw that all the birds were in a string formation headed for what looked like a freshly bulldozed Firebase, just short of the top of a mountain. In studying the Firebase for a moment, it occurred to me that there was higher ground to the south of the new base.

Militarily speaking, whoever holds the higher ground has the advantage, and it appeared to me that this Firebase was at a disadvantage. I punched the other guys saying, "Look where they put that freaking Firebase."

"Oh shit, I don't want to go there."

We were nearing the final approach to the FB when our bird suddenly took a hard bank to the right and headed straight back over the floor of the valley. Again we were screaming at the gunners—

"What the hell are we doing?"

As we could see the other craft in our group beginning to land on the base, we are now going the opposite direction! I didn't like the looks of the base, but I didn't like flying out over the open valley like a plump duck ready for harvest either.

Finally, a door gunner hollered out, "A chopper has crashed, and we are going to rescue the crew."

About that time our craft began circling in a descending spiral toward the ground and, soon enough, we could see the downed H-1 laying on its side, smoking, with four men waving their arms at us. Our pilot circled around and, finding a small opening in the elephant grass, put her down about a hundred yards from the crash site.

They say that your butt puckers up real tight when you're really scared. Well, you couldn't have pounded a straight pin into any of ours with a sledge hammer about then.

"Get out and form a DP around the bird!"

Oh shit, what next?

We push out through two-foot tall grass and stop near the edge of the rotor wash. The pilot kept the throttle going on the H-1, and all we could see was ten-foot elephant grass waving violently away from us. We held fast for a minute or two, when we began to hear shots fired in the direction of the crash site. Suddenly, the four crew members began to emerge from the tall grass, door gunners first, then the pilots. Each pilot seemed to take turns holding back, emptying his pistol into the path behind him, while the other reloaded. It was like watching an old western movie unfold.

Now, we had a real problem.

There had been six grunts packed to the hilt on our chopper, one humping a Pig and laced with extra ammo, as well as his ammo bearer. Now we have four additional crew, two of them door gunners who brought there M-60's and their ammo boxes with them.

All of us are quite anxious about getting back on board with our original crew with their two M-60's. Okay, that's fourteen men; six with full field gear and five M-60 machine guns with lots of extra ammo.

It must have looked like an intense Chinese fire drill for about a minute, as everyone scrambled to get on board.

I ended up in a *Kimuchi* squat directly behind the pilot, my hand over my left shoulder with a firm grip on the tubular frame of his seat and my right arm hanging onto the rucksack frame of Sgt. Brooks, who was standing on the skid, unable to fit into the craft. One or two men were also standing on the skids on the opposite side, unable to fully board.

The pilot quickly jacked it up to full throttle and allowed the rotors to gain maximum RPM's before easing up on the collective. It seemed like we sat there a very long time, then, like a ton of lead, the bird came up about a foot, gyroed for a moment, up another foot, gyroed, and repeated this until we were about 15 feet off the ground.

I heard the crack of a gun and turned to see the co-pilot's arm, pistol in hand, pull back from the window. Then he starts screaming—

"SHOOT! SHOOT! EVERYBODY! SHOOT! SHOOT!"

In order for the chopper to move forward it needed to transition, tilting the main rotor forward, lowering the nose and raising the tail of the craft, until forward movement began. Again, it seemed like an eternity before any speed was gained. Meanwhile, we could hear that old familiar sound of an AK in fairly close, just before the door gunners opened fire. Soon, anyone that could point the barrel of his gun out the doors was emptying their clips into the tall grass.

The bird crested a small knoll as the rotors blades acted like a giant weed whip against the elephant grass, and the runners and fuselage looking like a motor boat parting it back, the engine roaring, rotors whopping, men screaming, guns blazing, hot brass shell casings ejecting from the guns and bouncing off everything and everyone as we gained altitude, circling back over the downed helicopter.

As we ascended out of the danger zone, the flight path was not back in the direction of our original destination. Forty-five minutes later, we arrived somewhere on Camp Eagle and landed. I was so stiff from being in that cramped position that I could not get off the bird. Two of the guys helped me to the ground, where I laid for several minutes straightening back out. Meanwhile, the crew found 12 bullet holes in the fuselage, and one of the door gunners had a graze across his wrist.

You should have seen the looks on the faces of the ground crew as all the empty shell casings rolled off of us, the cargo bay and onto the tarmac.

Our original crew began to explain what had happened.

The co-pilot already had his 38 pistol at the ready while waiting for all of us to climb aboard. When the chopper finally started moving, he spotted an NVA who broke through the tall grass, and was about to raise his AK-47 in our direction. He fired, and the gook dropped. Then, as we gained a little altitude he saw many more headed our way, and he signaled for all to shoot.

The co-pilot said he had immediately called in air strikes from the "High Flies" to destroy the downed helicopter, and that the jet pilots had confirmed there were many NVA in the vicinity and had laid down fire at them. Artillery strikes were also called in and blasted the area even more.

We also learned that two of the H1's that were dropping our guys off on the Firebase, headed our way and followed us all the way to Eagle. Apparently the gauges and instrumentation were indicating a serious mechanical problem from the bullets that hit us. Had we been forced to land, we would have been picked up immediately.

Fast forward once again to August 2009.

A good friend, Jim Hunt, a Marine helicopter pilot who flew H-1 gun ships in Vietnam in 1970, was at a VFW meeting when he loaned me a copy of his *VHPA* (Vietnam Helicopter Pilots Association) magazine. I had been questioning him about certain helicopter terminology for this book. I noticed in the magazine that many of the letters to the editor were from people trying to find old comrades they served with in Vietnam.

I thought perhaps by sending a brief, but descriptive, account of that harrowing helicopter ride that it might ferret out a member of the crew. The editor accepted the article and request, then published it in the September/October 2009 issue of the magazine.

Well, on October 5th, I received an e-mail from a Mr. Richard Green who remembered the incident quite well, as he was the co-pilot that day. We corresponded several times as he filled me in on information we packs would not have known about the flight.

He informed me the pilot was a WO (Warrant Officer) named Larry Moak. I have now had the opportunity to thank them both for their skill and bravery that day. At the time, it was just all in a days work, for them and us!

It was about 6:00pm and we grunts were thinking that it was too late to take us back to that God-forsaken Firebase, and that we may have some good rear echelon food and nice digs for the night—*Not!* They transferred us to a different crew and bird, and within 30 minutes we were headed back to that damned Firebase.

We landed back on what we soon learned was Firebase Airborne and found third platoon with only enough time to lightly dig in for the night. I was totally fatigued enough to sleep. But, I didn't like it there and wanted to be anywhere else. Even the jungle would feel safer.

During the next morning on May 10th, it didn't take much time to explore the base. It wasn't very big, but there were two gun batteries and mortar tubes, along with another complete company of men guarding the perimeter, our sister A-Company (Alfa Avengers) who had arrived on the 8th. The bunkers were still under construction and there were three steel connex containers sandbagged in near the LZ and used as communication bunkers. We were formed up quickly and told to pack only ambush gear and prepare to make recon patrols around the FB, which we did for the next four or five hours. We were back inside the perimeter in early afternoon and were told to saddle-up, as we were going on an air assault. Soon enough the H-1's arrived, dropped off troops from A-Company and loaded us on. Our flight took us due west, straight across the valley, into some low foothills just north of a really big hill numbered 937.

I was with the lead pack on the assault, possibly the second or third bird. We made our approach to the top of a small hill that looked like it had been dozed off for a FB a year or two before. Each bird took its turn, as there was only enough room to land one chopper at a time.

We moved in to land, and—*Here we go again*—the bird suddenly slammed to the ground, made a quick hop or two and started tipping up towards the nose.

Someone on the opposite side baled out, and I struggled to get out too. The door gunner struggled to push me back in, then hollered and signaled that they were going to try the landing again, as we bounce off the side of the hill and take flight. Next time around we landed in good shape, pushed off the LZ and connected with the point group, as the remainder of the company slowly landed at the LZ and joined our ranks.

Typical combat assault into the jungle.

We had learned during the day that the mission we were on was called "Apache Snow," that it officially started today and that what we saw back at the airstrip was only a part of the overall mission. The entire third brigade along with ARVN units were participating.

It turned out that this operation was the single largest air mobile assault of the Vietnam War.

19.
Firebase Airborne

It was already getting late, and we needed to NDP. We had only moved a click or so from the LZ, but the evidence of heavy NVA traffic was already showing up. We were on extreme high alert, using extra caution and quiet. In later accounts, I learned that on the same day, elements from the 3rd, 187th and 1st 506th Inf. 101st Airborne, had made assaults near the base of this 3,000-foot high hill, but on the far opposite side from us, and their outcome was much different from ours. May 11th and 12th were repeats, and evidence of the enemy was everywhere. None of us had seen anything like this before, but we did not make any contact with the enemy. But, on both nights the men on the perimeter thought they could hear movement, and it was decided to call in artillery.

Calling in artillery strikes near our NDP's was somewhat common practice, but this time the fire support must have been coming from 8 inch cannons. We could hear the shells coming through the air just milliseconds before the blast. The red leg was walking the rounds closer and closer to our perimeter. Some were being detonated by the trunks of the bigger trees, and I could hear big limbs, or even entire trees, crashing to the ground after the explosions. Some rounds went off so close that the shrapnel was slamming through our NDP. It was pitch dark, but the flash of the bursting shells brought light for a split second. It's hard to explain how loud and frightening it is, to be so close to exploding shells. But even with that, it was comforting to know that it would be very difficult for an enemy force to form an attack through a barrage of that magnitude.

Interesting patterns form when a time exposure is made of gunships bombarding enemy positions outside the perimeter of LZ Bronco. The gunships are from the 174th Assault Helicopter Co.
(from Screaming Eagle *newspaper)*

On the night of the 12th, our NDP was near a small knoll at the base of 937. The jungle gave way to bamboo thickets before reaching the elephant grass that covered the valley floor. From there we had some horizontal vision across the A Shau. It was a replay of the night before, with artillery recon being coordinated and recorded by red leg and Company Commander. If we were attacked, the artillery could be called in quickly and walked right around our perimeter.

It was another night difficult for sleeping. In the wee hours of the morning, the quiet was disturbed by explosions and gunfire echoing from the opposite side of the valley. In seconds, the radio traffic went crazy. It was Firebase Airborne, they were being attacked!

If any of our men were catching some sleep, they were awake now. It may have been a mile or two across the valley at this location, and the mountain range to the east, paralleling the valley, appeared as a black silhouette against a dimly lit sky. The explosions, spark showers and small arms tracers not only showed vividly near the top of that mountain, but the sound of them came clearly across the void.

Many of us huddled around the radios, trying to make sense of what was happening. We heard a very familiar voice multiple times, shouting orders and supplying information. It was our own Captain Graney who, we later learned, had his new assignment with T.O.C. (Tactical Operations Command) and was stationed in one of the connix boxes on the Firebase. Anytime the radio mike was keyed up, we could hear the explosions from the mortar rounds that were raining down all over the base. We heard the reports of gooks being inside of the perimeter, satchel charging the artillery cannons and every bunker they could get to. The fighting was very intense and very close.

There was absolutely nothing we could do to help the men on Airborne, but pray for their survival. All eyes were fixed on the sight as the noise and flashes increased steadily. Somewhere in the midst of that carnage, a young GI named Sgt. Robert Malecki, a rifleman with A-Co., was fighting for his very life, along with about 200 other men.

We began to see artillery being shot in from other fire support bases, pounding the jungle outside their perimeter.

It seemed like an eternity passed before we witnessed a killing machine we had only heard of prior to this, nicknamed *Spooky* by the airforce and *Puff the Magic Dragon* by the army, and it could truly spit fire. About an hour into the fight we first heard the fixed wing craft do a fly over. Signal flares popped up around the base, and the C-47 went into a steep banked turn and circled the sight, as if going around an imaginary race track in the sky. The airplane is equipped with, I believe, three electronically-driven 60-caliber gattling guns, otherwise called mini-guns. They all face in the same direction, out one side of the aircraft. When the pilot maneuvers the plane into the proper bank, the guns are pointing at the ground. They began firing one gun at a time for about a ten-second burst, shutting gun #1 off and immediately firing up gun #2 and so on until all guns are fired before returning to #1, thereby allowing each gun to cool down.

This was an amazing sight to see and hear in the dark of night. As the bullets rained down, the plane was moving forward, leaving an almost snake-like trail of red tracers that resembled a hose stream of red sparks coming out of the black sky. I could not see the plane, but I could hear it. When the guns fired, there was a noticeable delay between the visual and the audio. I could not distinguish individual rounds going off, but heard rather a continuous deep report that reminded me of the long, low fog horn reports from passing iron ore boats on the St. Marys River, south east of the Sault Locks, back home in Michigan.

It is said that a mini-gun can put a bullet in every square foot of a football field in less than one minute. This plane spent all of 30 minutes circling the perimeter of Airborne, starting in a larger circle and slowly working its way closer and closer to the perimeter.

By the time *Spooky* finished its last lap, the enemy must have gone into retreat, and the shooting slowed down. We learned later that the fight started at 0330 hours and ended by 0530 hours, and that we would be flown back to Airborne.

We had our gear packed and ready by the first light, made our way into the bamboo thickets and found a place to quickly cut an LZ.

We reasoned then, that we were not making contact because the NVA were staging troops for the attack. There may have been another reason, as well. Had we tried to go up 937, we may have had a different outcome. Hill 937, at the time, was just another mountain to climb, a little bigger than the ones around it but nothing we hadn't done 50 times before. We most assuredly would have climbed it, if Airborne had not been over-run. There were no plans for us to leave the jungle and, in fact, we were scheduled for an extended stay, positioned and staged to go up.

By 0700 hours we completed a quick LZ, and, within the hour, we were back on Airborne and witnessing the devastation. We were already unnerved, sick in the gut and nearly sleepless for days on end. Thank God, most of the GI's that were KIA had been taken away, along with most of the wounded, before we arrived. The smell of cordite was still lingering in the air and, it seemed like the smell of death was already creeping in. Dead NVA had been moved to a perimeter opening, but their bodies were all over outside of the perimeter.

There was no smiling or laughing going on here. Every man was stricken with that thousand mile stare. Some of the men that went through the attack were walking around like zombies.

We learned that there were 22 KIA and over 60 wounded.

Sgt. Malecki was among the KIA's.

You can go to *www.alphaavengers.org* for additional information and history. Also see *www.Icompanyranger.com/A Shau/A Shauarticle.htm* and *VFW* magazine also has an account of Firebase Airborne in the May 2008 issue.

We were immediately detailed to remove the enemy bodies to a safe distance from the base and bury them.

Bodies in the wire and in the tangle of vegetation pushed off the base were difficult to remove but, of course, necessary. Within a few hours we were all sent out on lightweight recon, our platoons splitting up and covering larger areas out from the base.

We were looking for NVA alive or dead, any equipment or

Robert R. Malecki.

papers, and, of course, we were probing the jungle for any forces preparing for another fight.

Between us, we found many S.K.S. rifles and bags of satchel charges. There were enemy bodies near and at great distances from the base. There were blood trails and evidence of bodies being dragged away. We observed the evidence of *Spooky* with areas so riddled with bullets that a fast escape became necessary for the NVA, and they left behind more than usual.

We had all seen plenty of Vietnamese people, as well as live and dead NVA troops. Generally speaking, they are quite small people. But many of these bodies were of big men, some possibly six-foot tall and heavy, almost fat.

Robert R. Malecki with A-Co. 2-501 Airborne.

    Most of them had short fresh haircuts, but they only wore loin cloths, not even shoes. They just didn't look like Vietnamese either. Some thought they looked more like Chinese. One way or another, these men were highly trained, highly motivated and on a very well-organized mission. One note of interest was that we found flashlights with the lenses covered tightly with the exception of a very tiny hole in the center. A sapper (infiltrator) crawling along the ground, making his way through trip lines and barbed wire, could prepare himself visually, blink the flashlight on for a fraction of a second, see everything in front of him for several feet and subsequently move that distance. A GI on guard from the top of a perimeter bunker would never notice, and the Alfa Avengers did not.

B-Co. was back inside the wire late in the afternoon and took on much of the bunker detail. Many of them were in shambles from satchel charges, RPG's and mortar round explosions. This was grim duty. Our guys knew that men died in these places just hours before, and they even found small body parts stuck here and there. Pat O'Leary had the misfortune of uncovering a jungle boot in the corner of his bunker. The problem was that, a foot was still in it. They promptly buried it down the hill. Sleep, once again was hard to find.

The next morning we were back out continuing the patrols. After an uneventful morning, we returned to Airborne. Third platoon was ordered to pack up and prepare to fly to a different base that afternoon, leaving 1st and 2nd platoons on that God-forsaken base.

Fast forward once again to 2008.

A fellow high school classmate and Vietnam veteran friend, Robert Dillenbeck, and I were at our local VFW post one evening. Robert had with him a copy of his 1968 year book from the 101st, which I took interest in because my yearbook was 1967 and didn't cover the major events B-Co. was involved in. I knew Robert was associated with the 101st, but we never shared stories about it in the past.

While leafing through the book together, we came across an account of Firebase Airborne, and Bob quickly said, "I was there the next morning after the base was overrun."

I said, "What? So was I!"

I asked him why he was there. He explained that he fixed and re-sighted artillery guns and that there were many guns that had been satchel charged and needed to be repaired "quickly." So, Bob and I most assuredly, were walking around on that base at the same time but did not know it. We shared stories about Airborne for some time after that, and our bond grew stronger. I also learned that Bob had received a draft deferment the same time I did, but was called back early in February 1968. For some reason we never crossed paths during the wait. It was probably for the best, as we would have most likely ended up in some kind of trouble with the law and spent those last months in "Stumps Motel" (jail).

20.
Eagle's Nest

In mid-afternoon we could hear the six helicopters moving our way. Third platoon prepared to load up and fly to its next destination. This was my fifth flight in six days, all of them in the airspace of the A Shau and all considered combat assaults. The pilots' tactical strategy seemed to be just "fly high." Our sortie headed south above the valley's east side. It was another clear day, and, despite the bitterness of war in that place, the twenty six miles of valley snaking down through the mountains was almost breathtaking.

The flight was short. We approached a tall skinny mountain with two primary peaks, about four hundred yards apart, with one about a hundred feet lower than the other and nothing on it but dirt. The primary peak was a small base with an LZ that seemed no larger than a postage stamp, but the pilots had no trouble setting us down on it.

Okay, this was more like it. I could hardly believe what I was seeing. I actually felt safe for a change and exploring that place, which was about the length of a football field but only half as wide, was a joy. First of all, this site had been occupied for a long time with the exception of a parapet wall built of a hodge-podge of stones, bricks, blocks and mortar. It was about twenty feet long, five feet high and on the south slope of the mountain facing west, and it appeared to have been built recently.

They were small but well-built bunkers around the perimeter that one platoon and a handful of permanent party could man. Our first task was to deploy to quarters, and I ended up in the strangest bunker I'd been in yet.

When the base was built, engineers flew a small 'dozer up there and somewhat flattened off the peak, which ended up like a long, skinny saddle. In the small of the saddle, the 'dozer apparently turned at ninety degrees to the longer direction of the base and pushed hardened earth, like soft sand stone, out over the east slope.

The resulting trough was about 30 feet long, eight feet wide and six feet deep and sloping up at each end, to allow the 'dozer to exit up the slope near the center of the perimeter. The middle 15 feet was then covered with PSP and two layers of sand bags. To enter, all you needed to do was walk down the earthen ramp, duck under the PSP, step onto the wood pallet floor (with large gaps between boards), and you were "Home Sweet Home."

Before the day was out, I explored every inch of the place. I felt more secure every minute, even though the only armaments guarding the place were one 80mm mortar tube and a gas engine powered Quad 50, like the one on the truck back at Pohl Bridge. This one, however, was mounted on a flat platform of heavy squared timbers with a heavy steel cable fastened around it, then pushed nearly off the edge of the slope at the northwest corner.

The 80mm tube and three-man squad were sandbagged into a shallow pit about eight feet in diameter at the opposite end from the Q-50, with a view of the lower camel-hump of this mountain. I mentioned to one of the tube squad how secure the place appeared to be, but that the secondary peak of this mountain was within mortar distance from us. He just smiled, quickly summoned one of his partners, spun the adjustments on the tube and hollered "Fire in the hole."

"Thump," then a several second delay and the round exploded dead center of the flattened dusty top of the second peak.

He said, "We have every inch of that hump memorized and we fire rounds like that on a random basis day and night. We can have a round anywhere on it in seconds."

So he had just demonstrated. They pitched the mortar round canister over the side of the perimeter where it tumbled down to a resting place, and went back to reading their books.

Typical Quad 50.

A third defense was the altitude of this peak. It had very steep sides, little vegetation on the valley side and very little on the eastside for the first one or two hundred yards. There were also five or six laps of barbed concertina wire placed fifteen or twenty yards down from the edge (concertina wire, when in place, is like slightly stretched out slinky coils). But the thing I liked the most was the fact that anyone who stayed there threw their C-rat cans over the side. I kid you not. There must have been one or two million cans, bullet cartridges and mortar canisters thrown over the side, all the way around the perimeter. Cans and small metal debris had rolled down the banks for a hundred yards in some places and were two feet deep in others. The most stealthy of sappers could never negotiate his way up, undetected.

Finally, sleep came easy that night, as it probably did for the remainder of third platoon. My original issue air mattress was holding air most of the night, despite several homemade patches. Life was good!

The next morning, May 15th, I woke up to bombs going off in the distance and headed out to investigate. The explosions were coming from the opposite side of the valley, nearly due west. I moved to the parapet wall where there were several pairs of high-powered binoculars on tripods set up and aimed at the mountain on the opposite side. I took the liberty to use a pair and take a look for myself. The top of the hill, which I recognized as 937, was showing some signs of damage to the triple canopy forest that grew there. Artillery bombing continued sporadically all day, with the occasional assistance of A-4's, F-4's or A-7 jets, dropping out of the sky at some hellish speed, drilling their 500-pound bombs into the top of the mountain and quickly disappearing again.

During the day an H-1 landed, shut the engine off, and four high-ranking officers climbed out. At that point I understood two things about the parapet wall. One—it would keep you from being blown over the side when a chopper landed at the nearby LZ. Two—the height was just so that a even good sniper would have a very hard time shooting one of the brass standing nearly motionless at the binoculars.

This confirmed that our command had had great knowledge of this area for a very long time.

Sometime during that day, word came down to me from Captain Franzinger and through Lt. Bohden, that a replacement medic was being dispatched to 3rd platoon and that I was to report to Camp Sally for R&R when he arrived. Oh My God! After nine months and 14 days of near constant field duty, I was happy.

Very happy!

I found a nice pile of sandbags where I could just sit down, hang my arms at my side, take a few long slow breaths and just let some of the tension drip away. There were several conex boxes on the base, and one was T.A.C. (tactical air control) station. I got to know the communications operator well because I made several inquiries every day as to the arrival of my replacement. The other two were warehouses for food and water. The permanent party guys on this outpost were treated well with plenty of food, books, magazines and one can of hot beer each day, not bad at all. Helicopters came and went each day for one reason or another.

On the 16th one of them dropped off a duffel bag full of assorted cigarettes. They were divided up to anyone who wanted them, and I ended up with about a dozen packs. These were regular cigarettes, not the little six pack boxes from 1945 C-rats, and they were fresh.

The bombing on 937 continued all day, maybe intensifying some as the day went on. I could actually see spots of dirt through the foliage, and I wondered what in the hell was going on there!

I began to discover one small problem with our little hunk of paradise. I was running out of things to do and, anxious for my replacement, getting bored. Some excitement came that evening when the men in the armor detachment manning the Q-50 announced that they were going to do a random recon by fire, as they did about every other day. I had the opportunity to see one of those things operate back at Pohl Bridge, but our view was looking toward the business end in the dark and several hundred yards away. To truly appreciate one of those vicious machines you need to be up close to the operation end and see where the tracers go.

Three men walked out to the precariously placed machine gun, each carrying two boxes of ammo, placed them on the platform and then made one additional trip for more, for a total of 12 boxes. They started a gas engine mounted under the gunner's seat that provided the mechanical power to fully manipulate the weapon. One man removed a tarp and barrel covers. The other two opened all the ammo boxes, attached one box to each of the four machine guns, flipped the first round of the ammo belt into the chambering mechanism and loaded the guns.

Within a few minutes the engine was warmed up, and the gunner climbed into the seat. He tested the two articulating movements the machine could make, barrels moving up nd down from about 30-degree negative of horizontal, to nearly straight up. The entire platform above the wood pallet could rotate 360-degrees. It could do this in a very fluid and fast manner, tilting and swiveling simultaneously. The primary intent of this particular machine gun was for anti-aircraft, but in this case, it was also suitable as an anti-personnel weapon.

Let me provide a few statistics about the 50-caliber round, chambered in a long gun built for snipers. It has a proven accuracy of 1.5 miles, but the projectile will travel up to eight miles. It will also shoot through a half-inch steel plate or just about anything else that gets in its way.

The ammo bearer gave the gunner a thumbs up signal as he aimed the barrels down the slope and pulled the trigger. The machine started barking big time as he raked bullets through the lower tree lines, anywhere in the sight line of the gun. Keep in mind, a 50-caliber machine gun will fire three to four rounds per second, a red tracer bullet every fifth round—and there were four guns firing at once. That's about 850 rounds-per-minute—a lot of lead flying down the mountain.

Meanwhile, the ammo bearers, who were standing beside

the swivel base, were hanging fresh boxes of ammo onto the guns and clipping the fresh belt to the one about to run out, while the operator was blasting away at anything that may look like a target.

About a minute into the recon by fire, smoke from the burnt gun powder and gun oil (gasifying as the barrels got hotter and hotter) engulfed men and machine in a cloud of smoke. It was obvious these guys knew what they were doing. They ceased fire long enough to allow the smoke to clear, then turned the gun across the valley. They looked at each other for a second and then—rock'n roll!

The gunner worked the top of Hill 937 for another minute and emptied all 12 cans of ammo. Watching the path of the tracer rounds was incredible. They shot two miles across the valley, close to three at the summit. There was a visible arc in the trajectory, but nearly a flat path. Some of the tracers ricocheted off solid objects on the mountain and went soaring off into the sky for miles.

When the recon stopped, the crew cleaned away spent cartridges from the smoking quad and kicked them over the edge. My fingers were in my ears most of the time, and when the volley stopped, I could hear the brass tinkling down the side of the slope.

Just before dark, when the guns had cooled down some, the crew cleaned the guns, brushed and swabbed the barrels with oil, then covered them again until next time.

On May 16th, the bombing of 937 continued. We had no idea that the I/82nd Airborne and the 1/506th Airborne were on the opposite side fighting entrenched NVA and losing men fast every time they tried to gain ground. The brass flew in and the brass flew out of the nest, as the earth on the mountain slowly became more visible.

I had little work to do, and my guys were all in good shape and now resting. Oh sweet rest! No showers, but good rest.

That evening, I noticed that the dozen packs of cigarettes I was given the day before, and had so carefully placed on a shelf

I dug out from the side of our hardened earth home, were nearly all missing. What the heck! I would have been embarrassed to ask any of the six guys sharing our trench in the ground home if they had taken them, because anyone who smoked had more packs than they'd seen in months.

That night I was pulling guard duty, radio watch, from 0120 hours to 0200 hours. It was pitch dark, and I heard a noise in the upper corner of our bunker. I slowly found my flashlight, aimed it toward the noise, turned it on, and "Oh My God!—"

The biggest rat I'd ever seen was staring at the light, frozen in his tracks. What was worse, it was holding a full pack of my cigarettes in its mouth! The only thing I could think of to do, was to standup slowly and work my way across the pallet while holding the light directly on him. My plan was to get close enough to punch him with my fist while clutching the flash light. The plan was working well. I had nearly pulled back to make the punch, when my foot practically went through a gap in the pallet boards. The noise was sufficient to scare the animal back into a hole it had dug by the PSP roof, dropping my pack of cigarettes along the way.

With all the discarded food cans around, it was not surprising that rats were around. But this critter was like a chihuahua on steroids, only longer. I tried unsuccessfully to find the rat and his cache the following day. I wanted my smokes back. So, for what it was worth, I plugged his entrance hole.

Aside from the intermittent bombing across the valley, it was quiet and boring on the Nest. More so for me, I suppose, who was anticipating an exit from the war zone, if only temporary. I can see now how some soldiers—given a constant dose of boredom and isolated from the real action—could turn to drugs.

Many did during the war, but keep in mind, for every GI that came home with a drug habit (mostly pot) there were probably ten college students doing the same thing. As I mentioned earlier, our unit was isolated 95 percent of the time, making it nearly impossible to acquire drugs in the first place. Also, it would have been a rare individual indeed who would be interested in being high while stalking the enemy.

Certain Firebase duty was different, however. If some of our guys felt safe, and someone managed to buy some weed (most commonly through permanent party on the base), they might pass it around to those interested, and those who were not just looked the other way.

I tried it myself on several occasions, and it's like our Good Lord quotes in the Bible, *Try my spirits and see if they are of me*. Well, pot only caused me to become paranoid. I just couldn't see any fun in it, so that was that. I never tried it again.

Around mid-day, at least two different helicopters arrived, bringing four or five high brass each. They gathered at the communication conix bunker. They remained quite static at the connix for an hour or so, then all began to move toward the parapet wall, some looking up as they moved.

My curiosity was gaining momentum, and finally, I couldn't take it any more. I walked over to one of the officers, gave a quick salute, my name and rank, then asked, "What's happening here today?"

Surprisingly, the officer explained that they were about to drop a really big bomb on top of Hill 937 across the valley, and I should take the time to alert the others on the Nest as they might just want to watch.

It was a very clear calm day in the valley, which may be the reason they chose this particular time for their objective. Many of the men gathered and made themselves comfortable with a view to the west. We were advised of the drop time and that it was going to be a 10,000 pound bomb dropped from a B-52 by parachute. The bomber was flying at a very high altitude. When I could finally see it's tiny vapor trail, it was already long past the target. It may have been as much as 15 minutes before we could see a tiny dot in the sky, slowly descending, and another 15 minutes before we could distinguish what it looked like.

If my memory is correct, it had three white parachutes suspending a black box or cylinder. At over three miles I couldn't distinguish the shape. It looked as though it was in slow motion as it reached the top of that big hill and must have landed slightly over the far side, as the chutes disappeared from sight. I really cannot accurately describe what I saw, but in an instant it looked like all the air on the entire top of the mountain was compressed into the shape of an inverted, ragged bowl, a half mile across and a half mile high, the light being practically blocked out by the intense compression and revealing its shape for a split second. It was like a balloon in this bowl shape, being inflated almost instantly, hesitating for an instant, and then deflating just as fast.

Then a cloud of sticks erupted in the same shape, growing larger and larger.

I shouted, "They are not sticks, they are entire trees!"

They were huge trees, hundreds of them, cartwheeling away from the point of impact. You could see debris raining down from the sky as the secondary bowl shape went higher and higher, eventually turning into the shape of a very angry mushroom.

Sound travels about 1,125 feet per second. The distance was about 13,000 feet, so it took nearly 12 seconds for the sound to reach us, enough time to actually forget there was an explosion.

Then, the shockwave of compressed air hit us.

We staggered backwards as the intense cracking, reverberating boom ripped past and echoed through the mountains behind us. The shockwave hit hard enough to shake tin cans and spent 50-caliber rounds further down the slope, and they tinkled down for several minutes after.

You could actually have compassion for the enemy after witnessing that bomb go off, and the top of 937 grew ever more bald.

On May 18th, day five on Eagles Nest, I made my daily trip to the radio connix to ask the same question, "Are there any replacements coming today?"

This time the answer was, "Yes."

"Will a medic be with them?" I asked.

"Yes," again.

Oh, Dear God, I had waited a long time for that news.

I made the report to the platoon leader, made the rounds to see all the guys, shake hands, a few hugs, and "We'll probably see y'all in about two weeks."

I packed up my ruck and took a little extra time to make sure the catastrophe bag was in top shape, as I was considering loaning it to my replacement.

The morning went by quickly, as the air strikes and artillery continued to turn Hill 937 into a balding old man. The brass were sure interested in destroying that piece of real estate. The chopper arrived and several fresh new uniforms with fresh new gear stepped off. I met the first one off the bird, my replacement – Specialist Carl Sneed from Tulsa, Oklahoma. He had arrived in-country on May 5th and had gone through the same incoming P-Training back in Bien Hoa as I had.

Our conversation took place on the LZ, while leaning against the helicopter as it idled, rotors at a slow spin. I did the best I could to brief him about B-Company and third platoon, offered him my catastrophe bag and explained its use. He accepted and we shook hands. I thanked him for relieving me and said, "See you in a couple weeks!"

The bird headed straight for Sally.

21.
R&R

It was a great ride back to Camp Sally, and the view from the helicopter, as always, was stunning. Many miles of jungle-covered mountains grew smaller as we headed east toward the coast, mountains to hills, to rice paddies and eventually the coastline of the Gulf of Tonkin.

I no longer remember if there were others on the flight or not. If I were not alone, I felt alone anyway. I was very happy for the opportunity to get away from the field and away from the war. I had waited nearly three months longer than normal for R&R, so I deserved the break, needed the break, but somehow there were strong feeling of guilt in leaving my comrades back at the "Bad Place."

Sally had really changed, with very nice wood-frame barracks and buildings. The battalion medical building was new and included some sleeping quarters, new furnishings, nice shelving and was well stocked.

I made my way to battalion HQ, cleared the paper work for R&R and settled in at the aid station. And—oh yes—there came a sumptuous trip through the chow line and a sit-down meal, followed by a 30 minute shower. Then I was off to the NCO club for a few cans of cold 25-cent beer.

The next morning, May 19th, was spent on an early trip to

the shower house, on to the chow hall for an honest-to-God breakfast (the last one was in the fall of '68 at Culco Beach). I also hunted down a fresh "new' (meaning clean) uniform and made a trip to the barber.

That afternoon, I checked the flight schedules to Da Nang Airport and the motor pool for southbound convoys. Nothing was available for a day or two, but that did not bother me at all.

The next 48 hours or so was spent stashing my field gear in a back corner of the aid station, acquiring all the appropriate travel papers, writing letters, lying in the sun and with many hours at the NCO Club. I had the opportunity to meet a rather feisty, young farm boy from Iowa, Dan Hefel. He had orders for B-Co., but for some reason was on-hold in joining up. Dan was being used for every odd job in the company including shit detail, and was trying to absorb as much beer as possible before being sent out.

I was constantly hearing stories of incredibly good deals on sound equipment, radios and cameras at the PX's. So I hunted down the one on Sally with the intent of making some good deals. I found the place, walked in, and the shelves were empty, save for toothpaste, brushes, soap and some miscellaneous junk. I went to the clerk, "What the hay? I thought a GI could buy some high quality sound equipment here?"

In the typical jerk wad attitude that came from many REMF's (rear echelon, you figure it out), he answered back "You just need to be here when a new shipment comes in."

"OK, when would that be?" I said

"Anyone's guess," he answered.

Over the next 60 days, I figured out why the shelves were always empty.

I vegetated the remainder of the day, content with being at Sally for however long it took to head south. I was totally unaware, that while I was enjoying the good life that day, B-Co. had been air assaulted back to the north side of Hill 937.

It took two more days of duty-free time before I caught a chopper going to Camp Eagle, which was much closer to Da Nang than Sally. Travel to Bien Hoa could be considered fairly safe, but the entire country was a war zone, and staying armed remained a necessity.

I stashed my helmet and pistol belt / shoulder harness at the aid station. I took my aid bag, sleeping gear, a couple of C-rats, one canteen, two clips of ammo, my M-16, a new pair of sunglasses, (my only purchase from my third trip to the P.X.), a new military baseball cap and the fresh uniform I was wearing.

I landed at Camp Eagle mid-afternoon, fortunately in an area controlled by other battalion elements of the 101st, and checked in at the dispatch before hoofing out of the area. There were no flights to Da Nang that day.

I sought out directions to the motor pool and found out that Camp Eagle was a fairly large base. But humping that light pack on open, flat, dirt roads was almost enjoyable. The motor pool had a truck headed to the Da Nang airport the next day, so, what now?

No worries, I had the Eagle patch on my shoulder and I was in Eagle Country. I headed out until I found a group of guys who resembled ground pounders. I introduced myself and told them I was hitchhiking to Bien Hoa for R&R, but was stuck here until tomorrow. One of the guys said, "Shit, come on with us, we're headed to the chow hall and we have extra bunks in our hooch."

Many stories were swapped that evening, but none of us were aware that B-Co. 2-501st had battled for the last three days, along with many other units, to finally take the top of Hill 937.

The deuce-and-a-half traveled to Da Nang the next day, on a very nice, freshly black-topped road. I kept a clip of ammo in the M-16 but did not chamber a round. I continued to keep a watchful eye on people and terrain, but no one else seemed concerned.

Arriving at the airport, which was actually a public facility guarded by ARVN troops and used by U.S. Military, I found it had been totally rebuilt during the nine months since I had landed there the first time. The place was simple but quite modern looking, constructed mostly of open air, flag stone walls and partitions, with heavy beams supporting cantilevered roof sections with seating underneath.

How did all this happen?

The military air dispatch had a C-130 headed for Bien Hoa, but it was not scheduled to depart until later that night. This time the wait actually got boring, but I was well used to that. As time passed, the staging area I was in slowly filled up with ARVN brass, civilians, GI's and a Korean USO entertainment band.

At ten or eleven o'clock that night, our transport arrived. Passengers and cargo unloaded, it was refueled, and the collected group begun to file up the large ramp under the tail of the plane. The entire rear of a C-130 folds down like a tail gate on a pick-up truck, making it very easy to get on board quickly. There were no seats, and the walls were just a gaggle of wires, pipes and riveted air frame. The floor was very large plates of flat aluminum with a roller system underneath that moved when we walked on it. I was quite happy having my ruck as a piece of furniture to sit or lean on as everyone squeezed on, along with musical instrument cases, baggage and miscellaneous cargo. Before boarding, all the GI's were told to remove clips, clear their chambers and keep the barrel of the gun pointed at the floor at all times.

The tail gate went up, and the lights went out. Oh boy. Did they go out! Aside from a few very tiny colored instrument lights it was pitch black in that cargo bay. The plane taxied out 100 yards or so, the pilot cranked her up and we took off. A bunch of us learned immediately that we had a small safety problem. The aluminum pallets were able to move forward or backward about two or three inches, not a big deal, except they moved independently instead of in unison. As the plane headed up, the rear pallet rolled back, then the next and next, creating a gap across the floor for a second then slamming shut like a guillotine, and I was on one of the seams.

The flight lasted about two hours, and every time the plane tipped for or aft, the metal pallets went "thud-thud-thud-thud."

They kept me alert during the flight. We arrived in Bien Hoa in the middle of the night. I slept on a wood bench under the giant pavilion canopy and thumbed a ride to the 101st unit rear in the morning.

A lot of new construction had taken place, but I recognized the rear area where I went through "P" training the previous year.

After reporting to HQ, it was like a production process preparing for R&R. I had previously applied for Australia with Hong Kong as a backup. My timing was such that I was to go to Hong Kong. That day we went to a huge storage facility and exchanged our war gear for our duffel bags containing a fresh khaki uniform, low-quarter dress shoes, civilian pants and shirt. A barracks was provided, along with information for anything we might need, including a brief tutorial in regards to the country we would be visiting. They even had a supply system in place to provide new ribbons and military patches for our uniforms.

We were required to travel in military khakis but needed to switch into civilian clothing as soon as we secured our rooms at the hotel. I was anxious to get into my civies and tried them on the first chance I had.

What the heck! I could not get my legs into the pants nor button the plaid short sleeve-shirt more than halfway up! The sneakers fit, but were covered with a thin green mold. I honestly thought that this goofy hot humid country had caused my clothes to shrink, and I cursed the place for it.

A commercial airplane (with very nice seats) took us to

Hong Kong International Airport the next day. A shuttle took us to a prearranged hotel, very large and very nice. Upon check-in, we needed to exchange our military-issue money for Chinese money. The exchange rate must have been very good at the time, as I ended up with much more than the 460 dollars I came with. I requested the hotel to hold most of the money and made withdrawals as the five-day, six-night vacation continued.

I met a GI (I think his last name was Hoining), and we were getting along good on the flight and back at Bien Hoa, so we decided to hooch up next door at the hotel. While I was waiting for Hoining to register, I noticed a very large and ornate set of scales with a sign that that said, "Weigh yourself for a penny and receive a fortune."

Something about my civilian clothing was bugging me, so I headed over to the scales with my new money, popped in the correct coin and stepped onto the platform. Now, when I left for the service I was about 135 pounds, and after about six months of military training I was about 145 pounds. The giant dial finally stopped at 175 pounds!

"What?" I thought, "this machine must be out of whack!" and I beckoned someone else to try it.

Several GI's weighed themselves as I inserted new coins, and they all said that the scales seemed about correct for them.

There was no way I could have gained 30 pounds humping that jungle, I thought, as I dropped another coin and stepped back on. But sure enough, I did. No wonder my civies didn't fit! What the heck do they put in those C-rats anyway?

I found after returning home that I had also grown another inch-and-one-half to a lofty five-foot-ten-inches, making me the single tallest member of the Flory clan at the time!

We headed up to our rooms. I walked in and set down my small bag of things and, "Oh——Oh!—thank the maker!" A bed!

A real nice bed with real sheets and overstuffed pillows!

Did I mention the shower? A shower with hot water!

For a while, returning to the war zone was not foremost in my mind. I put a civvie belt in the khaki pants, slipped on a pair of red ball sneakers, put on the short-sleeve plaid shirt with the top three buttons undone and headed out to find a suit.

The lobby in the hotel contained a mall with several clothing stores and men's shops. I brought a pair of wing tip shoes and rented a suit from Sir Tailors until I could be fitted for a new one the next day.

Hoining and I rendezvoused with several other guys and headed out for supper and on to the night clubs. The food was fantastic, and the beer, mixers and stories of our tours flowed as we eventually found a club with a good band, dancing and lots of girls.

We danced and danced. I eventually met a girl with the good old American first name of Daisy, who spoke reasonably good English. We ended up together, every minute that she was not working, for the entire week. We went to many different places in the city every afternoon, very nice dining places every evening and clubs every night. There were cabs available, but we traveled almost everywhere by rickshaw. The men pulling them really earned their pay.

One night she asked if I would like to go to Kowloon, on the opposite side of the bay.

"Why not, how do we get there?"

We were on the waterfront where there were many large commercial ships moored. She led us to a place where there were several small sampans at the bottom of a steep stairway off the dock. She negotiated briefly and waved us on board. Six in all got into that small water craft. The wrinkly old captain started a "putt, putt" engine and cast off.

It must have been more than a mile across the bay, and

there we were, bobbing through the waves in the midst of huge ships, long after dark. We laughed all the way over, found a club, had a few drinks and laughed all the way back.

Dinner with Daisy.

It must have been about day four, when the thought of returning to the war crept in. I probably tried to kill the thought by administrating extra doses of alcohol. The other guys were starting to grumble, also, as some had as much as six months remaining on their tours. I was now feeling fortunate that I was down to about 65 days.

We were due to fly out about May 30th. The hotel had a great service for shipping all your purchases back to the states, and everything went into the box except my brand new top-of–the-line Polaroid camera. It was staying with me. Riding the shuttle back to the airport was mandatory, so Daisy took the morning off from work to meet me at the airport for goodbyes. It had been a wonderful week. She was truly a wonderful girl, and certain aspects of the

Asian culture still amaze me.

On the flight back, I reflected on the fact that I had literally been plucked out of jungle warfare, fighting Oriental people for the better part of a year and, in an instant, was deposited into a huge unfamiliar city, full of Oriental people, and simply turned loose!

However, everything worked out fine. American GI's are highly adaptive to any environment.

The author with Daisy on R&R.

Back in Bien Hoa, we reversed the drill, packing the duffel for storage and retrieving our jungle gear. There was a flight dispatch office right there in the 101st area, and I signed in on the roster for northbound flights. Again, we hitchhiked, taking whatever the next available means of travel was as long as it was going our way. This time it took five days before I could catch a transport back to Da Nang.

It was probably the last day of May, and I found that I was temporarily stranded at the unit rear. The first couple days seemed nice. No one messed with the R&R guys at all, no duty whatsoever. I had written letters to everyone I had addresses for, but mail being sent to me was going to Sally.

I feared the thought of going back to the field, but in my ADD world (Attention Deficit Disorder) it is an absolute necessity to be busy at something. I reckoned that going back to the jungle would beat this boredom any day. By day four, I was wondering if anyone back at 2-501 HQ was asking where the hell I was!

Could I be in trouble when I got there?

The unit rear was large enough to have a great NCO club, with live music every night. Vietnamese musicians and singers were doing thir best to reproduce all the magic rock'n roll songs of the '60's. Some were quite good, some not so good, but it was fun none the less and reminded us of being back in the "world." The club also had civilian women working, tending the bar and tables, so the scenery was good. However, there were some rather large MP's posted nearby, who would be happy to make a pretzel out of you for an attempt to touch one of the women.

On the fifth of June, dispatch had a flight going to Da Nang, and there was room for me and several other guys heading north.

For joy, this C-130 was primarily for personnel transport and was equipped with lawn chair-like woven nylon seats. I sat beside a newbie destined for an infantry unit, and was able to provide him with useful information—but I tried not to scare him too much.

I was to learn soon that the 101st abandoned the top of Hill 937 on June 5th and headed down the mountain to ferret out any enemy holdouts around the base and in the valley. The NVA had not taken kindly to our having destroying their prize base camp.

I was able to catch a deuce-and-a-half almost as soon as I checked the motor pool and headed north again. Going through Hue was great. It was hard to believe that only a year earlier it was the property of the VC and NVA, and that the city was in shambles. Now it was quite beautiful again, bustling, alive.

The big surprise came when the truck exited the city on the north side. The road was a mud bog through rice paddies when I arrived, then an improved gravel road six months later. Now it was five feet higher than the surrounding farm land, fully paved with yellow caution stripes down the center and white stripes on the edges and enough shoulder on the side to contain a stalled vehicle.

How did all this get done?

Several of us jumped off the truck at the front gate of Camp Sally and humped to our respective areas, as the "twice-and-a-half" continued north to Quang Tri. I went straight to HQ and reported in, having some fear that my butt was in a sling. With a sigh of relief, I found there were no wanted posters out for me.

Another surprise came to me when I showed back up at the aid station. Six or seven medics were hanging out, two of them were replaced from B-Co. Captain (Doctor) Cook was now in charge of the 2-501 aid station, and he told me that there were plenty of extra medics for the entire battalion and that it would be highly unlikely that I would be required to return to the field.

Sometimes we may not realize just how much anxiety can be built up in us, until it is suddenly released. I think I stood speechless for a moment, stepped back out and ducked into a bunker, tears bursting out of my eyes. The news was far better than my release for R&R. I regained composure, and my next thought was B-Co.

Where is B-Co.? What are they doing?

It's a paradox, to be so happy and relieved at not having to go to the field and, at the same time, to feel anxiety and guilt for not being with your comrades.

At my first opportunity, I boogied back over to HQ to find out where my buddies were. The clerk started out by saying that they had been part of a joint effort to assault "Hamburger Hill" back on May 19th, and several men were lost during the three- day battle to the top.

"Hamburger what?" I replied.

"Hill 937, now they call it Hamburger Hill, lost a bunch of guys taking it, it's big news all over the country!"

He continued with a list of KIA's. Some I knew, some I didn't. One stood out however, and it gave me a chill, the guy that was self-inducing jungle rot on his shins, Louis Johnson. I think about him to this day. (Myself and Dave Reinheimer, went to visit his grave site at Jefferson Barracks National Cemetary, St. Louis Missouri, on July 12th, 2011).

A day or so later I crossed paths with Sgt. Carrara, 2nd platoon. He was recovering from small wounds he acquired during the assault. He told me about some of the losses and a bit of heroism.

He told of Sgt. Armendariz being in an ambush element one night when trip flares were triggered. The guys touched off several claymore mines and almost immediately began receiving small arms fire. Their position was quickly overrun and several guys were killed. Sgt. Armendariz was shot in the leg and had shrapnel in his gut, but managed to lay over a radio and play dead.

Please read the accompanying insert I found in the *Screaming Eagle* newspaper, shortly after that. (Armendariz was present at the 2007 reunion in Oregon, and still has a limp, but it was so, so good to see him again.)

Our clerk also told me that the hilltop had been abandoned, and that B-Co. and other units were now making search and destroy recons out from the base of the mountain.

Patrick Armendariz, 1969.

    Trust me on this, it was the grunts that named Hill 937 "Hamburger Hill,"—not the media. It was actually a medic by the name of James Thomas, with the 3/187th Airborne; the cardboard sign was made by a grunt named Edward J. Hinery, from a C-rat box.

    There is an excellent article on the taking of Hill 937, in the June/July 2008 issue of *VFW* magazine which includes a photo taken by the men of B-Co.

    It was probably bizarre that I felt left out of the action, but, in reality, it was truly fortunate for me to have been delayed so long for R&R.

    May of 2009 marked the 40th anniversary of the taking of Hill 937. I still have a strange feeling of guilt for not being there, not being with my unit, or with the guys at a dark hour.

    Is that crazy?

Wounded Troop Fools NVA

A SHAU VALLEY — Short-timers in Vietnam enjoy telling new arrivals "war stories," most of them fantastic but false. Spec. 4 Patrick M. Armendariz of Burbank, Calif., however, has a tale that's fantastic but true.

Armendariz is a member of B Co., 2nd Bn., 501st Abn. Inf., operating in the A Shau Valley near the Laotian border.

Half of his platoon was on ambush about 500 meters southwest of Dong Ap Bia when three trip flares went off. The element began blowing its claymore mines and almost immediately started receiving small arms fire, satchel charges and rocket-propelled grenades. Concentrated return fire silenced the enemy temporarily, and Armendariz' fire team was sent out to sweep.

Outside the perimeter, the team was pinned down by heavy machine gun fire, preventing the rest of the element from reaching the trapped troopers.

Armendariz found himself lying on a radio surrounded by NVA soldiers, with shrapnel in his side and a gunshot wound in his leg. He was still conscious but pretended to be dead, and the NVA took little notice of him.

When the enemy soldiers moved away to engage the Screaming Eagle reinforcements, Armendariz attempted to call his company on the radio. He succeeded, and began passing information on the exact number and disposition of enemy troops.

The radio was making noise, and the enemy soldiers turned and looked at him every time he made a transmission. But they seemed preoccupied and, for some reason, left him alone.

All through the night, as the platoon attempted to get to Armendariz, he kept them informed of the enemy's situation.

Finally, the company called in gunships for assistance. As they began to fire up the surrounding area, the enemy deserted the hill.

At daybreak, the company found Armendariz at the top of the hill, in the midst of the deserted NVA positions, still on the radio.

A medevac was called, and Armendariz is now recovering at the 95th Evac. Hospital in Da Nang, with a war story to beat all war stories.

Article from Screaming Eagle *newspaper.*

Hill 937 – "Hamburger Hill" taken by Ed Wick, with B-Co., on or about May 21, 1969. Jim Duke at left. Note bayonet holding cardboard sign to tree stump, with black silk shirt hanging on the bayonet.

22.

Short-Timer at Sally

The aid station had living quarters with about four bunks for Captain Cook and his primary aid, Doc Murray, along with Paul Pawlak and Doc Farrell. The remainder of us were in a barracks a few rows over. The only thing remaining of the tents on those wood-frame, corrugated tin roof buildings was canvas, rolled up outside, above the screens that went 360 degrees around the building. The canvas could be rolled down to cover the bug screen in monsoon rainy season.

All the barracks had sandbags stacked neatly around the full perimeter, high enough to protect a man sleeping on a cot if a rocket or mortar attack came. There were also heavy-duty bunkers in between the rows of housing and near any structure people might be in. They were not fighting positions, just places of safety.

I had a net-covered cot, my same old original air mattress, a small desk with lamp, and a foot locker. For what I had become accustomed to, the plywood floors were as good as ceramic tile. It was hot, but otherwise living was okay. I managed to keep slightly longer hair for R&R and got away with it here, too.

Our aid station was overstaffed by at least double. The captain was diligent about keeping us detailed out on miscellaneous jobs and taking turns on duty at the station. Even though there were infantry units coming and going from the camp, it was mandatory that all permanent party do night guard duty. We were able to rotate this detail also, and it really wasn't all that bad, anyway.

The author at his hooch, Camp Sally, summer 1969.

The bunkers were absolutely elaborate, two floors high with sleeping quarters separate from the forward watch area. Food and snacks were available, and I could make coffee. It was always "lights out" for the entire camp, but I could use a flashlight to go to the privy. Most of the bunkers had a starlight scope in the loft, so you could see anyone approaching from a half mile away. Four men were in the sleeping quarters and two on watch at a time. As a perk, the walls were wallpapered with clippings from *Penthouse* and *Playboy* magazines.

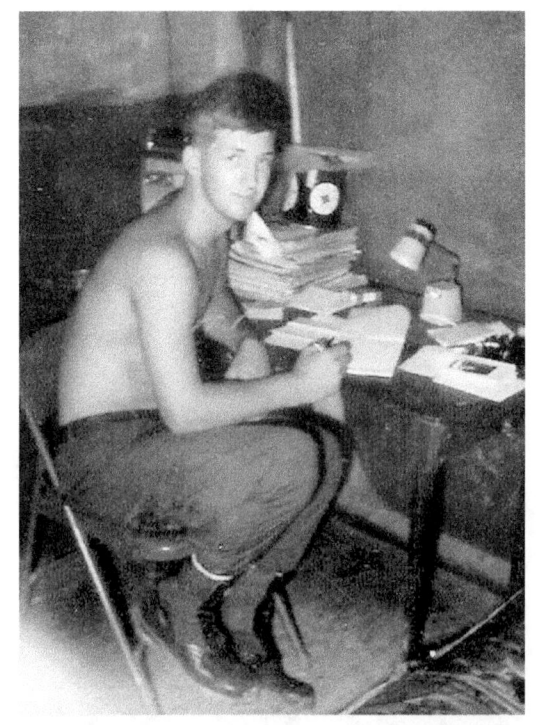

The author's barracks area, Camp Sally.

B-2-501 Aid Station, Camp Sally.

All those pulling guard were riflemen, but each bunker had an M-60, plenty of ammo, command over four or five claymore mines and the starlight scope. Batteries of howitzers were spaced out behind the perimeter bunkers and some eight-inch cannons on tracks. They would keep you awake if they were firing a support mission, but for us medics it didn't matter much because we could just sleep-in the next day.

Sitting on an 8-inch track Howitzer.

I had time to freshen up all my field gear, which needed to be kept ready for field duty should the call come. I had nice pens, paper, envelopes and time to write better letters, as well as to take pictures with my new Polaroid camera and send them home. I requested the family not to send any more care packages, as I had everything I needed there at Sally.

It was the evening of June 12th, and I was now marking my short-timer's calendar again. You must remember, there are no weekends or weekdays in the war zone, just days—one less day!

I was trying to keep track of B-Co. by stopping from time to time at headquarters and asking a few questions. The clerk, Bob Colombo, had plenty to report on that day. B-Co. had continued pulling recon near the base of Hamburger Hill and had thwarted an all-out attack that day with multiple KIA's and WIA's.

What I heard next tipped me into the nether world for a while.

Both Captain Franzinger and Carl Sneed, the medic who replaced me, were killed at the same time by an RPG explosion. I do not know if I have reconciled this in my mind or not, as thoughts of those two return fairly often, yet today. I learned at our 2007 B-Co. reunion in Clatskanie, Oregon, that Phil Hazen (1969-70) reported directly to Captain Franzinger and witnessed the action as it unfolded. Also, that Jim Duke assisted another medic in trying to save them. Hearing it all in detail, even though it was 40 years later, has helped to bring closure. Reunions for veterans who have witnessed the bad stuff are truly wonderful events.

On June 13th, my 21st birthday, while making the next "X" over the date, I happened to notice that it was also Friday!

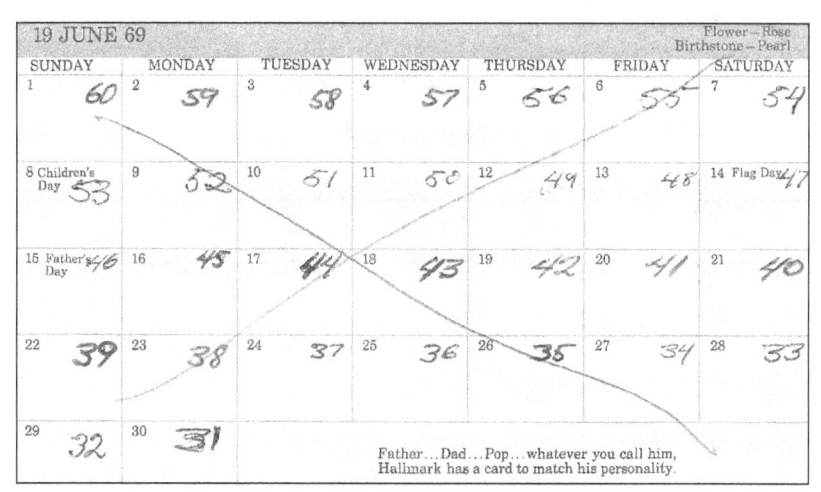

Countdown or Short-timer's calendar. 48 days remaining on Friday, June 13—the author's 21st birthday.

Oh Boy! Turning 21 on Friday the 13th in Vietnam! What are the chances?

I'm not superstitious, but it annoyed me a little anyway. I chose to just ignore it, and it turned out to be a very good day. Nursing a little more heavily on "Mother Beer" didn't hurt either!

I had the good fortune of crossing paths with Dan Hefel once again, as he hadn't joined the Company yet and was on "gofer-boy" detail. Old Dan had help now, however, in the form of an additional Bravo recruit by the name of Leo Hiller from Pennsylvania. Leo being an uncommon name, we referred to each other as "the other Leo." We continue to trade the phrase in correspondence and at reunions, to this day. Their "rear echelon" jobs were coming to an end the next day, and we spent time talking about what a great company they would be joining, and that, if they watched their butts and kept their heads down, we would see them back in the "world" in a year!

During the month of June, I also qualified officially for the unofficial term of "Short-Timer." In the ranks, one often displayed his status to a passing GI by holding his hand about head high and fingers in a fist, with the exception of the thumb and first finger, with a specific gap between them. You might start with about two months remaining, with a two-inch gap, at one month, a one-inch gap, 15 days equals a half-inch. But at one day you hold your fingers with a tiny crack between them, the fingers held directly in front of your eye as you address someone.

The next six weeks are mostly a blur to me now, with the exception of almost daily trips to the P.X. I hit a shipment day and purchased a reel-to-reel tape player with speaker system and head phones, which I sent home after using for about a month.

Doc Cook was having trouble keeping us hidden and decided to send us to Culco Beach, three medics at a time for six days. I went the last week of June, then again about the third week of July.

The coastal areas and cities were so secure at this time that it was no longer necessary to carry a weapon or wear a steel pot while being trucked down Highway One through Hue to the dock site. But we stayed armed anyway.

We had no duty whatsoever at Culco Beach, now renamed Eagle Beach. We ate good at the C.B's chow hall, enjoyed long nights at the NCO Club, and long days in the sun, sand and surf. We also felt free to feel like we deserved it.

I need to back up for a moment and write about my good friends, Dan Wakefield and Gary Welch, who were on Eagles Nest with me. But, of course, they ended up making the assault to the top of Hamburger Hill.

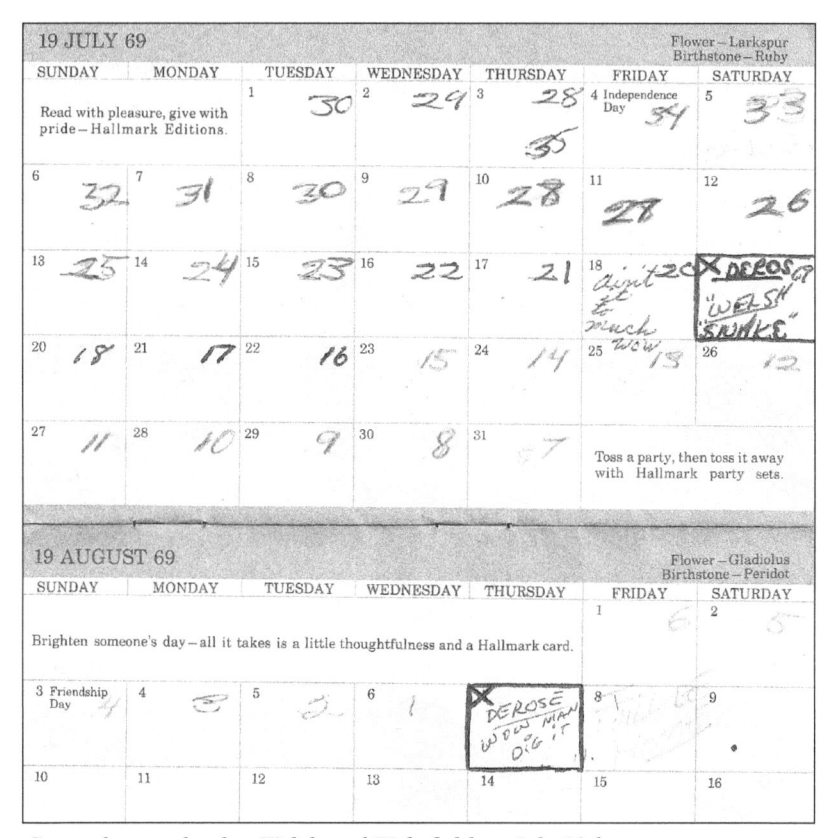

Count down calendar. Welch and Wakefield on July 19th.

Lt. Bohdan Kopystianskyj. He also survived Hamburger Hill, the aftermath, and many more months of field duty. We were reunited at the Branson reunion 2011, where he arrived nursing a broken collar bone from hang-gliding. He is still "Airborne!"

Well, once the hill was fully secured, the high brass began coming in from day to day, praising the troops and pinning on medals. The 2nd Brigade's CSM Daniels (Command Sergeant Major) thought it might be a good time to do a little recruiting. He announced that anyone who re-upped for six more years in the Army would be immediately removed from the field and given a job in the rear. Dan and Gary talked it over and decided it would be a good idea, especially because they only had about two months to go and were wondering if their good luck might run out in some firefight. So, they took his offer and were almost immediately taken back to Sally.

Now, back to mid-June, Dan and I crossed paths at the NCO Club, and he confessed what he and Gary had done. I ragged on him some about it, but what was done was done. And we decided that an increase in Pabst Blue Ribbon would cure the condition.

Dan was assigned as driver for battalion XO Boil, and Gary went to the motor pool, as he was a proven mechanic. We were all together again in much better conditions and spent most every night sucking down the suds and telling true-life war stories to the RIMF's and newbies. It was the 4th of July, and, with the obvious absence of the enemy, it was party time Sally style. Dan, Gary and

I started early, as most did, and by early afternoon we were feeling no pain. Some jeep driver who had came down Highway 1 from the north came into the motor pool and told us about a place about seven or eight miles back north where a bunch of prostitutes were doing business under a bridge. He said a Vietnamese kid was washing jeeps for two bucks each as a decoy for the women.

We held an alcohol-influenced conference. Gary decided to pass on this one, but he would forge the paper work to get us out the gate.

"Okay, yeah! Okay, lets go!"

Dan fired up the XO's brand new jeep, not a 100 miles on it yet. He threw in his M-16 and one clip, we cleared the gate and headed north.

The cruising speed on that brand new jeep was about 50 mph, and Dan had the pedal to the metal. It wasn't quite like doing the quarter mile in my old '57 Chevy, but just the two of us headed down an open road felt damn good.

Highway 1 south of Camp Sally.

After about twenty minutes, we were on Highway 1, but things were looking just a tad sparse out there, and we contemplated turning around. Then we saw activity on the west side of a bridge close ahead. We pulled down in, and, sure enough, there was the kid washing jeeps. There was only one problem, there were at least ten jeeps ahead of us.

About 15 minutes went by, and we moved up about two jeep spaces as the alcohol buzz began to wear off. Dan, being a point man, said "I think we had better pull a recon and scout out what's going on under the bridge."

Using a little well-honed stealth, we made our way to a small knoll about 30 feet from the bridge. Peering over, we saw multiple layers of cardboard all over the ground under the bridge, GI's and naked Vietnamese women. Two of the women were doing the *kimuchi* squat in the muddy river, splashing their hind parts back and forth.

Dan and I decided we would be better off with a nice cold can of Pabst, hopped back in the jeep and went straight back to Sally. It was very hot that day, so we stopped at the NCO Club and tipped four or five cold ones before heading on to the motor pool.

The motor pool was not much more than a patch of dirt, one third the size of a football field. Steel posts with two runs of barbed wire were stretched tightly around the perimeter to mark its boundary. Alongside a garage building for mechanical work was a long reinforced pit dug down near the side of the mechanic's hooch, for changing oil or whatever a mechanic might do if standing under a vehicle. The pit ran alongside the path that led back to the parking area, and Dan, being maybe a little more inebriated than normal, drove the jeep straight into the pit, bending up the driver's side front fender of the XO's brand new jeep.

Gary was still hanging out at the mechanics garage, but wasn't in much better shape than we were. None the less, between the three of us intoxicated country boys, a 6 x 6 truck and chain, we pulled the jeep out and parked it. You will need to consult with old Dan "the Snake" Wakefield if you want to know what trouble it caused him, but he may not remember.

I remember Ol' Gary saying over and over, "All I want to do is buy a '57 Mercury and cruise it back and forth down the main street of Garber, Iowa."

When the song *Mercury Blues* by Alan Jackson came on the country stations, you can guess who I thought of.

Dan and Gary ran into bigger trouble within the next two days, however, when they found out that the re-up papers that were sent to the states had subsequently been returned to Sally HQ for lack of certain signatures. C.S.M. Daniels summoned the two of them to his office to acquire the signatures.

Dan said, "You mean those papers are not binding?"
Daniels replied, "No fellows, not until you sign right here."
Dan said, "Shit, I'm short now, I'm not going to re-up."
Gary said, "That goes for me too!"

In later years, Dan told me that the C.S.M. turned beet red, spit, sputtered, cussed them out, called them every name in the book, and said, "Pack your field gear right now, report to the LZ in two hours, you're going back to the bush until the day you leave the country."

All I knew was that I couldn't find Dan or Gary for the next two weeks and thought they had DEROS (Date Eligible to Return from Over Seas) without saying good bye. On July 19th they showed back up at midday, tear-assin' around the compound trying to get DEROS papers signed so they could head south to Bien Hoa on their actual DEROS day.

Dan explained to me later that the C.S.M. contacted their platoon leader and ordered him to keep the two of them on point every day until their time was up.

Dan did as he was ordered, but he had one last trick up his

sleeve. He demanded to carry an M-60 with Gary as his backup and ammo bearer. He said, "Before my two weeks were up I had four ammo bearers because if I saw so much as a butterfly flap a wing I'd burn up a box of M-60 ammo into the jungle."

Dan and Gary survived the war.

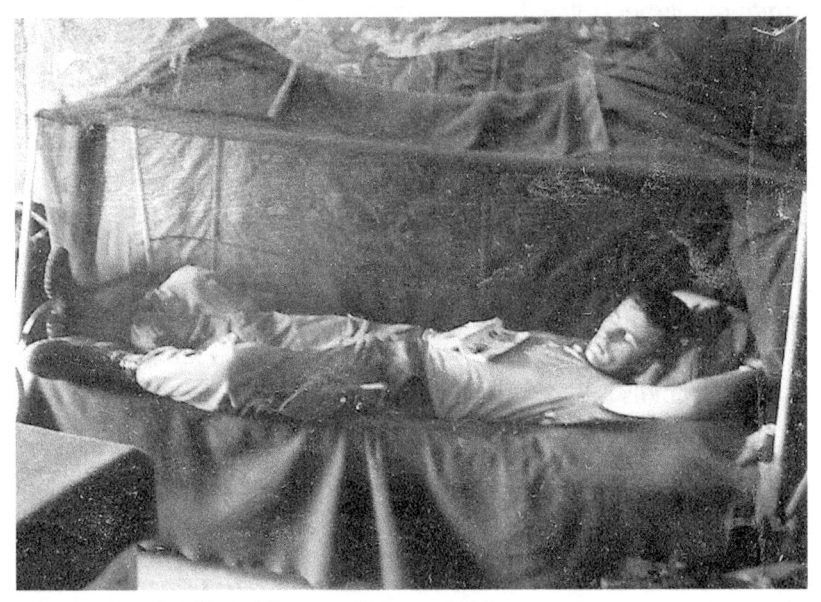

Doc Murray, 2-501 Aid Station, Summer 1969.

My old friend Moose showed up at the aid station one day, with stories of his R&R in Hawaii. He explained how one day he was at a lounge near the hotel pool, talking to a couple of Marines. One asked what he did in Vietnam, and being a bit inebriated at the time, said he was a human flame-thrower. He volunteered to demonstrate, and they were all to willing to watch. But when he let go with the flame, one of the Marines was too close, some of the lighter fluid landed on his shirt and caught fire. Moose said he reacted quickly and pushed the Marine into the pool to put the fire out. He said that the Marine jumped back out of the pool and hit him quite hard, so he put him back into the pool and walked off.

August 6th was some 19 days away, and most of my buds, except fellow medics, Michael Edwards and Paul Pawlak, were gone. We worked the aid station together when we could, talked about the gory days and the glory days in the field, but mostly about going home and what we were going to do when we got there. I suppose that was something we all did from the time we arrived until the day we headed home.

The author and Paul Pawlak at Camp Sally Aid Station.

There wasn't much action in the aid station day to day, with the exception of a sick man who came in from the field. We needed to pick him up at the LZ and almost carry him to the aid station. Doc Cook came to the conclusion that he appeared to have symptoms of malaria, which we had no way of treating properly. We ordered a dust off and sent him to Da Nang Field Hospital as fast as possible.

My thoughts went back to my first days with B-Co., when Doc Summers sent an artillery forward observer back to the rear, who I only remember as "Skinny Red Leg." He apparently had several relapses of malaria. News came back to the field several weeks later that he did not survive the last bout, which caused everyone in the company to be serious about taking the anti-malaria pills that we gave out weekly.

101st Airborne Combat Medic

The author at 2-501 Aid Station, summer 1969.

Happy Hour at Sally, 1969. Back row: Larry Muller, Unknown, Dennis Peterson, Jim Delgiorno, Bob Columbo (Clerk). Front row: Doc Ayala, John McCammom, 1st Sgt. George "Top" Schorr.

Time passed slowly, but it passed. Our company clerk, pay master, and others of the fully professional men that supplied our company and battalion were now helping me put all my paperwork in proper order, so I could leave without a hitch. I cannot recall a time that the same group had let B-Co. down in any way, from mail and care packages, payroll, food and water, ammo, explosives, medical supplies, chainsaws or axes to notification of R&R.

If it were possible—many times even dangerous—they would get it to us.

On August 4th I received the final paper to clear the post.

On the morning of the 5th, I nabbed a chopper to Da Nang and quickly caught a flight to Tan Son Nhut Airbase. Not where I wanted to go, but it was south.

During the flight, I reflected on my last day at Sally. It seemed bittersweet. I was so thankful to be there those last weeks, I thanked our Maker every night for that blessing. But my time was legitimately up, I had papers to go home, on time, unhurt. I was so glad to leave.

Back on the 3rd, I had felt there was a little unfinished business to attend to. I learned through my constant visits to the P.X. that the attendant and a few of his cronies were snapping up all the good electronic equipment and cameras prior to being displayed on the shelf and making a nice business of sending it all to their friends back home.

I paid a visit to the P.X. about closing time. No one was around, so I took advantage of some of the training I received at Fort Sam and put the sales clerk into a few physical positions that he was not accustomed to. I politely explained that from now on, it would be nice if he were to retain a few things for the grunts who came in week by week trying to find a deal. He seemed agreeable, but I wasn't sure if he would follow through. I switched holds on him, causing slightly more discomfort and asked him where a good old boy like him might hang out back in the states. He was quite thorough with his address, and I noticed the short delay must have been keeping him from a visit to a piss tube. Poor REMF just couldn't hold it any longer.

I disappeared into the Sally lights-out condition, knowing I would be long gone in the morning if he tried to hunt me down. I don't know if he reformed or not, but I felt better. He unwittingly "messed with the Medic."

When the C-130 landed at Tan Son Nhut, the hanger resembled the condition at DaNang, in that it looked somewhat civilian.

At one o'clock in the morning, there weren't many people around, and it became difficult to find out where to head next. I finally found some GI's and explained that I needed to catch a ride to Bien Hoa.

They said, "Oh you need to go to Camp Alpha."

"Okay, where is that?"

"About a mile or two down that road. You're not going to find a ride now, going to need to hoof it. Just look for a little guard shack on the left. The guard will help get you there."

"Thanks fellas," and I was on my way.

I was packing nearly all my original gear, because it all needed to be turned back in at the 101st unit rear on Bien Hoa. Unlike R&R, my ruck was full of personal items, no grenades or the like, but I did carry two clips of 5.56mm ammo and my M-16.

I headed out, humping down the road, as the already dim lights of the airport faded behind me. I hoofed it for about 20 minutes. It was so dark I could hardly find the road. Then I began to see tiny lights off to the right, several hundred yards up the road. As I got closer, I could see it was a hamlet. Then a dog barked, then another. I continued moving forward but began to hear voices. The distant voices were speaking Vietnamese.

My entire being went into high alert. I slid a clip quietly

into my M-16, chambered a round and shifted the selector switch from safety to full auto. I stood in confusion for a moment, had I been directed the wrong way?

Did I go the wrong way?

Did I somehow walk off the base and not know it?

I rehearsed the details and was positive I was traveling in the correct direction. I must also be past the point of returning. I assumed the night-firing position, gun butt at center chest, left hand outstretched supporting the fore stock, first finger pointing straight down the barrel, right hand on the pistol grip and finger on the trigger.

While moving at a slow but meaningful pace, another 15 minutes passed. Finally I saw a beam of light from the top of a pole in the distance. I stepped up the pace until I had a full view of the outhouse sized shack at an intersection in the road.

I shouted out, "GI approaching!"

An answer came back, "Come on up."

Breathing a sigh of relief, I continued to the shack and introduced myself and explained what I had been told to do. He said I'd come to the right place.

He explained that a jeep would be coming along soon, delivering coffee, and that the driver would take me where I needed to go.

"Is this all on Tan Son Nhut, I asked?"

He looked at me funny, "Oh yeah, this place is big."

"Okay then," I said, "No need to have this thing loaded," as I pulled the clip and ejected the chambered round.

"Good idea," he replied, "You will only shoot civilian workers or GI's around here."

While waiting for the jeep, he explained that the area I passed in the dark was indeed on-post housing for civilians that worked within the confines, many of them families of men in the

Army of the Republic of Vietnam who were fighting for their country alongside us. I have been thankful every day since that no one came close to the road that night.

A short time passed, and the jeep pulled up, delivering coffee and snacks to the guard. The driver told me he had several deliveries to make on his route and asked if I wanted to ride along before going to Camp Alpha. I told him I was in no hurry and would ride with him the remainder of the night if he wanted. So off we went.

As it turned out, the intersecting road followed the perimeter of the airbase, with concertina and barbed wire laid out row after row up to the edge of the road, where it became part of a 10-foot fence. It was a massive deterrent for any invader. The perimeter bunkers were about 100 yards apart and were very large two-story fortresses that were over 100 feet back from the wire. Each one had a driveway. There was no vegetation for 100 yards on either side of the road and none between bunkers.

As we drove along mile after mile, making deliveries to each bunker, I got a sense of the size of the base. As we rode along, the driver explained that his route only covered about 25 percent of the perimeter and that it took about two hours to simply drive around the base in a jeep.

Daybreak came, and the driver headed for the interior of the base to a group of barracks used for housing transient soldiers from all units and divisions who were making their way home, to R&R or just arriving in the country.

It was Camp Alpha.

I went directly to the chow hall, and, shortly after, buses were loading up. I hopped on one headed for Bien Hoa. The route went through part of Saigon and was extremely busy and crowded. The roads were filled with pedestrians, heavily loaded motor bikes, tiny cars and VW buses. The people dressed more colorfully in the city; black silk pajamas were few and far between.

After the two-hour, very interesting, bus ride, we arrived at the 101st unit rear, which I now knew quite well. I was able to quickly navigate the out-processing procedure. Again, it was like a production line. I went from station to station, building to building, turning in equipment, retrieving the duffel bag—and of course—the military never passes up an opportunity to give you a few more shots to maintain your good health.

There were two things that I found hard to turn back in: my helmet—why, I don't know, it was like an old friend—and my M-16. I had possession of that gun for a full year, and for nearly ten months it was never more than arms length away. I carried it every day, all day long, in the ready and relaxed positions. I slept with it every night, cleaned and oiled it constantly and used it in defense of our perimeter and flanks many times. I reflected on the thought that my training and use of this M-16 probably made my CO status a moot point. I viewed the status quite differently now as well, in that I never met or knew of any man during my tour that expressed a true desire to kill. My life experience tells me that, other than the truly sick, all Americans are basically conscientious objectors.

As the clerk took possession of the weapon, the ragged hole through the forestock came into view. 20/20 hindsight rushed in.

Why didn't I swap the forestock before leaving Sally?

It was a great memento, and I let it slip away. At each station, there was always a clerk recording that particular transaction and keeping your records straight. At one of the clerk stations, while waiting for the attendant to do his thing, I noticed a very large and prominent scar on top of the right side of the clerk's head. I thought, that looks familiar, then I noticed his familiar face.

I said, "Hey Dude, I know you, I patched you up out in the jungle, when a sniper tried to take you out by the LZ."

What a great reunion that was, short, but great none the less. We exchanged a few thoughts about the incident and how he ended up down here at the unit rear. When his wound healed, the powers that be apparently took pity on him, seeing just how close he had come to sudden death, and just gave him a position in the rear.

We were holding up the production process line, so I moved out, but I do hope that veteran reads this account some day and contacts me.

The author's M-16 (left), pictured alongside an AK-47.

It was a busy day, and that evening I sorted through all the gear I had, so I was not carrying anything unnecessary. The only thing that would not fit in my duffel bag was a brand new pair of jungle boots, which I wanted to take home in the worst way. I went to the NCO Club for a few brews before turning in, but nothing could outpace the rush of going home. I did not sleep a wink.

The bus was to leave early the next morning for the Bien Hoa Air Terminal. I had taken my last warm shower while in-country, under that 10,000 gallon sun-heated tank, had eaten breakfast at the chow hall, put on my freshly-starched (ha ha!) jungle fatigues that I had already worn for three days, and waited for the bus.

The buses dropped us off at that enormous flat-roofed, open air pavilion that I had now arrived at twice and departed from once for R&R. This time however was different. I knew exactly what the program was, I knew where everything was, and I knew this should be the last time I'd ever see this place.

I found a spot on the maze of wooden benches that seemed as close as possible to the spot I was sitting when my name was called to report to the 101st Airborne. Sitting down, I turned my head to the left and found the marquee sporting the Screaming Eagle icon, and tried to reflect on what I now knew about one of the most famous units in military history.

I no longer remember how much time passed before the most beautiful airplane pulled up in front of the pavilion area. It was a DC-8 stretch, and it was my "Freedom Bird."

As it had been with us at Cam Rahn Bay, the occupants were held inside until ARVN military brass did a walk-through inspection. After about 30 minutes, fresh new troops from the states, in brand new jungle fatigues, began walking down the mobile stairway to the tarmac. They slowly came down the stairs at the front and the stairs at the back of the exceedingly long airplane.

About 380 fresh new troops, forming two long lines from that plane to the canopy, began finding seats in the expanse of long wooden benches of the staging area. I watched the expressions on their faces. Few with a look of confidence; many with the look of worry mixed with fear and a little confusion, all concerned about what was to come next.

What happened next could only come from the imagination of a truly dumb-ass high brass who never so much as got dirt on his spit-shined boot. Two lines were formed for boarding the plane, and a couple of guards were posted at the head of the lines. One of them was ordering each man to remove his cover (hat) and was inspecting haircuts. From time to time a very red-faced GI would head back toward the pavilion and soon enough it was my turn.

"Soldier, you will get that hair cut before you board this plane," said the rear echelon buck sergeant with the brand-new starched jungle fatigues (I found out where all the new ones went).

"You have got to be shitting me," I said, "I had it cut two days ago. Come on, I'm going home today."

"Get out of this line now, or I will call the MP's," he said.

That piece of REMF dung was messing with the Doc!

I took two steps to the left, snapped to attention, looked him dead in the eyes, fire coming out of mine, and said, "I will do as you ordered, but keep in mind, if this causes me to miss this flight, I will be very close to your AO until the next plane comes!"

He raised his hand, pointed and gave accurate directions to the nearest barber.

Fortunately for all involved, I and many others made it back to the plane in time. But it was those acts of sheer stupidity that kept me from staying in an army that I was actually beginning to enjoy. You've got to think about that buck sergeant, however. How did he write home to his best girlfriend and explain what he was doing for the war effort? You think he lied about his duties when he got home?

Can't you just hear the voice of his girlfriend, "Oh honey, you were so brave during the war, forcing all those nasty old veterans to shave their heads before returning home."

"Oh honey, did you get a medal for that?"

Had I been ordered to do that job, I would have chosen

a court martial and the brig first. I think I was at the point of hyperventilating, before finally getting on that plane. It seemed like forever, getting nearly 400 G.I's on board, and even longer getting everyone seated. But, at around 1000 hours, the plane taxied out and took off.

Travel voucher from 101st in Vietnam to Fort Sam Houston, Texas.

The wheels barely left the runway when resounding whoops and hollers broke out from every man. The spirit was very high.

The plane was headed for Yokota, Japan, and as it pulled away from the airspace of Vietnam, the pilot made the announcement, and the cheers began again. It took several hours to reach Japan for the first fuel stop, which took about two hours. Uncle Sam was not worried about any of us trying to sneak away on the return trip, and we were allowed to roam the airport.

I found a jewelry shop and spotted a gold-colored Seiko watch that was an exact match for the silver one I purchased on R&R. I had plenty of money, so I bought this one too. The next stop was to be Anchorage, Alaska – about eight hours of flying time. My silver watch was set for Vietnam time, so I kept it that way. I advanced the new watch as we traveled, but needed to turn back the calendar by one day when we crossed the International Date Line, which kept us on August 7th.

It was evening in Alaska, but it was light enough to see the panorama of the snow-covered mountains along the coast and a backdrop to Anchorage. During this two-hour hold-over, most of us went out onto an observation deck and soaked up the scenery, the comfortable mid-70 degree temperature, the incredibly fresh air— and the fact that we were now on U.S. soil.

Our next flight was headed for California, with another eight hours of flying time. I tried to sleep but could not. In thinking about it, I hadn't actually slept since leaving Sally. It could have been nearly 60 hours, but the excitement was keeping all of us active and talking.

The pilot announced that we were about to enter the continental United States and would soon be able to see the lights on the coast of California. We landed at Travis Air Force Base, northeast of Oakland, just after daybreak.

We were led from the plane directly into a large aircraft

hanger and ushered into several different rows of tables with attendants on the opposite side. We were ordered to dump the contents of our duffel bags and anything else we were carrying, so it could be searched. I doubt like hell they found any contraband, but it sure slowed us down in trying to get home.

As we finished the inspection, they conducted what I will call a very light-duty debriefing that included advice about avoiding the hippies that might be hanging around the airports. We were directed to the mess hall for breakfast, and I might add, the Air Force employed good cooks. As we were chowing down, I noted the time on my original silver watch. We had breakfast in Bien Hoa on Thursday morning, August 7th, and we were having it again on Thursday August 7th—24 hours later! Flying back in time across the International Date Line will mess with your head!

After barely finishing chow, we were ushered onto buses and sent on a two-hour scenic tour from Travis AFB to the Oakland Army Terminal. It was August, hot and dry in California, and the rolling hills we passed were covered with very dry grasses. The bus driver made it clear that if anyone was caught smoking, the bus would be halted for one hour for each and every infraction. It was a pain, but anyone could see the place was a beautiful tinder box, and one spark could touch it off.

Oakland Army Terminal was more like a giant office/warehouse building, taking up a city block downtown. The buses stopped at the curb, and we marched inside. This was a fast-paced production process. Everyone was measured for dress green uniforms, including: service cap and all patches, ropes, ribbons, name tags, poplin shirt and tie. While the uniforms were being made ready, paperwork and payroll were brought up to date. A roster of airlines, airports and cab companies with phone numbers was made available, along with a wall full of phones.

I buddied up with several other guys who were headed for

Chicago, and we made standby reservations on an American Airlines plane that was flying out about 8:00 pm. I cleared my last station, called a cab, called home to my parents with the arrival time (the first time I spoke with them in a year) and headed for the airport. Which one, I no longer remember, but the terrain going there looked just like San Francisco.

All went well until our cab clunked-out about halfway there and would not start. The cabby radioed for a pickup, but it took an extra 30 minutes to get there. We were starting to lose the window for our flight.

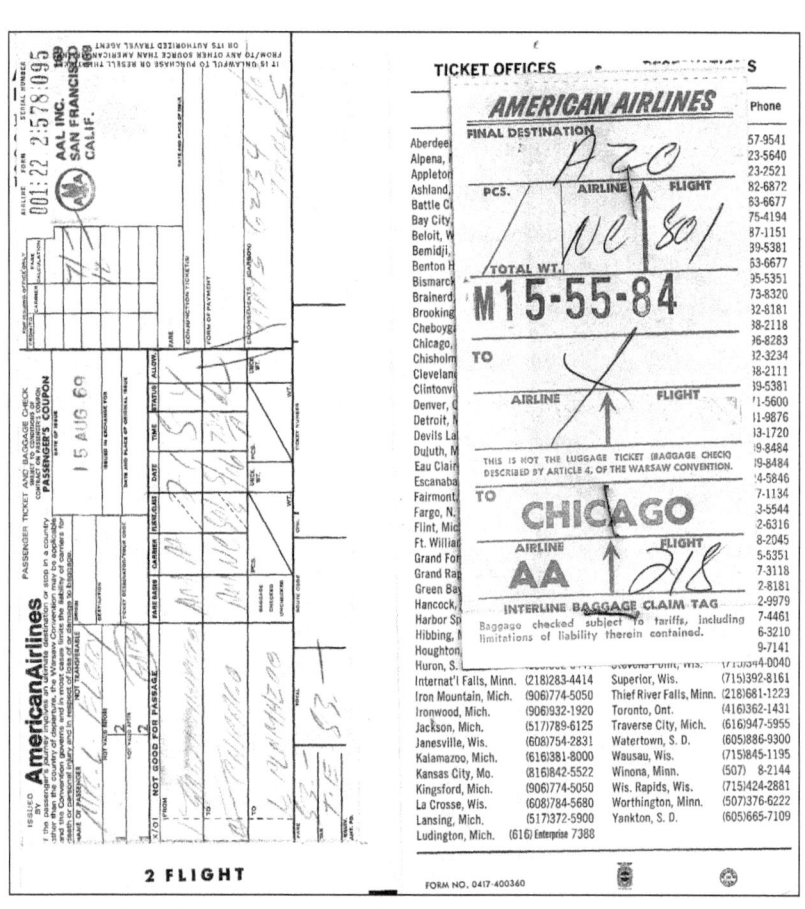

Gate pass from San Francisco to Chicago.

After arriving at the airport, we needed to find our way to the flight line while sprinting down the hallways with fully-loaded duffel bags. When I added my old uniform to the bag back at the Army terminal, there had not been enough space to pack the new pair of jungle boots. So I tied a knot in the laces and hung them around my neck. I was losing pace with the other guys, having the boots banging around, so I jerked them off my neck and pitched them at the side of the corridor. I was not going to let them stop me from catching this flight.

We arrived at the boarding site just in the nick of time, only to have the attendant say that all the standby seats in coach had been filled. A stewardess was standing nearby and confirmed the condition, "That's true," she said, "but we just happen to have enough room for three soldiers in first class."

"OOOOhhhh," came a sigh of relief.

We boarded the plane and had a great flight until we arrived at O'Hare Field in Chicago. In those days, O'Hare and many other large airports were experiencing more flights than they could handle, and we were put into a flight pattern circling the city for an additional 30 minutes.

I needed to advance my gold watch again, this time, three more hours. It was about 0400 hours, and the Kalamazoo connection was supposed to board at about 0500 hours. That gave me time to call home, estimating an arrival time of 0700 hours Michigan time, on Saturday morning (It was once again useful for me to include the day of the week).

Two of us that took the flight from California were still together. We both boarded the North Central plane. I was headed for Kalamazoo, and he was going to Lansing, with one stop in South Bend, Indiana, in between. The plane taxied out quickly, only to join what looked like a convoy of other planes, nose to tail, following each other through a maze of turns, waiting for its turn to take off.

Gate pass from Chicago O'Hare to Kalamazoo.

    The airport was full of planes and all we could do was wait for our turn to leave. I was on the left side of the plane in the window seat and found that if I laid my head against the portal, I could see down the side of the plane. Any time we turned a little to the left, I could count how many planes were ahead of us. Suddenly, I saw the lights alongside the runway zinging past about 50 feet below. Thinking that I had dozed off for a few minutes, I nudged my partner and said, "Hey dude, we're finally taking off!"

He said, "No, No—we're landing in Kalamazoo."

"No way," I said, "the plane is supposed to go to South Bend first."

He said, "We did—you slept through the whole thing!"

Sure enough, we were descending onto the runway. I had no intention of sleeping through this part of the journey, but it had been three full days of sleepless time, and I could not blame myself.

The plane landed, slowed its speed, came to the end of the runway, turned around, slowly taxied back to the terminal and made an easy 180-degree turn to the right. I could see my entire family lined up behind the fence. The engines shut down, and it took a while for the ground crew to push the portable stairway up to the plane. I sat there in silence for a while, looking at the faces of my family, who were looking at the door of the aircraft. I gestured to my partner to see them, and it was time to exit. We stood up, looked at each other, shook hands, and he said something that has stuck with me for a lifetime. I use this small, but oh-so-important phrase with every overseas veteran that I possibly can.

He said, "Welcome home brother."

I made my way to the bottom of the stairway, and my plan was to bend down and kiss the ground. But my sisters, Sandra, June, Susan and Bonnie sprinted the distance and had me in their arms before I had the chance. I quickly abandoned the plan as we made our way through the opening in the fence where I could pick up and hug each of my younger brothers, John, six years old, and Paul, five years old, then Mom.

Oh Mom, I couldn't hold my feelings any longer . . .

I composed myself like a soldier. It was Dad's turn. We shook hands. Dad was not a hugger, but I pulled him in with my left arm and held him close while shaking his hand and said, "I made it Dad, I made it."

I no longer remember the events of the day, other than the

ride home in my Dad's four-door Rambler, meeting with other friends and family and getting my first look at the pontoon boat Dad had been building all summer. I was impressed with his work, quite impressed. I unpacked gifts of silk Oriental cloth for Mom and my sisters and trinkets for my brothers. I asked Dad if he would like to have the silver Seiko watch (they were very expensive at the local jewelry stores). He was very happy with the watch and wore it until he passed away nearly 25 years later.

My cousin, Bill Flory, was due to return from Vietnam on August 15th, and I couldn't wait to see him and let the partying begin. I did not spend as much time with my parents as I should have during the next 35 days of leave time. I was back in the "world," 21-years old, in the heat of the rock'n roll, free love generation with a story to tell—and a chip growing ever larger on my shoulder.

I was totally unaware that a new silent war had just begun inside my head, and the proverbial angel on one side and the devil on the other would duke it out on a near-daily basis for the next ten years.

They are still there, in a quasi-truce with no peace agreement, because, on occasion, they jump back in the ring and go at it.

My wife Ann will be happy to attest to this.

23.
The First Ten Years

While on leave from Vietnam, I needed a car and started shopping almost immediately. Within a day or two, I found one I just had to have in the neighboring town of Paw Paw. I set out to find some racing-striped muscle car but ended up thumping down the cash for a luxury car with muscle, a dark sky-blue 1967 Chevy Caprice Classic two-door hard-top with a black-vinyl roof and lots of power gadgets. This car had a 396 cu. in. V-8, Holley four-barrel carburetor, and a 400 automatic transmission. It was faster than anything I had ever driven, and all it needed was gas and wax. I had intended to class up my act a bit if I survived the war.

This car was a good start, and due to the fact that none of my civilian clothing fit, I also needed to buy a complete new wardrobe.

I could not have been more happy about being home, but it was just so different. My family provided wonderful support, but I doubt that I took very good advantage of it. Cousin Bill was the only one around who I could relate to, but he was in the same frame of mind that I was.

About the third week of leave, one of my good friends with B-Co., Al Kontrabecki, from Niagara Falls, New York, showed up. He was still on leave but had headed out early for his next duty station, and it wasn't that far out of his way to stop at my place and stay for a few days. It had only been a month since we'd seen each other, but he was a sight for sore eyes.

We partied hard, and I introduced him to Bill and other friends. It was a confirmation that we were back in the "world." Al was a really great guy and a good storyteller. We have exchanged a few letters and phone calls through the years, but he has avoided reunions so far.

While processing out of the war zone, I had been asked what duty station I would prefer back in the U.S. for finishing out the remainder of my active duty. I requested Fort Sam Houston. I liked it there. It was much warmer than Michigan, I was familiar with it, and there was lots to do. My wish had been granted.

Leave time passed quickly, and I packed up the Caprice and headed for Texas in early September. My parents were probably glad to see me go. I had time to think on the two-day trip down there.

When reporting in on base, I made it clear that if I was assigned to some hospital ward that I would probably go AWOL (Absent Without Official Leave), and that I'd seen enough of that sort of thing. Again, my wish was granted. I was assigned to A-Co., which was a detail company made up of men like me who had limited time remaining in the service. A-Co. did every detail and off-the-wall job on the entire post that required manpower and diversified talent.

It was basically an 8 to 5 job with something new to do every day. Much of the base was dedicated to providing a basic training for doctors, dentists and specialists who were coming into the army as officers, and even they were required to have infantry and weapons training.

Everything about the army is structured. I needed it then, and it was good for me. I enjoyed being a soldier during the day and was quite proud to be wearing that Eagle patch on my right shoulder. I partied hard when I could but had calmed down enough to start thinking about what might come next. I truly enjoyed the Army, but the pay was downright lousy, despite the free food and lodging. Living on about $70 a week was impossible even for a single guy.

I found an advertisement in the orderly room offering tuition for educational classes off post. One was for a design and drafting class offered by San Antonio Tech. I signed up for the one-night per week class and acquired a diploma from it before leaving Texas.

I also signed up for military driving school and was licensed for many vehicles including the deuce-and-a-half, all of which came in handy with A-Co. I also pulled occasional night guard duty.

With A-Co., you damn well had better be in formation and standing tall at reveille, sound off for roll call, get your assignment for the day and do your job. There were occasional barracks details and night guard duty, but after five o'clock and on weekends, we were just a bunch of happy-go-lucky GI's waiting for ETS (Expiration Time of Service). I had an upper bunk on the second floor of our barracks. Everyone had a bunk, a foot locker, a wall locker and that was it.

One night while sitting on my bunk, writing a letter or doing homework, I kept hearing some unusual activity going on downstairs. I had heard it on other nights, but this time it got the best of my curiosity, and I went down to investigate. I stood just behind the stairwell wall, out of sight, and listened carefully for a moment, then peeked around the corner long enough to confirm my suspicion.

There was a quiet, spindly kid, maybe a bit of a derelict, who lived on the first floor. He stayed to himself, and I never paid much attention to him. Another short, stocky man, who also lived on the first floor, was doing all he could to make the kid fight him. About 15 other GI's had moved bunks out of the way and were perched here and there watching the show. I stepped into the room, dressed only in white, military, boxer shorts, as the kid fell to the floor and rolled into the fetal position as the man kicked him.

No one even noticed me as I moved closer to the action. So outraged I could not feel my body, I saw an opening as the short guy recoiled from a kick. I moved in quickly, hit him hard in the center of his chest with the palm of my hand and knocked him back several feet. I looked straight into his eyes and said, "Stay right there, It's my turn now."

I backed up to the kid, reached down behind me, grabbed his upper arm and pulled him to his feet. I brought him around to my side and instructed him to step down into the shower room and get himself cleaned up, while never taking my eyes off the short guy.

I then moved slowly toward the offender. Fire must have been coming from my eyes as I screamed, "OK asshole, let's continue the show."

He immediately pissed his pants, backed up between some of the other guys, fell to his knees and whined, "I can't fight you!"

I addressed him with a battery of four-letter words, then turned to the other men on the bunks, slowly pacing the length of their arena, and shouted, "Any of you God damn gapers want to jump bad, now is the time, but there will be blood and broken bones."

No one moved as I stood fast, surveying every eye, and I screamed again, "If I hear so much as a rumor that someone hurt that dumb kid, it will be very bad for them."

"Now, get the f—k up and put this f—ing barracks back together."

I backed down into the shower room to check on the kid and told him to continue to mind his own business, that no one would mess with him again. I could see the gapers were obeying my orders as I returned to my bunk. I sat, shaking like crazy for a long time, partly from the adrenaline rush and partly from knowing

I could easily have gotten my ass kicked bad had several of those guys jumped me. Later I found that the aggressor had befriended the timid guy and protected him.

My father had ingrained in me from my childhood, never to instigate a fight, and I have been successful at abiding by his rule. But that night I discovered that I had become fearless for a just cause.

Don't mess with the Veteran Medic.

San Antonio was an amazing place to be stationed for a 21-year-old country boy with a few bucks in his pocket and one hell of a confidence builder in his recent past. It took about a month to get to know where the best haunts were and have some new buddies to hang out with. There was no end for things to do, within the city or out.

In less than three hours you could be in Mexico, or Corpus Christi, swimming in the Gulf of Mexico. I must admit too, that in my travels before and after, I have never seen a place where their were so many absolutely beautiful women. They seemed to like GI's and all of us spent as much time as possible chasing them. The parties raged nearly non-stop for the entire six months I was there.

I ETSed from the military on February 28, 1970, but needed to stay in San Antonio for an additional week to finish my class and get the diploma. It seemed like a much longer drive heading home, and the further north I drove the colder it got. I had been in warm climates for the better part of two years and was unaccustomed to the cold.

I moved back into my old basement room at home, agreed to pay mother rent for food and laundry and went looking for work.

I found another government law was working well. If you left a job because of military service, the employer had to hire you back. Before the week was out, I was back with Jessup Door working full time (I have remained fully employed for the last forty years, never having drawn unemployment).

Bradley Jimmerson, 60 Gunner, severely wounded March 13, 1968 during TET. Bradley's wife Cathy started the B-Co. website in February 2001 and continues to be webmaster.

The class at San Antonio Tech had gone very well for me, and I was determined to use the GI Bill to continue my education. I shopped around the local community colleges but found that classes would not be starting for another six months. So I enjoyed the time with little responsibility other than my job and helping my parents with whatever odd jobs they needed done on weekends. Otherwise, I was hunting for the next party.

In August, a friend shared information about a mechanical design and engineering course being offered at Parsons Business School in Kalamazoo and starting the fall semester. The two of us registered for the class and were accepted. It was to be the equivalent of an Associate's Degree, with a diploma upon completion.

The classes met four nights each week, Monday through Thursday, for four hours each night. The course was to last for 15 consecutive months, but in the end it took sixteen.

Unlike high school, my motivation was completely different, and I consistently earned a four point average through the course. Oddly enough, the slide rule was part of the curriculum and Ken Massy, our primary professor, taught the use of it. However, he used a (new to the world) portable calculator by Texas Instruments that was about the size of a large, thick slice of bread. Although relatively small for the times, it would not fit into your pocket. It would do common math functions but nothing really special, and it sold for about $125.

In 2010 money, that would be about $650, and none of us students could afford such a novelty. Funny thing, by the time the course ended, I could buy a pocket-sized calculator by Texas Instruments with twice the functions as Ken's for $15.

Incidentally I never used the slide rule again after the class.

Sometime that fall, I encountered an old friend, Jim Chabitch, as we stood on the sidewalk at the stoplight waiting for the light to change. In the course of the conversation, Jim mentioned that his sister Ann wasn't seeing anyone at the time and that I should give her a call.

At some later time I did call her, and the conversation went on for half an hour as she was thinking that she was talking to an ex-flame. When she realized who was on the phone with her, she was so embarrassed that she agreed to a date set for the following weekend.

We had that first date, but it was about a month before I called and we dated again. Then it was about two weeks, then every week.

It was a very strained relationship, as we were both in school and working. We couldn't even talk on the phone from Sunday night until Friday night. But despite all the hassle on May 1, 1970, we were married. Ann was already pregnant, and on June 17th, the baby decided to come four months early. She was the smallest preemie to survive in the Bronson Hospital Neonatal Care Unit at the time.

Little Lisa weighed only one pound and twelve ounces at birth. Think of that relative to seven sticks of butter!

Ann and I grieved her impending death for days, but she fooled us and all the odds, and was released from the hospital 91 days later. The three month's wait had its own blessing, in that Ann was able to finish school and become a licensed cosmetologist.

It was probably during this time that Ann and I began to learn who one another really was, and had conditions been different, we may have headed in opposite directions. Lisa was the glue that held us together, as we soon had the devastating news that she had Downs Syndrome. There was no way of knowing where her mental abilities would plateau, but they certainly would at some point, and she would need assistance in living the remainder of her days. The doctors were correct, she plateaued at about the two year level, never learned to speak even one word and was nearly blind. As I write this, she's healthy, but needs care 24/7.

Over the following six years, we developed enough nerve to have two more children, two more daughters. Both became scholastically exceptional, amazing young women and my best friends.

Meanwhile, Ann and I did everything we could physically and mentally to train and teach Lisa to be all that she could be. By the time she turned ten, the entire family was suffering far too much. I think I would have rather put her in the ground at the time, but, instead we placed her in group care. We continue as her guardians, see her, guide her care and tend to her needs every month or so. Her care has always been the very best.

Did Agent Orange have anything to do with Lisa's problems? It is extremely rare for two healthy young people to have a Downs child. However, the VA does not recognize Downs as a side effect of the chemical.

Rebecca and Elizabeth both acquired four-year degrees from Hope College in Holland, Michigan. Elizabeth is currently a psychologist in Las Vegas. Rebecca uses her arts degree successfully, but is currently a stay-at-home mom, raising two amazing grandsons.

I can only talk about the first ten years in retrospect. I knew that there were other things going on inside my head, but a great deal of life was coming at me at the same time. I just didn't dare allow the *woe-is-me* side to take over.

For the first couple of years, explosive sounds would unnerve me, and it was a bad idea to touch me if I was sleeping, but that wore off. I was unable to hunt for nearly 20 years, mainly for fear of other hunters in the woods. Some are simply pure idiots, and most have no idea what a 12-gauge slug can do to a person.

Most of that fear has worn away, and in retrospect, those early years were used wisely. Even though there was never a time I didn't feel like there was an ever-present dark shadow in the background or that there were always two paths to follow. How easy it would have been to slide into the *woe-is-me* world—and I even had an excuse, a good one. However, there were times that I thought I could drink all that Miller Beer could produce, but I only caused them to put on a second shift a time or two.

In the 1980's, the political debacles of the war were being revealed, the baby-killer bull shit, right along with it. The Vietnam veterans were being fully exonerated and accepted.

In 1986, a neighbor, Jake Kluch, a WWII vet and former POW who had been shot up badly by a German machine gun and captured, explained to me that he could no longer physically carry the POW flag in the 4th of July parades. He told me he would be proud if I carried it for him. I joined the VFW and have carried his flag in the parades and at Memorial Day services ever since. God now rests his soul.

Through all of these good years, God has provided for me, and I thank him for his generosity on a regular basis. I have truly tried to live life to the fullest, to give a day's work for a day's pay, and I travel this great country with my family as much as I can. We built our final home from the timber on our land. We dance when the music plays and laugh as much as possible. I learned to play the guitar and sing with the honky-tonk bands. I have run five marathons, shaken hands with President Bush, spent 22 years involved in local government, 25 with the VFW and fight like hell if a cause is right. I jump on the trampoline with my grandsons, squeeze them, tell them that I love them and try to teach them the rules of LIBTYFI (leave it better than you found it).

When it's time to tip a few pints, I always tip one for our lost comrades. I never, ever dreamed that I would one day write a book about it all, but after I finished the initial draft, I sought help in editing it from a good friend, David Tate, who is the director of the Van Buren County Library system (Michigan). Dave said he couldn't do it, but he had a friend by the name of Larry Massie who might be interested and called me one day to meet him. When we sat down to have a look at the draft, I noticed he had a Paratroopers jump wings badge on the lapel of his sport coat. I pointed at it and smiled, and he said, "173rd Airborne, Vietnam, 1965."

We welcomed each other home, thanked one another for our service and, well, here we are.

Attending my first B-Co. reunion in 2003 was one of the truly good things I have done for myself and, as it turned out, for Ann, as well. It was as if the wives were all veterans too, sharing their battle stories about us. Again, regardless of status, we are all equal there, draftees, RA (Regular Army enlisted) privates, specialists, officers and military lifers. It's a level playing field, and it is wonderful.

Hosting the 2009 reunion was an absolute joy, but standing at the podium addressing those men and their wives in my own home town, 40 years after the fact and with 32 years having had no idea where any of them were, with the exception of Dan Wakefield, was a strange feeling indeed.

It was about 2003 when the movie *Saving Private Ryan* was released. We went to see it on the big screen, and I believe it was an extraordinarily accurate depiction of the landing at Normandy with the story line and subsequent action of trying to find private Ryan behind enemy lines. Of course, the fact that they parachuted in with (you guessed it) the 101st Airborne was very good too. At the end, we were jerked back to the present time at a cemetery near Normandy full of GI's killed during the invasion.

The old version of Ryan looked at his wife and said, "Tell me I have lived a good life. Tell me that I have been a good man."

He needed to know if he had lived honorably for those who died. Those words took the breath from me, as I realized I had been trying to do the same thing all along, and if I was trying to do it, then tens of thousands of other Vietnam veterans were trying to do it too. I am certain that we are succeeding.

When we are made to persist, to complete the whole tour, that is how we find out who we are – Tobias Wolf

24.
REFLECTIONS

As Americans, we need to salute the men and women in the armed services, all branches, those that fought in the foreign wars, those that were stationed overseas in peaceful places and those that never were required to leave U.S. soil.

The thing that we may not fully comprehend is that when they raise their right hand in the swearing-in ceremony and don the uniform, it matters not what branch of service they are in, they do not have any idea where they may end up or what might happen to them.

> DEFINITION OF A VETERAN
> *A Veteran – whether active duty, retired,*
> *National Guard, Reserves or Coast Guard –*
> *is someone who, at one point in his life,*
> *wrote a blank check made payable to the*
> United States of America *for an amount*
> *up to and including his life.*
> *– Author unknown.*

I was a country boy, without knowledge of the world and with only a curiosity about a far off war. I had no thought whatsoever of the military and very little chance of ever volunteering for it. But when the call came to me, I did not shirk it. I went to do my duty and joined the military service, even if in an abstract way.

I was sent off to war and assigned to one of the most recognized and famous units in U.S. military history. The 101st continued to uphold its reputation, receiving both U.S. and the Republic of South Vietnam presidential unit citations for meritorious actions against the enemy.

The June, 1970 issue of *Time* magazine referred to the 101st as the suicide battalions. Then, out of all the well-documented battles and campaigns of the war involving many other hardcore units of the Army, Marines, Air Force, Navy, ARVNs, Australian, New Zealand and ROK (Republic of Korea) units, my unit ended up involved in the most remembered battle of the war, "Hamburger Hill," which also became the actual turning point of the war. That turning point took off in opposing directions, and I will try to give my take on those later.

I cannot guess how many times I escaped harm during my tour. At recent reunions, the '68-69'ers have estimated involvement in some 12 to 14 out-and-out firefights, four sniper attacks, four boobie trapped areas (that we knew about), countless *punji* pits (they were ineffective), one friendly-fire incident, one mortar attack and 36 combat air assaults.

Who knows what other accidents could have happened? The sky is the limit on that! Remember Agent Orange?

B-Co., 2-501, lost 68 men killed from December 1967 to May 10th of 1972, and I could have been in that group just as easily as not. The unit as a whole, had 4,011 KIA, 18,259 WIA—and seven Medal of Honor winners during the unit's tour.

Some of my escapes were by obvious twists in timing or the skill of other men. Some may call it luck, but I do not believe in luck in the traditional sense, as if some mystical force governs it.

Luck, for the most part, is created by us when we put ourselves in a position for good or bad things to happen. The remainder is purely accidental—you have a bad accident or a good accident.

I am not saying that God does not have a plan for us, either. I believe that He does in the end, but, meanwhile, He has left us pretty much on our own. My escapes may be known by the Man above, but He is keeping it a secret.

Strangely enough, I fully enjoyed most of my stateside time in the military. It's clean and organized, with a freshly starched uniform and spit-shined shoes every day, and a simple and rigid structure. I needed it and learned from that environment, and it was probably a blessing. Even stranger, 40 years later, I would not trade my war experience for anything, but at the same time I would never wish it on anyone.

One thing is for sure, I had an opportunity to be in the presence of some of the bravest men on earth, and these brave men – the American GI and Allied forces – *won* the physical war in Vietnam in every conceivable way.

The VC and NVA pulled off one hell of a TET (oriental new year) offensive on January 31, 1968. They hit us hard, but devastated themselves doing it. The VC were all but wiped out. Every single one of the battles in their offensive was lost except for one, in that they captured and held captive the American media.

B-Co. 2-501 was heavily involved in the retaking of Hue and lost many men. Bradley Jimmerson and John Heil were wounded badly but survived. They never miss a reunion (Bradley's wife Cathy has been our wonderful webmaster).

For a great explanation go to: *www.1stcavmedic.com/tet_offensive_of_1968.htm*

The TET offensive of 1969 wasn't much more than a fart in the wind, with lots of rocket and mortar attacks on larger bases, but that was it. Basically there was no TET in 1969 or after. The taking of Hamburger Hill and the entire A Shau valley in the Thua Thien province decimated the NVA's 46th infantry, which was alleged to be the North's most elite unit. At the end of 1969, the majority of the enemy were residing in Laos and Cambodia, sending raiding and harassment parties back over the borders to create firefights or lay siege to some Firebase. But they continued to lose every single fight. At that point, there was no reason why the South Vietnamese people could not have been a free nation, as they so badly wanted—and the USA and its allies intended.

Rules of engagement prevented pursuing them into these other countries, or even into North Vietnam, with the exception of sporadic bombing raids. By 1970, the rules of engagement lay squarely on the shoulders of the grunts. It is not unfair to say that, near the end of the "forfeit," a soldier needed to see blood squirting out of a bullet hole in the man next to him before he could return fire in defense.

I am in no way in favor of war, and no one can hate war more than a veteran, but if you are going forth to have a war, only good generals with good soldiers with full backing of their country can win it.

This war lasted so long, with the loss of so many young men and so much unrest in America, for what most of us veterans believe was caused totally by politicians that were indecisive, self-centered in their political gain—or stood to gain monetarily from it.

It's no different than having bean-counters in charge of manufacturing / production facilities. A-Company might last for a while, but failure is almost certain.

Hamburger Hill was the final undoing of Hanoi's ability to conduct a legitimate war against anyone.

As grunts, we would say, "Their dicks were knocked straight into the dirt!"

The Hill was the pivotal point for the media, which turned

from just lopsided reporting to legalizing outright deception and lies.

Try this, for example: a reporter wrote about a race between an American horse and a Russian horse, the American horse won but this is how it was reported:

> *The Russian horse came in second and the American horse came in next to last.*

All Americans need to sort out carefully what they are told on the TV, unscramble it, decide what they believe was left out and write their own news based on that.

About 60 GI's died taking Hill 937, but it appeared the media took into account all the military deaths in the entire country for the entire month, making it appear as though there were hundreds of men massacred. Reading their accounts would have you believe a major portion of our military had been wiped out. Then they set forth to create the baby-killer image, mostly from a single photo of villagers running from a burning hamlet, led by a naked young girl.

They claimed our GI's had no regard for collateral damage caused to civilians, vilifying returning veterans. I never witnessed any of that baby killer crap, nor have I encountered any other Vietnam veteran who has, either. Captured prisoners may have been roughed up at first, but I know that even the combatants were treated humanely.

Years later we found out that the burning village was actually caused by a horrible accident, when the ARVN airmen dropped napalm on the wrong target. Americans had nothing to do with it.

It was simply not necessary to tell an American GI to avoid harming civilians, they always have and always will do everything in their power to protect the innocent—especially babies.

From 1970 to 1972, more and more rules were depleting the fighting ability of our GI's. De-escalation (forfeiture) had begun, and all new rotating troops had nearly grown up with dissension toward the war. Even the system of draft took a bad turn for the worse with the "Lotto" system. It was all enough to drive GI's crazy, and in some cases it did. For many years after the war, if some vet or group of vets acted out in their own defense, they were quickly booed or passed off as some weak lost soul left over from the Vietnam conflict. It took more than 20 years to overcome that stigma and, in between, we bore that burden, too.

Now—as long as we are around—no generation of veterans will abandon another.

One last issue with the media is that as badly as they would love to continue bashing our GI's in our current wars, we will not let them do it anymore. There are a great many Vietnam vets in high places these days. The media want only to show photos of caskets and devastated civilians, never the good and even wonderful things that have happened as a result of the GI's work.

I was witness to unbelievable changes in the infrastructure and the positive attitude generated in Vietnam in just one year. We were there for nine years, and the good that we left was massive. I know that what we have done for Iraq and Afghanistan would take an entire crew of reporters, working 24/7, to try and keep up with the good things that are happening over there daily. But you will not hear much of it from the media. You will need to talk directly with the returning GI's if you want to hear that side of the story.

This is, of course, just the opinion of a guy who was a soldier once, someone who has *been-there-done-that.*

I currently live just a short distance from the place where I grew up, three miles out of the little town of Decatur and 30 miles in any direction from a town with more than 5,000 people. The isolation probably kept us all more innocent in those days, and everyone still needed his neighbors, all of them. There were many black families that lived in and around Decatur, with the town of Vandalia, about 15 miles to the south, said to have been on the underground railroad route.

The Rileys, who had a rest home just around the corner from us; the Overton boys, whose mother worked for the Rileys; the Gothard family who lived two miles north; the Lee and Roth families; the Harris's; and the many generations of the Goens families; the Gibsons; Slaughters and Kemps and more. We all grew up together. We went to school, church, fishing, swimming and to the movies together. Our parents worked at many of the same places, and if you dented your car, Art Slaughter could fix it up like new again. Prejudice never seemed to be part of our culture, it was not taught to me by my family or the community.

I was finally taught by two men in Vietnam.

Thankfully the years have taken away most of the memories of the constant verbal onslaught I received from these two men.

According to them, I was a fairly useless and stupid human being. They did not touch me physically, but if either one had the opportunity to bend a branch back, as you were humping through the pucker brush, it would be timed out to let go and swat me, if I got into range. My job took me away from the CP constantly, and if I left any of my things unguarded, something would happen every time. Prepared food may be contaminated with dirt, or tipped over and spilt out. Maybe all of my heat tabs would be stolen.

I will tell this now for the first time since then.

One morning as I was about to shoulder my pack, I spied something unusual on the upper webbing, about where it would rest against my right shoulder. Taking a closer look, I found that a small amount of human shit had been applied with a stick or whatever. The platoon was preparing to head out on recon. Tell me how, in this place, that I can quickly clean it off? I cannot scream or cuss loudly, I cannot prove who did it, and I cannot slow down the platoon. Fortunately, as a medic I carried bandages and disinfectants that removed the problem but wasted the supplies.

I did learn something from dealing with these two guys. Spontaneity and extreme patience, can both yield great dividends.

It was sometime after the war that I learned that Jim Crow laws still existed in the South at the time and what the Rosa Parks bus incident was about. For crying out loud, prejudice was being taught in the South and inner cities on both sides of the fence. It's no wonder there was unrest. Sergeant Battle and Private Wooten were just products of those places. I forgive them and hope that they forgive me.

At Reunion 2003, sponsored by Jim and Ruth Julien in Kansas City, Missouri, a man and his wife pulled up to the main entrance on a Harley with a very unusual paint job. A medium height, stocky-built, square-jawed guy stepped off the bike, pulled a bottle of homemade wine from one of the saddle bags and said, "Hi, I'm Dan Hefel."

My encounters with Dan while in-country were very brief, but it was him, alright, and before the reunion was over we all heard a most incredible story.

As he told it, around September he got very sick and was sent back to the rear where he was diagnosed with malaria and sent to the hospital ship USS *Hope*. He recuperated, then was sent back to the field and, within a few weeks, had a relapse. He went back to the medical ship, recuperated again and was sent back to Sally, where he spent some time convincing Sgt. (Top) George Shorr to keep him in the rear. He won his case by volunteering as a door gunner on our LOG birds and enjoyed being back at the base every night on a dry bed.

All went well until the fifth of February, when a new pilot was in the process of taking over the craft. The new pilot's first assignment was to take the bird to Da Nang for a new altimeter and to have the rotors repainted (black on the bottom, white on top). On the flight south, the new pilot explained to the other that since the A Shau was his new AO, he should take him for a quick tour to get the lay of the land before doing it on his own. With some reluctance With some reluctance from the pilot and crew, they took an unannounced and unscheduled flight straight up the center of the valley. It was a good flight, until the notorious A Shau fog blew in and blinded their return trip. The altimeter was not working, so it didn't take long to find the side of a mountain the hard way and crash the helicopter into the jungle.

Dan said that he woke up lying on a piece of the tail section, with burns on his wrists, one broken arm, and he could not make his legs work. He looked further up the hillside at a ball of fire he assumed was the remainder of the chopper. He was not sure how much time had passed, but it didn't seem too long before he realized he was looking down the barrel of an AK-47 and into the face of an NVA soldier.

It would be best to check out the narrative about Dan at *www.b2501airborne.com* under POW, but briefly, Dan and one of the pilots lived through the crash and were captured.

They spent weeks with the NVA as they were slowly taken to Hanoi, North Vietnam, Dan was carried the entire distance, as his back was broken. They spent the next 1,143 days in captivity, finally being released in March 1973.

It all sounded unreal until Ann and I visited Dan and his wife Sue at their home in Gutenberg, Iowa, and went through the album his mother made while he was a POW. Reading the telegrams sent by the Government to his family was really quite something.

There is no doubt about what happened to him!

Let me add one more note about the Tulsa Reunion. When Duke and his wife were giving tours through their new home that was built on the family ranch, his mother happened to be in the kitchen, and we were introduced.

She said, "Flory, my great, great grandmother's name was Esther Flory," (which happens to be my mother's name, too).

She lived in Ohio until she got married. I told her that my grandfather had lived near Defiance, Ohio. We exchanged phone numbers and, after returning home, I checked the genealogy book and found that Esther was my great, great grandfather's sister. So, Jim and I are like 6th cousins, twice removed!

"Huda thunk it!"

As one may gather from these stories, and from the stories from any other Vietnam veteran who was exposed to field duty, the helicopters were our saviors. They were absolute life support, in every respect. Yet today, if we hear the rotors of a helicopter beating the air in the distance, it brings chills.

Postscript to 2023 Edition

Now that you have read *101st ACM* (or *Transition to Duty,* which was its first published title), I invite you to enjoy, as I do, some of the many things I have been gifted with as a result of writing this book. I suppose I should start with the very first book signing at VFW Post 6248 in our home town of Decatur, Michigan.

It was a wonderful experience, with so many of the townspeople showing up in support, including our State representative at the time Eric Nesbit and several WWII veterans: Elmer Jackson, (more later) Ray Jansen, George Masurra and Chubb Adams, all of whom purchased books.

I did a short talk that evening, my first of many to come.

Over the next couple of years I was given opportunities to speak at many varied venues, mostly local or semi local: VFW's, American Legions, Rotary Clubs, churches, high school classes, militaria collectors, Elk and Moose Lodges and such. I had the opportunity to speak at a 101st Airborne Division Association National Convention In Nashville, Tennessee—not to pitch my book, but to thank them for pitching it for me. As a result of that event, veterans of the 101st acquired copies of the book, and one of them contacted me later. He was a Vietnam Veteran by the name of Lenny Kamensho, and we will tell his story a bit later.

The author with Eric Nesbit at the first book signing.

The most memorable of these speaking engagements started with our Schwann man Jason Wood, an Air Force veteran I had given a copy of the book to. Months later I received a call from Mr. John Wood, Jason's father, of Defiance, Ohio.

John was also a medic who was stationed in Japan 1969-70, treating Vietnam Vets returning to the States. As we talked, it seemed likely he had dealt with some of the GI's I treated in the field. John then loaned the book to veteran friend, Mr. Rick Booher, who contacted me and said he identified with the book so well, he thought I was writing about him. (This has happened many times).

Some time after that I received a call from Mrs. Brenda Arps, also from Defiance, Ohio, who had my book on loan from Rick. Brenda was the coordinator of events at Tenora High School, just North of Defiance. Tenora High has a tradition of going all out for Veterans Day, and she wanted to know if I would be the keynote speaker that year.

I accepted without reservation as my father was born and raised only a few miles from the school, and this would have been his 100th birthday.

The audience was about 800, students, parents, local veterans, faculty and two of my personal comrades from our Vietnam days who lived within driving distance – Craig Willcutt and Bob Layton, what a surprise!

Thank you Dave Reinheimer, for putting them up to it, but they did it out of comradeship. The talk lasted about 45 minutes and in the last 15 I slowly swapped my formal attire, revealing an OD T-shirt, donned a black leather vest and GI hat – both covered with patches and pins a veteran might wear.

They gave me a standing ovation.

At the podium at Tenora High. *Leaving the stage.*

Things were speeding up a bit at this time when my comrade Dave Reinheimer put me in contact with our sister, A-Co., 2-501, 101st Airborne (who also supported an excellent website). A-Company was on the perimeter guard when Firebase Airborne was overrun. After making contact with a Mr. Roger Barski, I was advised of their next FB Airborne survivors reunion, which I attended. I am so thankful that I did. I not only met many men who knew Robert Malecki, (the reason for writing this book) they knew exactly what happened to him.

They were also in contact with Jennifer Gains, she had made it full circle in coming to know what had happened to her uncle.

With Bob Layton and Craig Wilcutt.

These grunts had truly been traumatized during that event. One of them, Georg Buchner from Chicago, maintained a large-scale model of the Firebase, on two tables that he built over the years in a way that he could break it down and haul it to these reunions. It was amazing in detail. I also met and traded books with Mr. Sam Zaffiri, author of the book *Hamburger Hill,* the actual blow by blow history of the battle. Not the hocus-pocus version seen in the movie. Hollywood actually did a fantastic job of recreating the fighting events, but that is where it ended. The remainder of the storyline will irk the ass of any Vietnam Vet. For those of us who know it personally, we have hate for the producers. (More on Sam later.)

Above: Georg Buchner with model.   Below: Sam Zaffiri with the author.

I had heard for many years about a grand Vietnam Veterans reunion being held in Kokomo, Indiana, but was never able to attend one. Things changed after writing the book, and approaching retirement, it was time to find out what it was about. I joined the HCVVO (Howard County Vietnam Veterans Organization) as a life member, then found a group of 101st guys who had space for my class A motorhome and joined the event.

I was flabbergasted at what was there and what these Veterans had accomplished. It was an 80+ acre site divided into about 10,000 campsites (all full). It had facilities for everything and a continuing events program for a week.

My goal was to meet as many people as possible and sell as many books as possible. Selling was a door to door (campsite to campsite) tough job, but it led to meeting many more people than expected.

In our own campsite, there were many 101st, flags flying.

I met Mr. Ron Werneth, who was not a veteran, but a published author of military history. Ron was compiling individual history's of veteran Dog Handlers and I was able to offer the quiet and solitude of the motorhome for him to conduct interviews.

This worked for the next few years. Our B-Co., 2-501 reunion founder and president, David Reinheimer, met and stayed with me at the first two September events. Dave proved to be a much more energized and motivated book salesman than I, so we covered a lot of ground.

In one camp, an old vet looked at my hat and said, "101st, eh?"

"Yes sir," I said, as he handed me a challenge coin.

He said he and his dog were hunting and had sat down by a tree to rest, when he spotted something shiny in the leaves. It was the 101st Airborne challenge coin. He made a personal oath to give it to the first 101st GI he met, well, that was me. It's in my pocket always.

Left to right: Author and historian Ron Werneth with dog handlers Allan Mathews, Richard Boyer (deceased) and John Meeks.

101st Challenge coin.

Going from camp to camp, we would ask, "Permission to enter your perimeter?"

Of course we were always invited in—and usually offered food and libations!

In one, we met Nurse Jane. Jane served in Vietnam during

1968 and 1969, as a triage nurse at the Danang field hospital. She had a passion for 101st guys, as there were a great many processed through her unit. We concluded that there was no doubt she handled cases for men I had patched up and put on choppers headed for the Danang field hospital. We hugged and cried, hugged and cried.

Jane's copy was free.

The author with Nurse Jane.

At the end of the third day, that first year at Kokomo, Dave and I were on the home stretch headed for our own camp, pooped out, as we sighted a 101st flag in front of a rather large group of campers. They were with the 101st Artillery. After asking permission to enter their perimeter, we met Mr. Ralph Forbes. While putting the pitch on Ralph to purchase a copy of the book, I showed him a photo in my book of a 8" tracked artillery piece I was sitting on in Camp Sally. Ralph looked very closely at the photo, then called for his comrade Russ Withers to come view it.

They studied the numbers on the artillery piece and blurted out, "That's our gun! That's *Ass Kicker!*"

Ralph and Russ continued the story about *Ass Kicker*. In the summer of 1969, that particular howitzer was chosen by the 101st Artillery Brass to shoot the 300,000th round the unit fired in the Vietnam war. The gunners went overtime to clean and paint *Ass Kicker*, but the brass made them paint over the name for the photo event.

They also polished and painted the HE-round for the shoot.

On the big day, a half dozen high brass showed up as the gun crew created an extra long lanyard that all of them could grip a distance from the gun and all pull on a single command. As the last officer left the scene, the crew repainted *Ass Kicker* back on the barrel! Thanks again Ralph and Russ.

Right: Rear view of Ass Kicker *(HE-round with canister on table).*

Below: Russ Withers.

Below right: Ralph Forbes.

The new friends, comrades, developed during those seasons of HCVVO remain on going, especially Ron Werneth. (More with Ron later).

After the 101st National Reunion in Nashville, Lenny Kamensho, A-Co., 2-501 (mentioned earlier) contacted me and sent a packet with a story authored by A-Co., 2-501 member Perry Lewis. Perry's story was about the capture of the python and included photos. Perry told his story very well, but for the sake of brevity I will try to put in his words.

Perry had been away from A-Co. for a while recovering from wounds and upon return he was made squad leader as many of the men were wounded in his absence and replaced with cherries. After climbing a rather large and steep hill, the Company was setting up for NDP. Perry was ordered to take his platoon a ways back down the hill and set up an ambush OP for the night. He flanked their inbound trail to mask their return, but on the way down he found himself on a very slippery and rocky area, losing his footing.

He said he slid for a distance before sliding off a ledge and falling over 10 feet into a chest deep pool of water. The snake coiled deep in the pool would have been waiting in its lair for much smaller prey and with the dramatic invasion of its territory, it apparently took great offense. The reaction was violent as the snake immediately began hissing loudly as it blew water into Perry's face.

He said he went into hand-to-hand combat—well, hand-to-head combat—with the angry critter. He could also tell that he was standing on moving parts of the snake as it was quickly getting the best of him. His squad had made its way to the scene by then and began his rescue from this incredibly strong reptile. Perry said things changed quickly when he pulled his sweat towel from around his neck and wrapped it around the snake's head, blinding it. It went limp.

After a bit of radio traffic with his CO, he was ordered back to the NDP for the night and to carry the snake with them. On arrival they put this 18.5 foot Burmese Python into a nylon mail sack.

The next morning, it was airlifted to a place somewhere in the rear, which Perry never knew until he read my book—so now we have the rest of that story!

A-Co. with snake!

Back in our home town in Decatur Michigan, The VFW had been very successful over the years. Thanks to Bruno Dragan and a few other WWII veterans who refused to exclude, but welcomed the new Vietnam veterans into the fold, many joined.

In the summer of 1984 the VFW built its own Vietnam Memorial of black granite in the front yard of the post. On that memorial are engraved the names of three local men who were KIA in Vietnam. Clarence Gipson, James Sowa and Ron Vliek.

I knew the first two, but did not know Ron Vliek at the time. As it was, Ron's family had a Decatur address, but he went to school in the neighboring town of Hartford. Sometime in the first year after the book was published I received a call from a Mr. Ken Nelson, from Paw Paw, who wanted to meet with me. We set a time to meet at the Hard Times Restaurant in Decatur.

Ken had reservations as he began his story about knowing Ron Vliek. They met on the induction bus at the Courthouse in Paw

Vietnam Memorial at VFW Post 6248 Decatur, Michigan.

Paw, February 28, 1968, as it headed east across Michigan to the induction center in Detroit. They managed to stay together through basic and AIT for artillery and both became cannoneers.

Both received orders and deployed to Vietnam where they served on the same forward Firebase. I do not recall how long they served together, but it was close to a full tour when their base was attacked by a mortar barrage, and in the aftermath Ken found that Ron Vliek had been KIA. Ken still suffers with this loss. He also revealed to me that I was also on that same bus headed to the induction center, and he was correct.

Let's go back now to Elmer Jackson, WWII veteran.

While passing the front door of his corner plumbing store at the main intersection of Decatur, Elmer shouted out "Hey Flory, Come in here!"

With a correction in course I entered the store to sit at the family table. Elmer, whom I had known from my childhood, but knew nothing of his military service, wanted an audience. Having just read my book, he began confessing to me that, as a WWII veteran, he did not believe he could have endured what we veterans had to do in Vietnam.

Ponder that for a minute, as I have heard the same thing from several other WWII veterans.

As powerful as that statement was to me, for the first time since his war, he totally opened up and wrote down what he was charged with. Elmer traveled the same path as I had, except by train to the Detroit induction center, August 30, 1944. He took that one step forward and was *In the Army Now*. He and many others then traveled to Fort Hood, Texas, for basic and advanced infantry training.

The Battle of the Bulge had begun at that time, so training was cut short and they were all given ten days to report to Fort Meade, Maryland, for deployment to Germany.

The east coast was on his way home and he managed a few

days with his parents prior to reporting at Fort Meade.

He sailed, packed in very tight quarters on the *Queen Mary* – converted to a troop transport ship – to Glasgow, Scotland.

From there, many trains and finally trucked to the Rhine River, where he saw action for the next four months.

The war ended in Germany, but for Elmer, he was reassigned to graves detail, and spent the next six months touring many of the battle sites in a hunt for KIA American soldiers. They were successful, but I will omit the details of his story there.

No one in Decatur knew this, except maybe his wife. They lived among us, and still do.

Elmer Jackson.

Shortly after that I worked to convince Elmer to take the Honor Flight to Washington D.C., and provided all the paperwork needed. He went, accompanied by his eldest son. He was flabbergasted at what went on that day and raved about it until his passing in 2021. If I had never written the book, we may not have known Elmer's story! His full story is in the archives of the *Decatur Republican* newspaper.

The next WWII veteran lived farther away, but closer at heart, Leo Wojnoroski—the man I was named after. My father met Leo and his rather large family in the very late 30's, when Dad and his relatives were looking for hunting property in the Upper Peninsula of Michigan.

Friendships were cemented as WWII started and my father went to Bay City Michigan as a welder in the shipyards, while Leo and his brother Ray went to serve in the Army. They both saw heavy combat in the Battle of the Bulge, Leo being wounded two times and sent to the rear to heal.

Meanwhile, the 101st Airborne had made a jump behind enemy lines and captured the city of Bastogne and a very important bridge. The Germans took great offense, surrounded the city and swore no quarters if they didn't surrender. While under siege, resupply for the 101st was difficult. The 318 Regiment, 80th Infantry was tasked to break through the German lines and supply the 101st.

Leo Wojnoroski was with the 318th unit as they successfully broke through, but he was wounded the third time and sent home. I believe elements of the 2-501st, were in Bastogne at the time—my unit 26 years later!

I had known Leo more than 60 years and knew none of this until after he read a copy of my book. What is written above is just a portion of what he shared with me after that. This hero passed away a few years ago and I was able to give a brief talk about him and the true role models he and his family were. Then, to my absolute surprise, the funeral director invited me to drive the hearse. So I drove my comrade and namesake to his final resting place.

This next story may not be directly connected to this book, but it is definitely one that is worth sharing.

President George W. Bush was campaigning for his second presidency and was scheduled to speak at Kendall College in Grand Rapids Michigan. We were notified at VFW Post 6248 that there were five tickets reserved for us at the gate. It was short notice, so we needed to draw straws, if you will, to finalize the group to go. When the day came, we decided that if we were to see a president, we should be well dressed, so we donned our parade uniforms. On arrival, we found ourselves in a very long line as all were being searched. After a time some fellow in a suit and a little coiled wire stuck in his ear, looked at us and said, "Gentlemen, come with me."

He took us to the front of the line, put us through the search gate and on into the main doors to the auditorium. We joined other veterans in the foyer, but not dressed as we were. Shortly after that, a woman with a wire in her ear summoned us all to follow as she headed toward the front. We were excited at the possibility of being up close, when some guy in the half filled auditorium stood up and shouted out, "Thank you for your service!"

At that a group did the same thing and in an instant the entire place stood up and erupted in cheer and clapping. We were dumbfounded to the point of tears. We were all Vietnam veterans and had never received that kind of welcome. I still get chills when thinking about it.

The woman placed us along some gating near the front row and left. Shortly after another woman asked us to follow her as she headed toward the stage, up the stairway and put us in a bleacher directly behind the podium. We were outright giddy. In time the program began and when the President came on stage, he addressed each section in the auditorium, then turned, looked at the bleachers. He stood at attention and gave our group a solid salute. Wow!

At the close of the speech he turned to the bleachers and worked his way down, shaking hands with the first three rows. Sure enough, everyone of us shook hands with the President that day.

We did find out later that the National VFW frowns on displaying the uniform at political events. But after what happened that day, we would much rather post an apology than ask for permission.

I had a truckload of books, so I scanned down our B, 2-501 reunion roster and began sending free copies to all the comrades who had been at the reunions. One went to Mr Larry Trask who lived in Nashville, Michigan, just east of Kalamazoo, and only 60 miles from me. He and his wife came to their first B-Co. reunion sponsored by Ann and I in Kalamazoo in 2009. It was also the first year for Mr and Mrs Robert Butts from Detroit.

Robert and Larry had served together in the same squad and had their own reunion going on.

About a year later Larry called me in regard to a Mrs. Annie (Duffy) Woodmann, a friend of theirs, who had read his copy of the book and was deeply touched by it. She was hopeful to meet me one day, so we made it happen soon after. We met at their local VFW where Annie explained that her older brother, Jerry Duffy, had been KIA in Vietnam when she was very young, and how she remembered how devastating it was for her family.

Jerry entered the war as it was de-escalating and fewer KIA's were being reported. Jerry had been the only death in a full week, so *Life* magazine decided to run with it. The headline on the magazine read, "The Only Boy to Die."

A man named Dale Whitney was the reporter. The family and townspeople were interviewed. Neither the magazine nor Dale Whitney offered anything of comfort or value to the grieving family. Quite the reverse. Their intent seemed to be driving a stake through their hearts and anyone who may read the article.

The family suffered many trials after that. For Annie, she had no idea what her brother may have gone through as an infantryman until she read this book.

Later that year Larry called me announcing that our brother Robert Butts had passed away from an apparent heart attack. His wife Audrey was devastated, and asked if Larry and I could come to Detroit and attend the funeral. We not only agreed, but came prepared to talk about Robert. He was a black man who lived in the inter city of Detroit and their Baptist Church was also in the inter city – Robert had been a preacher there in earlier years.

Larry, his wife and I were the only white people there. Audrey did a wonderful job of introducing us to the congregation. At one point in the service we were asked to speak. I went to the pulpit in Larry's place, as he was feeling the effects of a light stroke that affected his speech. I first talked of the B-Co. reunion he and Audrey had attended and how they were the best dressed couple there.

I spoke about Robert in Vietnam and knowing him there. He was just one of those guys who bridged any gap between races and was respected by all the men. Then I read a letter drafted by Larry, that told of Robert's heroism in saving his life during the Tet battles of 1968. Larry was fighting from a bunker when it was hit with an explosive round, caving in the bunker. Larry managed to make his way out, but in a daze he ran toward the enemy. Robert pursued him and pulled him back to a safer place, and for doing so he was awarded the Silver Star.

I watched the faces of this congregation as I was telling Larry's story of Robert and realized that they had no idea what he had done and that he was a true hero. We donated several books to the Church for anyone who wanted to know more about his service.

Rest in peace Robert Butts, our comrade, our friend.

I also sent books to other relatives, friends and veterans like

Richard Green and Larry Moak, the helicopter pilots *(Chapter 18)*.

Both were grateful, then Larry called later wanting ten additional copies for his family and friends! He said he had been telling these stories for years and thought that most people didn't believe him. When he found his story written in my book, he could point to his name and say, "See!"

Jim Hunt *(Chapter 18)* was a chopper pilot and member of the VHPA (Vietnam Helicopter Pilots Association). They have annual reunions, and a few years back it was scheduled to be in Washington D.C. Jim and His wife Sue asked if Ann and I would care to travel there with them, and we agreed. I learned that Larry Moak would also be there and we finally met face to face. Seeing all the D.C. monuments and the "Wall" for the first time was a moving experience. I left a sealed copy of the book at the base of the wall where the most B-Co. 2-501 KIA's were listed.

Larry Moak with the author, standing in front of a Huey.

Above: Jim Hunt and Ann Flory at The Wall. Note the space in between them is my time in-country, August 1968 to August 1969. KIA's during that period were 7,468.

Left: I left a sealed copy of the first edition of this book (originally published as Transition to Duty) at the wall. My personal tribute to those who gave everything.

The author with Jim Hunt in D.C.

    Larry had friends in high places there in D.C. and scheduled a private tour of the Capitol building. We entered a nondescript building about four blocks away, took an elevator down several floors and proceeded through a labyrinth of hallways ending in the Capitol. We traveled in the building, apart from the regular visitors. There were six of us, we sat in the Capitol chamber in complete silence and pondered where we were. We thank you Larry and friends.

    Our return trip back to Michigan took us close to the memorial of the fourth plane crash of 9-11 and we decided to visit it. I have been to Ground Zero in New York twice, but this desolate place is more solemn yet.

The author with his wife Ann, together with Suzy and Jim Hunt at the Flight 93 National Memorial near Stoystown, Pennsylvania.

We have been blessed with the B, 2-501 reunions we have been able to attend since our first in Kansas City, Missouri in 2003. There was Tulsa, Oklahoma in 2005; Clatskanie, Oregon in 2007; Kalamazoo, Michigan in 2009; Branson, Missouri in 2011; Great Falls, Montana in 2013; Reno, Nevada in 2015; Springfield, Illinois in 2017 and St. Paul, Minnesota in 2022. (2019-2021 we could not get together due to Covid). All have been powerfully healing and greatly expanded our geographical knowledge of America.

At the 2017 reunion we had a new attendee, Colonel Pierce T. Graney, *(Chapter 5)* who I had visited at his home in Mexico Beach, Florida, and who wrote the foreword to this book.

In the watering party ambush, six men were wounded, one KIA. Dave Reinheimer was RTO for Graney at the time and had been sent down with the detail to fill canteens *(Chapter 16)*. He was subsequently wounded and sent home, never filling Tom Graney's canteen.

Left to right: David Reinheimer (WIA), David Krautscheid (WIA) and Tom Graney, receiving his canteen after 48 years.

    I want to go back to Sam Zaffiri, author of *Hamburger Hill*, the blow by blow historical account of that battle. Sam explained that during his research, he found a June 27th, 1969 issue of *Life* magazine dedicated to death in Vietnam and particularly aimed at the battle of Hamburger Hill.

    The magazine's entire cover was filled with small head shots of military men. The issue was titled "The Faces of Dead in Vietnam – One Week's Toll." Their focus was "The Hill" and the claim was 240 dead. The actual history says 63 died during the 10 day battle (two of them were from my company).

Leo meeting with Steve and Sandy Johnson prior to the 2017 reunion. Steve was the fifth man wounded in the watering party massacre, (page 206).

They were all precious lives, deserving absolute respect.

My take on the read was that *Life* magazine neither had respect for the dead nor their families. Again, collateral damage for their goal is acceptable to them—but for anyone else it's not Especially if it is military.

The 240 KIA's seems to match the count for the entire country for the entire month. The tactical command of that operation used all of their talents and intel to conduct that military operation, which was a success. The A Shau Valley was then ours.

Sam Zafirri spent years carefully researching this battle. His work is factual and it's historically accurate. However, any jerk journalist can foist a ruse on the American people, lie about any subject they want, cause the deepest pain to anyone they want, and not only get away with it—but actually get paid for it.

It's easy to have great disdain and distrust in American big media. They have completely earned it.

This next story again reinforces the very reason I wrote this book.

When Jennifer Gaines was looking for answers, I was able to help fill many of them for her. In this case, Mrs Mary Farrell, wife of Vietnam Veteran Jim "Doc" Farrell *(Chapter 22)*, found answers and closure she did not expect.

I have mentioned Dave Reinheimer, who has worked tirelessly to contact all the men who served with B-Co. 2-501 Airborne, from December 1967 through April 1972 and invite them to reunions. His invitations went out to our comrade Jim "Doc" Farrell, who for his own respected reasons, chose not to join these events.

In 2013 Dave's invitations went out as usual to all known addresses. My book was new to the company at that time and Dave included information about it and my contact information in the invitation letter.

On November 26, 2013, I received an e-mail from Christofer Farrell, one of Jim's two sons. The family had received the reunion invitation. Christofer explained that his father had just passed away from cancer and he was very interested in a copy of the book. I corresponded with Chris via e-mail and sent him a copy, which he shared with his Navy Veteran brother Jimmy Farrell.

I received wonderful letters from them both. Their father, like many veterans, never shared much of his war experience, now they knew. I also sent a copy to Mrs Mary Farrell. She read the book and wrote the following letter:

November 30, 2013

> *Mr. Flory,*
>
> *I am the last Farrell you will hear from- Jim's wife and Jimmy and Chris's mom. I just wanted to take a minute to thank you for the kind words you wrote about my Jim to his sons. We have always been a close family, so Jim's passing was very hard*

on all of us. Not only was he an honorable person, he was a wonderful husband and a great father.

Recently (after 10 years of trying to have his records corrected) The Dept. of the Army admitted they made a mistake and corrected Jim's DD-214 discharge papers, to show that he was a recipient of the Purple Heart. He had the medal and the certificate showing his RA number, but they finally added it to his DD-214 form. Upon further review they also awarded Jim the Army Good Conduct Medal (first award) Vietnam Service Medal with Three Bronze Service Stars, Presidential Unit Citation, Republic of Vietnam Gallantry Cross with Palm Unit Citation, and the Republic of Vietnam Civil actions Honors Medal First Class Unit Citation.

I wonder how many other veterans have been overlooked for these awards?

I am sure these "posthumous" awards will add to Chris and Jimmy's pride for their Dad, and give them a better understanding of his gallantry, and your book will answer many questions for them. So once again, thank you for taking the time to write your story, I am sure that many people will benefit from your words.

Sincerely,
Mary Farrell
Proud wife of a 101st Airborne Vet.

I have received many such letters, e-mails, texts and conversations. I am thankful.

I am also thankful that my mother, Esther Flory had the opportunity to read TTD and she did so twice. But, I am most thankful to the Father of us all, who has been with me and us through it all.

Blessed!

This next and last story I consider one of those "Full Moon" experiences, meeting Joe Galloway, co-author with Colonel Hal Moore, in writing *We Were Soldiers Once... And Young* which became a movie released in 2002 that starred Mel Gibson as Colonel Moore and Barry Pepper as Joe Galloway.

According to the authors at least 75 percent of the movie was authentic, (For this the authors are revered by veterans), the rest is Hollywood.

Being interviewed by Joe Galloway.

In most Hollywood versions of the war, the only thing authentic is the word "Vietnam."

Quick review of the movie: Colonel Moore is in the throes of the first large scale sustained battle in the war thus far, and he is desperately trying to get more men and supplies in by helicopter. One of the supply birds that make it in has a civilian reporter climb off, Joe Galloway. Col Moore is upset as he needs fighting men—not an embedded reporter—and puts Joe in a fighting position with a weapon for the night. The battle was the La Drang Valley, fought by the 1st Cavalry. (True stuff!)

The Department of Defense had commissioned a project documenting the 50th anniversary of the Vietnam war and had been at it for about two years of a four-year project. Their primary method for gathering information was through audio-visual-oral-histories, and Joe Galloway was the guy conducting the interviews.

These interviews were to be forwarded to the National Archives as a permanent record. Joe was to conduct interviews in Chicago and knew Ron Werneth (mentioned earlier) from his military history writing. Joe asked Ron if he could recommend Veterans in the area for him to interview, and he certainly did. Through this Ron contacted me. I in turn contacted Roger Barski, Chicago resident, (mentioned earlier) and Jim Hunt (helicopter pilot, see Appendix I).

We were all given interview opportunities.

Ann and I traveled to Chicago on interview day, and as the first for the day, I had a chance to simply chat with Joe and just absorb the moment. I knew that Lieutenant John Cecil Driver *(Chapter 13)* was with the 1st Cavalry during the La Drang Valley battle and I asked Joe if he knew him. He smiled and said that he did. We actually had a tiny bit of history.

Thank you Ron Werneth for that experience, and for your relentless effort to persuade me to do this again.

And thank you Mick and Diane Prodger at Elm Grove Publishing, our fantastic new publisher.

There you have it (for now)!

Leo "Doc" Flory

In case you wondered what our minimum pay was in 1969
E-4 Basic   214.20
Hostile Fire   55.00
Foreign Duty   13.00
Total $282.20/Mo
On call 24/7 - 365 = hourly wage was approx. $0.03/hour

APPENDIX I — A CHOPPER PILOT'S MIND PICTURES

For every chopper there is a pilot, co-pilot and crew, who in our eyes, represent the bravest men on earth. Thousands died doing everything they could to protect us or serve us in some way.

Below are some written memories from my good friend Jim Hunt, Marine chopper pilot in Vietnam.

I am proud to add his writing to this book.

MY MIND PICTURES FROM VIETNAM

Some have faded over the past 33 years, but these are as clear as the day they were taken.

The sound and sight of Main Rotor Blades from my UH-IE beating the sky into submission.

The ever present smell of JP-4 (helicopter jet fuel) when the engine starts.

The beautiful dark green of the mountains and the breath taking beauty of the country flying at 2,000 feet in our I Corp operating area around Da Nang.

The sound of an Oriental band trying to sing American songs without their accents.

The sight and sound of Puff the Magic Dragon *(C 130 Gunship with mini-guns) with its solid red line of tracers, at night, and then the muffled guttural growl that followed slightly after seeing the huge fire hose like, red line reach the ground.*

The feel of a 68-degree night when you're long used to a 120-degree day.

The sight of beautiful young Asian women in traditional oriental clothes.

The sight of all the stars on a pitch black night on the flight line when looking straight up and pretending for a few moments you were back home on the farm.

The faint rumble of a B-52 Arc light way off in the distance, then shortly after taking off in my UH-IE and seeing the huge long line of dirt clouds while flying at 1,500 feet.

A boy (young Marine getting much older) whispering into the radio that his unit has enemy contact all around them and requires a Helo emergency extract immediately.

Trying to find a Marine unit at night for a Medevac pickup, when they couldn't even use a strobe light for fear of tipping off the bad guys.

Getting the call for an emergency Medevac pickup, getting the brief and the Helo off the ground in record time. Then getting the call part way there, that it has been downgraded to a Permanent Medevac.

Whoever it was had died in that 6 minutes.

Lying in the top bunk at night hearing incoming rockets explode in the distance down by the flight line. Then looking at the floor and seeing my short time roommate crouching on the floor. Then wondering, should I be down there too. I still have 10.5 months to go.

The loud chatter of my four forward firing M-60 machine guns, and then the relatively quiet single M-60 firing from my door gunner. Just after turning hard away from my target and then hard-back level so he can continue to fire, while my wingman rolls in hot on the target. As I climb for altitude to come around and do the same thing again and again.

The sight at night of green tracers reaching up towards my gunship from an enemy 51-caliber machine gun, slow at first, then very fast as they pass by. Someone says they remind them of what beer cans on fire might look like at night coming at you.

The sparkle of the rocket trails at night from the seven rockets I just sent to the ground.

Looking out of the door window of my gunship at the tree line on the ground, watching the tracers coming straight up at my window, ever so slowly at first, until they get close, then passing just underneath with lighting speed. Also knowing that in between each tracer there are four armor-piercing rounds.

The way the unconscious Marine looks when loaded into the back of my gunship, stripped to his under shorts, passed out from heat stroke, my door gunner pouring a canteen of water over him. Then flying back to the 95th MED. Max airspeed, at 5,000 feet instead of 1,500 feet, because it is cooler for the Marine, also knowing it is much safer from small fire at 5,000 feet.

The Navy medical corpsman being loaded into the back of my gunship by his Marine buddies. He is smoking a cigarette, one of his feet bloody and bandaged. The other foot is missing, with the stub wrapped in a bright red bandage, moist with blood. Once he is in the back, my next thought is can I now fly the heavy gunship out of the Landing Zone and over the small trees and bushes in front of me.

Shooting rockets so close to the ground that they stick in the ground and mud with the rocket motors still burning, and don't explode because they did not hit anything hard enough to set off the warhead.

Marines on the ground directing your rocket fire so close to them, that when they key the radio mike, and say you're right on target, you can hear the rocket explode in front of them through their microphone.

Getting so drunk at the O'Club after a bad day, or a good day, that you can't find your hooch that night to sleep it off.

The sound of a young Marine's voice slightly as he radios up to my gunship, asking how badly wounded their Lt. is, as he was just picked up by the Medevac Helo's I provided gun cover for. I contact the Medevac CH-46 by radio, and the pilot then talks to the Navy Corpsman on board. I get the information and reply back that he should live. The Marines radio operator's reply a thank you, as his voice breaks more, saying that the Lt. is good people, and his men wanted to know if he was going to make it.

Looking for two of your squadron pilots and friends lying in an emergency ward and not being able to find or recognize them because of their burns and injuries from the helicopter crash. The second time walking through the 20-bed ward you find them, because they are the only two in the ward that still have both arms *and legs.*

The worried call from a Marine unit's radio operator on the ground in deep shit, wondering if your three gunships can stay long enough until all of them are lifted by the CH-46 from the side of a mountain. I call back and assure him that we will be there until all are out.

Making a split second decision to place your best friend, who is the pilot in the number three gunship in the most dangerous position to cover a hovering CH-46. This is because you know he is a better pilot than the pilot in the number two gunship. You cannot take his spot because your gunship has to control the area nearest to the CH-46 and provide communications to the other aircraft in the flight of five aircraft.

The time I flew the freedom bird home (name called the passenger jet that flew troops out of Vietnam back to the states) from Da Nang. All the passengers cheered and clapped as the big plane cleared the runway and climbed out over the South China Sea.

I am in the middle of a gun run, (all four M-60's putting out over 2,400 rounds a minute) and the target was some bad guy that had pinned down a convoy on the Hi-Van Pass. My gunship is approaching red line airspeed, and I plan to pull off in seconds. I then feel the controls are stiff, like they are starting to freeze up. They won't respond to my normal touch. Quickly I look for hydraulic failure, warning lights, and see none. Then I notice that my new co-pilot is frozen on the controls, collective, cyclic and rudders. I calmly tell him to let go, nothing happens. I calmly tell him louder to let go, nothing happens, I then yell like hell at him and he releases his grip. The gunship then responds normally, and I pull off target above red line airspeed. The aircraft is handling normal, but the entire air frame and rotor head will now have to be inspected by maintenance crews.

I am flying a low level Visual Reconnaissance Mission in a UH-IE dirty slick with two pilots, two door gunners and one aerial observer. The A.O. wanted to go back and look at some trails on a mountain ridge line. I start my climb back up, gaining altitude, to slowly reach the point he wants to see, in the distance that I have available. I have planned my turn and exit away from the mountain in case I could not climb fast enough. I misjudged the amount of room I have to turn along the side of the mountain, then have to bleed off airspeed and turn sharper, pulling max power. The helicopter would not climb and began a descent. I pulled in more collective, which over taxed the engine, and the rotor turns decreased until the low RPM warning light and horn came on. I was forced to lower the collective and nose the aircraft over to pick up speed and slow the rate of descent. I saw an opening between two trees. The airspeed had increased, and the aircraft was responding and starting to climb slightly. One tree on the right was taller than the left one. I rolled the helo upon its left side, rotors missing both trees. The chin bubble and right door gun hit the top of the tallest tree, breaking out the chin bubble, and some leaves were stuck in the flash suppressor on the barrel of the machinegun. I landed and looked for any other damage and found none. I flew back to the Marble Mountain Air Base okay. That night in the O'Club over some drinks, my CO asked me what happened. I told him I ran out of airspeed, altitude, and ideas all at the same time. Ten hours later, I was back in the cockpit flying my next mission.

– J. L. Hunt, USMC (Retired)

APPENDIX II — A POEM BY ELIZABETH FLORY

To a Medic father
who fought and healed with pride.

"Justifiable Sacrifices"

Yesterday I was racin' cars, crashin' bars, and skippin' stones.
Now I repair broken bones and mangled flesh.
Surrounded by jungle trees, moral tests, and enemies.
My drafted prison for strangers to be free.
Hospital walls of exotic plants and glowing moss.
Boys become "Docs." Battles and lives won and lost.
Military issued fatigue from bearing my red cross.
We pray to opposing Gods that rewards equal the cost.

Runnin' through steel showers and mine fields.
As my mind steals solitude in the face of death.
My Blood thumps in my chest, taking calculated risks to assist,
When errors are fatal and metals buy another breath.

How can humanity reside in the insanity?
Scrubs replaced by army combat fatigues.
Do I dare to admit the culture intrigues?
Ten Commandments broken by a soldier's creed.

Tin can rations don't feed a broken soul.
Thunder and lighting ringing in my dreams.
Like R rated scenes from horror films on continuous repeat.
I called shotgun and got the front seat.

We shall stand with our enemies when we atone for our sins.
I attempted to heal others in the beginning and myself in the end.
Only this warning I wish to send:
if we want to continue murdering our children, let war be a trend.

APPENDIX III — ROBERT "UNCLE BOB" MALECKI

My name is Jennifer Gaines, a niece of Robert Malecki.

In early 2008 I began a journey to know my Uncle Bob... the problem is I had no idea where to start. Growing up we never talked about him. He had always been just a picture and a folded flag on the wall. I think it was too difficult for my Dad to bear.

Quite frankly, as a child, I probably wouldn't have given him the attention he deserved anyways. By the time I was old enough to comprehend the enormity of his life and sacrifices, I felt like the window of opportunity had passed to ask. All I was left with was the little information I had about his service in the Army, and it turns out that it was more than I needed.

My journey has taken me places that I never dreamed possible. I have met the most incredible people along the way — every one of them willing to help me above and beyond what I could have imagined. In a couple of short years I have met and talked to some of my uncle's best friends from basic all the way to the very FSB where he died. I have heard some of the stories that he talked about with his buddies, seen the pictures of him that were taken in Vietnam, and I know what his future aspirations were when his tour was over.

My journey is in no way finished... I still occasionally run across someone else who knew my uncle, but now it has opened the lines of communication a little with my Dad and that is just another gift that I have been given through all of this. This is a short bio that my Dad sent to me and I think it is more than I have heard regarding my uncle over the course of my whole life:

Born Robert Richard Malecki, December 31, 1944, Chicago, Illinois (2 years 3 months older than me). I was about 7 and he would have been 9 when our mother died.

We grew up taking care of each other, although he did most of the taking care of. Dad went to work at 5 and came home at 7 or 7:30. We barely saw him most weekdays. You couldn't do that today, but I like to think that it was a kinder time, even in Chicago. He went to St. Genevieve Catholic Grammar School, St. Patrick H.S. and took up civil engineering at the University of Illinois, Champaign-Urbana, after high school (1962).

Civil engineering didn't work out, and he went to Wright Jr. College to bring up his GPA. He re-enrolled at Loyola University (probably one of the few influences from me in his life since I was already at Loyola) in Business Administration and graduated cum laude *in January, 1968.*

He was hired by Illinois Bell as a management trainee before graduation. He got an apartment in Northlake, Illinois, and came home every weekend for our weekly softball and/or football game (more later).

He was drafted in June or July 1968 and then went to basic, AIT, Vietnam and home (remind me to let you read his letters someday). We played 16" softball or touch football in the parking lot of St. Gens every weekend and every other chance we got. Bob could hit the softball further than anyone I ever saw play there. It was a good half city block ending in a two story kindergarten building. We finally had to ban him from swinging away as too many games were ended with our only ball being on the kindergarten roof.

Our touch football was on concrete and not as pretty as the Kennedy's games. We would have been better off playing tackle on dirt than "touch" on cement with a brick wall two feet inside one end zone.

I'd lose a pair of glasses a month in football season and most of us limped or worse through the rest of the week. As teens the games continued every week although we played softball in park leagues more often than with just our group,

I had met mom at Loyola of course, so she knew Bob a little. We even double-dated once or twice. A million moments always come to mind, nights talking about life, our futures, girls, school, and so on, but I was intending to give you a fast biography of Bob, not a trip down memory lane.

I truly believe from everything I know and have heard that every soldier was part of a true "band of brothers" including my uncle, and I am eternally grateful for the sacrifices that each and every one of them has made.

All my love,
Jennifer

APPENDIX IV — STATISTICS

These statistics were taken from a variety of sources to include: *VFW* magazine, the Public Information Office, and the HQ CP Forward Observer – 1st Recon April 12, 1997.

STATISTICS FOR INDIVIDUAL IN UNIFORM AND IN-COUNTRY VIETNAM VETERANS:

- *9,087,000 military personnel served on active duty during the Vietnam Era (August 5, 1964 – May 7, 1975)*
- *8,744,000 GI's were on active duty during the Vietnam War (August 5, 1964 – March 28, 1973)*
- *2,709,918 Americans served in Vietnam, this number represents 9.7% of their generation*
- *3,403,100 (Including 514,300 offshore) personnel served in the broader Southeast Asia Theater (Vietnam, Laos, Cambodia, flight crews based in Thailand and sailors in adjacent South China Sea waters)*
- *2,594,000 personnel served within the borders of South Vietnam (January 1, 1965 – March 28, 1973). Another 50,000 men served in Vietnam between 1960 and 1964*
- *Of the 2.6 million, between 1-1.6 million (40-60%) either fought in combat, provided close support or were at least fairly regular exposed to enemy attack*
- *7,484 women (6,250 or 83% were nurses) served in Vietnam*
- *Peak troop strength in Vietnam: 543,482 (April 30, 1968) 312*

CASUALTIES:

- *The first man to die in Vietnam was James Davis, in 1958. He was with the 509th Radio Research Station. Davis Station in Saigon was named for him*
- *Hostile deaths: 47,378*
- *Non-hostile deaths: 10,800*
- *Total: 58,202 (Includes men formerly classified as MIA and* Mayaguez *incident casualties*)*

- *Men who have subsequently died of wounds account for the changing total*
- *8 nurses died – 1 was KIA*
- *61% of the men killed were 21 or younger*
- *11,465 of those killed were younger than 20 years old*
- *Of those killed, 17,539 were married*
- *Average age of men killed: 23.1 years*
- *Total Deaths: 23.11 years*
- *Enlisted: 50,274; 22.37 years*
- *Officers: 6,598; 28.43 years*
- *Warrants: 1,276; 24.73 years*
- *E1: 525; 20.34 years*
- *11B MOS: 18,465; 22.55 years*
- *Five men killed in Vietnam were only 16 years old*
- *The oldest man killed was 62 years old*
- *Highest state death rate: West Virginia – 84.1% (national average 58.9% for every 100,000 males in 1970)*
- *Wounded: 303,704—153,329 hospitalized + 150,375 injured requiring no hospital care*
- *Severely disabled: 75,000 of which 23,214 were 100% disabled; 5,283 lost limbs; 1,081 sustained multiple amputations*
- *Amputation or crippling wounds to the lower extremities were 300% higher than in WWII and 70% higher than Korea*
- *Multiple amputations occurred at the rate of 18.4% compared to 5.7% in WWII*
- *Missing in Action: 2,338*
- *POW's: 766 (114 died in captivity)*
- *As of January 15, 2004, there were 1,875 Americans still unaccounted for from the Vietnam War*

Draftees vs. Volunteers:
- *25% (648,500) of total forces in-country were draftees. (66% of U.S. armed forces members were drafted during WWII)*

- *Draftees accounted for 30.4% (17,725) of combat deaths in Vietnam*
- *Reservists Killed: 5,977*
- *National Guard: 6,140 served: 101 died*
- *Total draftees (1965 – 73): 1,728,344*
- *Actually served in Vietnam: 38% Marine Corps draft: 42,633*
- *Last man drafted: June 30, 1973*

Race and Ethnic Background:

- *88.4% of the men who actually served in Vietnam were Caucasian; 10.6% (275,000) were black; 1.2% belonged to other races*
- *86.3% of the men who died in Vietnam were Caucasian (including Hispanics); 12.5% (7,241) were black; 1.2% belonged to other races*
- *170,000 Hispanics served in Vietnam; 3,070 (5.2% of total) died there*
- *70% of enlisted men killed were of Northwest European descent*
- *86.8% of the men who were killed as a result of hostile action were Caucasian; 12.1% (5,711) were black' 1.1% belonged to other races*
- *14.6% (1,530) of non-combat deaths were among Vietnam blacks*
- *Overall, blacks suffered 12.5% of the deaths in Vietnam at a time when the percentage of blacks of military age was 13.5% of the total population*
- *Religion of dead: Protestant – 64.4%; Catholic – 28.9%; other/none –6.7%*

Socio-Economic Status:

- *Vietnam veterans have a lower unemployment rate than the same non-vet age groups*
- *Vietnam veterans' personal income exceeds that of our non-veteran age group by more than 18 percent*
- *76% of those sent to Vietnam were from lower middle/working class backgrounds*
- *Three-fourths had family incomes above the poverty level; 50% were from middle income background.*
- *Some 23% of Vietnam vets had fathers with professional, managerial or technical occupations.*

- *79% of the men who served in Vietnam had a high school education or better when they entered the military service. 63% of Korean War vets and only 45% of WWII vets had completed high school upon separation*
- *Death by region per 100,000 of population: South – 31%, West –29.9%; Midwest – 28.4%; Northeast – 23.5%*

Drug Usage and Crime:

- *There is no difference in drug usage between Vietnam Veterans and non-Veterans of the same age group. (Source: Veterans Administration Study)*
- *Vietnam Veterans are less likely to be in prison – only one-half of one percent of Vietnam Veterans have been jailed for crimes*
- *85% of Veterans made successful transitions to civilian life*

Winning and Losing:

- *82% of veterans who saw heavy combat strongly believe the war was lost because of lack of political will*
- *Nearly 75% of the public agrees it was a failure of political will, not of arms*

Honorable Service:

- *97% of Vietnam-era veterans were honorably discharged*
- *91% of actual VietnamWar veterans and 90% of those who saw heavy combat are proud to have served their country*
- *74% say they would serve again, even knowing the outcome*
- *87% of the public now holds Vietnam veterans in high esteem*

Interesting Census Statistics —
(and those who claim to have "been there"):

- *1,713,823 of those who served in Vietnam were still alive as of August, 1995 (census figures)*
- *During that same Census count, the number of Americans falsely claiming to have served in-country was: 9,492,958*
- *As of the Census taken during August, 2000, the surviving U.S. Vietnam*

Veteran population estimate is: 1,002,511**
- *During this Census count, the number of Americans falsely claiming to have served in-country is 13,853,027. By this census, FOUR out of FIVE claiming to be Vietnam vets are NOT!*
- *The Department of Defense Vietnam War Service Index– officially provided by the War Library – originally reported with errors that 2,709,918 U.S. military personnel had served in-country. Corrections and confirmations to this erred index resulted in the addition of 358 U.S. military personnel confirmed to have served in Vietnam but not originally listed by the Department of Defense. (All names are currently on file and accessible 24/7/365).*
- *Isolated atrocities committed by American Soldiers produced torrents of outrage from anti-war critics and the news media while Communist atrocities were so common that they received hardly any media mention at all. The United States sought to minimize and prevent attacks on civilians while North Vietnam made attacks on civilians a centerpiece if its strategy. Americans who deliberately killed civilians received prison sentences while Communists who did so received commendations.*
- *From 1957 to 1973, the National Liberation front assassinated 36,725 Vietnamese and abducted another 58,499. The death squads focused on leaders at the village level and on anyone who improved the lives of the peasants such as medical personnel, social workers, and school teachers.*

– Nixon Presidential Papers.

---

* The Mayaguez incident occurred in May 1975, one month after the Vietnam War officially ended. An American cargo ship, the SS *Mayaguez* and its crew were seized by the Cambodian Khmer Rouge Navy in international waters. United States troops suffered severe losses and casulties in the resulting rescue mission.

** This number is difficult to believe, losing nearly 711,000 between 1995 and 2000. That's 390 per day.

APPENDIX V — UNIT ROSTER

First Name - Middle Initial - Last Name - Years Served - State (if known)

Luis V Abreu (71-72)
Larry J Acuff (70)
Jack F Adair (67-68) CO
Charles E Adams (69)
Ernest R Adkins (70)
Denver Daniel Albrecht, II (69-70) AZ
Paul Aldoupolis (70-71) MA
James R Allen (67-68)
Mickey D Allen (71-72)
Teddy L Almond (67-68) GA
Michale B Altizer (69) VA
David M Anderson (67-68)
Richard W Anderson (68-69) WA
Willie F Anderson (71-72)
Fernando Andrade (69-70)
Darwin T Apple (71-72)
Richard A Arbogast (67-68) MS
Patrick Armendariz (68-69) CA
Winford D Arthur (71-72)
Henry H Ash (68) MS
Steven J Askin (70-71) NJ
Dick L Auld (71-72) TX
Ronald J Babin (68-69) LA
Joseph M Bacchi (68) NY
Daniel Baker (69-70) TN
Robert K Baldwin (68-69) MI
Larry J Banks (69) OH
Walter E Banks (67-68) TX
Jeffrey M Barnett (71)
Shelton J Baxter (68)
Robert L Beasley (67-68)
James T Beavers (68) AZ
Gary Becker (71-72)
Larry D Belcher (70)
J P Bell (71-72)
Jeffrey E Bennett (70-71) WA
Russell A Benson (68-69) MA
Donald J Betzen (69-70) KS
Victoriano Biddle (69-70)
James E Birch (67-68) FL
Arlyn E Bjerke (70-71) MN
Lenard Blachly (69-70) WA
George E Blackwell (68)

Raymond E Blanchard (70)
James F Blanco (71-72)
Glen P Bockelmann (68-69)
Francis K Bohn (67-68)
Jimmy Bouffard
Walter P Bouman (68-69) AZ
Warren F Bowland (69) DC
Steffen Boyd (67-68) PA
Robert J Bradford (68) PA
Russel Brami (67-68)
James J Bray (69-70) WI
Raymond M Breaux (70) LA
Thomas Bremer, Jr. (71-72)
Ronnie J Bright (69)
Harvey H Brind (68) NY
Ron Bristow (69-70)
Charles W Brooke (69)
Ora E Brooks, Jr. (68) VA
James A Brown, Jr. (69-70)
Melvin R Brown (69-70) GA
William J Brown (68-69) NJ
Willie M Brown (67-68)
Frederick L Browne, Sr. (68-69) PA
James E Brymer (67-68) TN
Gerald Buchanan (70-71) FL
Jeffrey M Burnett FL
Peter Bustamente (71-72)
Robert L Butts (68-69) MI
David H Byers (69-70)
Jose F Camacho (70)
Larry Camby (71-72)
Gerald Camp (69-70)
Frank B Campbell (67-68)
William J Campbell (69-70) SC
Frank Cannon (71-72)
Jerry G Cannon (69-70) GA
Vincent D Capadula, Jr (72) NY
Glenn A Carlson (71-72)
Kenneth T Carlson (67-68)
Rodney Carlson (67-68)
Thomas W Carnahan (71-72)
Leonard A Carpenter (69-70) WA
Rodney R Carpenter (70) FL

Wellman Carr (67-68)
Wayne R Carrara (68-69) NY
David Carter (69-70)
James E Carter (68-69) FL
Anthony Castro (67-68)
Roke A Castro (71-72)
Thomas A Cavanaugh (68-69) FL
John Caylor, III (67-68) GA
Jon Chaffin (70-71) CA
Terry Channel (70) OH
Corbin L Cherry (68-69) NC
Darrell J Choate (69-70)
William A Christensen (68-69)
Gerald S Clark (68-69)
Harold U Clark (71-72)
James A Clark (67-68) GA
Matthew T Clark (68-69)
Robert A Clark (69-70) VT
David B Clausius (67-68) TN
Donald R Clayton (71-72)
William Clegg (67-68)
Gary W Collins (68-69) NY
James M Collins (71-72)
Larry L Collins (67-68)
Sidney C Collinsworth (68-69) TX
Robert W Colombo (69-70) NJ
Edwin R Colon (67-68) FL
Donald E Colvin, Jr (67-68) WA
Garrell L Conner (69-70)
Orville E Cooper (67-68)
Jerry D Copeland (69-70) AR
Patrick H Corder (68)
Robert C Corning (71-72) GA
George R Cosby (67-68) GA
Emanuel Coston (71-72)
Christos M Cotsakos (67-68) FL
Walter Counts (69-70) IL
Gary E Cousins (69-70) TX
Larry O Cowley (68-69) TX
Gary A Crocker (68-69) MO
Jessie B Croley (68-69) TN
Clyde E Crossguns (68-69) MT
Carson R Crouse (68-69) MO
John P Cuches, Jr (70)
Wayne Cummings (71-72) TX
William B Cunningham (69-70) OH
George David Dalbey (68-69) MO

Terry Dallegge (70) NE
Billy E Damron (69-70) OK
Melvin Davis (69-70)
Charles M Dean (68-69)
Gerald A Deboy, Jr (69-70) AL
Norman L Dehart (69-70) AZ
James H DelGiorno (68-69) NY
Floyd G Devine (68) TX
Merle R Dewitt (68) ME
Richard Dexter (69-70) VA
John A Difazio (71-72)
James C Dillard (68-69)
Stanley B Dilworth (70) CA
Michael V Dipinto (70) FL
Alfred E Doby, Jr (71-72)
James M Donnelly (68)
Clifford Doucette (67-68)
Canes G Dowd (67-68)
Mark E Doyle (71-72)
Thomas A Drake (68-69) NY
Douwe P Drayer (70-71) NY
Daniel Driscoll (68-69)
Paul M Drusky (68-69)
Frank Duarte (67-68)
Frank L Duchow (68-69) WA
James M Duke (68-69) OK
Rafael Duran (71-72)
Robert Durning (71-72)
Michael F Dyer (68) KS
Michael R Dzikas (69-70) CT
Emmit Eaddy, Jr. (71-72)
Brian M Eckert (67-68) MA
Lawrence F Edmundson (71-72)
Bobby R Edwards (67-68) TX
Mitchell R Edwards (69) AR
William R Edwards (67-68)
Jay F Eilers (70) ID
Gene Elder (67-68)
Richard J Eldred (67-68) MI
Carl A Eldridge (67-68)
William W Erbach, Sr. (67-68) VA
James Gary Ervin (68-69) FL
James L Estes (68-69) MS
Richard N Evans WI
Robert J Evans (69) CA
Howard E Farmer (67-68)
J B Farmer (67-68)

James Farrell (68-69)
Gary C Farrow (68-69)
Isiah Felder (68-69) SC
Karl R Feldthausen (68-69)
Daniel J Fender (67-68) IL
Ron Fenstermacher (68-69) PA
Paul H Ferguson (68-69)
Ralph E Fike (71-72)
Scott C Filipek (71-72) WI
Vander S Fleming (68-69)
Charles P Fletcher (68-69)
Leo R Flory (68-69) MI
William R Foote (71-72)
Stephen W Forsstrom (70-71) SC
Samuel B Foster (68-69) MO
Everett Gary Fowler (69-70)
Ronald Fraley (70)
Michael A Franc (71-72)
Douglas E Franklin (71-72) TN
Charles Wade Franks (69-70) AL
Michael A Franz (70-71)
Robert D Froreich (67-68) MI
Gene Fry (67-68) GA
John Fuit (70)
Paul E Gagnon (69)
Jesus T Gallardo (71-72)
Capriano Garcia (71)
Donald W Gardiner (67-68)
Lawrence H Garver (70)
Reed A Gash (68)
George W Gaskin (71-72)
Brent L Gatherum (68-69) UT
Richard L Geiben (69-70)
Leslie C Gentle, Jr. (71-72)
Bobby W George (69-70) TX
Charles J German (69-70) ND
Robert L German (68-69) ND
Jack P Glendenning (71-72)
Andy Glover (70)
Ronald W Goff (68) CA
Willie J Goff (69)
Hazzie Leroy Goggans (67-68)
Fernando T Gomez (67-68) TX
Jose Gonzales (68)
Edgar O Gonzalez (67-68)
Jose M Gonzalez, Jr. (69)
Manuel A Gonzalez (71-72)

Donald L Good (68-69) PA
James W Goodridge (68) TX
Harry T Gossage (67-68) CA
Tim Gould (68-69) AL
Pierce T Graney (68-69) FL
Jimmy Grant (70)
William E Graves (69)
Ancil G Gray (69)
Stanley R Greenia (68-69) FL
Douglas C Grier (69-70) NY
Richard Griffin (69-70)
Jimmy Griffith (71)
Frank S Griggs (67-68) NY
Robert R Grigsby (68)
John L Grondona (68-69) CA
Carlis R Gross (68-69) KY
Allen F Grotzke (69-70)
Robert Grotzke (69) WI
Lee B Grubaugh (71-72)
Martin M Guardiola, Jr. (71-72)
Alvin C Guenther (67-68)
San Juan Guevara (67-68)
Orson Gunderson (70-71)
Keith A Guthrie (67-68) LA
Michael V Gutierrez (71-72)
Cpriano Gyrcia
Edward M Hackenburg (69) PA
Charles Hackney (69) NC
Ottis T Hafford (68-69) TN
Alan K Hall (67-68)
Samuel A Hall (69-70) NC
Richard Haller (68-69) OR
Mark S Hallgren (68-69) IL
James D Hallums (68) TN
Phillip S Halyard (69)
David J Hamilton (69)
William J Hamm (68-69)
Edward Hanley (69-70)
Roger G Hanna (68-69) CA
Mark G Hannan (69-70) OH
David R Hansen (71-72)
Tommy R Hardy (68)
Larry K Harrah (71-72)
Charles Harris (69-70)
John A Harris (67-68)
Percy Harris (69-70)
George E Harvey (67-68) AR

Paul G Hastings (70) UT
Joseph Hasty (67-68)
Monte Haughland (69-70) CO
Gerald R Haussler (71-72)
Daniel D Hays (69-70) GA
Philip V Hazen (69-70) OR
Jerry W Head, Jr. FL
Robert Hearn (68-69)
James R Heath (71-72)
Terry L Heaton (70) MD
Randall E Hedrick (71-72)
Dan Hefel (69) IA
Terry J Heig (70-71) MO
John L Heil (68) PA
Darrel D Heinsohn (68-69) OK
Anthony Heiter (68)
Frank D Hengesbaugh (68-69) FL
John F Hensley (69-70)
Jose Hernandez (69-70)
Juan J Hernandez (70) TX
Sipriano Herrera (67-68)
Damon Herrington (70)
David W Herron (69-70) NH
William H Herron (67-68)
Vladimir Hessler (69-70)
Thomas F Hessling (70-71) FL
Jackie Hibbard (68)
Frank Hill (68-69)
Tommie M Hill (67-68) FL
Leo J Hiller (69-70) PA
Frank H Hilley (68-69) CA
Ronald E Hinkle (68-69)
Henry H Hintz (67-68)
Jerry Hively (71-72)
Billy L Hodges (68-69) NC
Harold W Holdren (68-69) FL
David D Holland (69)
James A Holland (67-68) IL
Alton R Holmes (67-68)
Jack W Holsten (69) NC
Michael F Horigan (68) OH
Larry Hoskinson (67-68)
William G Hoskinson (68-69)
William G Hough (68-69)
Terry L House (71-72)
Michael L Howard (71-72)
Wallace Howell (71-72)

Joseph W Hudson (68-69) NV
Dennis W Huffine (70)
James E Hughes (67-68)
George W Hunt (69-70)
Dwayne J Huseman (68-69) TX
Thomas W Hutton (70) MO
Charles M Hyatt (68-69) NC
Dale R Hylton (68-69)
Lloyd C Irland (69) ME
Wilfred J Jackman (68-69)
Dennis Jackson (68-69)
Earl T Jackson (69)
John W Jackson (69-70)
Lawrence Jackson (69-70) FL
Roy L Jackson (67-68)
William Jacob (67-68)
Kevin P James (68-69)
Oliver J Jennings (70) AL
Bradley N Jimmerson (67-68) NY
Edward J Johanek (71-72)
Grady Johnican (71-72)
Donald Johns (70)
Jackie L Johns (68-69) IA
George S Johnsen (67-68) TX
Alan Rusty Johnson (67-68) CA
David R Johnson (68-69)
Larry E Johnson (68)
Larry S Johnson (67-68)
Robert R Johnson (67-68)
Stephen W Johnson (69) IN
Brent Jones (71-72)
Donald R Jones (70)
James E Jones Jr (71-72)
Leandor Jones (70)
Richard F Jordan (70-71) NY
Thomas B Jordan (69-70) GA
Walter L Jordan (67-68)
James D Julien (68-69) MO
Sander R Jumper (70) IL
Tom Kahler (69-70)
Robert Kaiser (68-69)
Jack W Kato (70-71)
William Kaufmann (68-69) IN
Keith M Keiderling (70)
Steve Keithley (71-72)
Frank J Kelly (67-68)
Allen H Kendrick (71-72)

Douglas D Kennedy (69-70)
John C Kennedy (68-69) CA
Owen S Kervin (67-68)
Frank L Keyser (69-70)
Anthony Kieffer (69-70) OH
Ellard Kinney (71-72)
Gunther Kirschner (69-70)
David K Kissell (68-69) FL
Larry R Klamm (69)
David L Kloster (67-68) MO
Ralph Knerem OH
Thomas L Koenig (68-69) IL
David Kohanyi (69-70) IN
Lyle Kohmetscher (70) NE
Michael Komar (69-70)
Joel Komrosky (70-71) ND
Alfred J Kontrabecki (68-69) NY
Bohdan Kopystianskyj (69) NY
David H Krautscheid (68-69) OR
James R Krizan (71-72)
David L Kyle (67-68) PA
Warren S Lacy (69-70)
Herbert D Lampkin (68-69)
Williard J Langdon (71) GA
Guillermo E Lanzo (67-68) NJ
Luther Lassiter (67-68) FL
William F Laughlin (70) FL
Robert W Layton (70-71) OH
Thomas J Leahy (67-68)
Dennis J Lebrecque (70)
John J Ledesma (71-72)
John Lee Jr (67-68)
Adrian Lewandowski (69-70)
Michael R Lewellen (67-68) CA
James L Lewis (68)
Jimmie O Lewis (68-69) TX
William Lillard Jr (71-72)
Arthur A Lindell (70) FL
Joseph R Lindsey (71-72)
Jeffrey H Linkous (70) OH
William J Linsey (70)
Howard L Lockett (67-68)
Anthony Loiero (69-70) NJ
Carl L Long (69-70) MO
Douglas Long (70)
Joe C Lopez (68) AZ
Gary L Lowe (69) OR

Hector Perez Lugo (67-68) PR
Julius L Lutz (69-70) CA
David Madrigal (71-72)
Charles J Maguire (67-68) CA
George T Mahan Jr (68-69) NJ
Michael C Malone (69-70) MS
Gajus Marciulionis (71-72)
John W Marks (69-70) IN
John J Marlowe (70-71) FL
Clem Marquez (68-69)
Walter Marshall Jr (69-70)
James E Martin (67-68)
Michael C Martin (69)
Daniel A Martinez (70)
Jose A Martinez (71-72)
Ronald L Massey (67-68)
William L Matelski (68-69) WI
William J Matheson (70) GA
Ernest J Maxwell (69)
Freeman Maxwell (71)
Gregory Maxwell (69)
Keith S Maxwell (69-70) WI
Randall Mays (71-72) OK
Patrick McCambridge (70)
John H McCammon (68-69) CO
Thomas O McCleary (67-68)
Terry McClure (69-70)
Irvin R McCoun (68-69) MT
Thomas P McCourt (68-69) MA
Donald W McCullough (67-68) MA
Michael McDougal (71-72)
Ray K McGee (69-70)
Paul J McGervey Jr (68-69) TX
Philip M McGrail (68-69) MA
Gary V McGuire (71-72)
Johnnie McIntyre (67-68)
Jerry G McKinney (67-68)
John D McMahon (69)
Kenneth H McNitt (67-68) NY
Willie McWhorter (68)
Wayne N Medlin (67-68)
James W Meeder (71-72)
Dennis Meehan (71-72)
Ronald Mejia (68-69)
Richard F Mendel (71-72)
Robert C Merrick (69-70)
Norman R Miller (70-71) IA

Gerald Mikieiewicz (69)
Bobby Mitchell (71-72)
Gary A Mobley (71-72)
James Moore (70-71)
Jose L Morales (70)
Sergio Morales (71-72) MI
Albert A Morris (71-72)
Willie D Morris (68-69) NC
James R Motika (67-68) CA
Timothy W Muleern (71-72)
John P Mullaney (68-69) VA
Larry W Muller (69) IA
James W Mundy (68-69)
Edward C Munson (71-72)
Roger W Murphy (67-68) OH
Aaron Myers Jr (71-72)
Richard A Myers (68-69) OH
Samuel H Myers (67-68)
Stephen M Nalley (70-71) IN
Douglas R Naruo (70) CA
Richard A Nation (68-69)
Billy R Nelson (67-68)
Danny Nelson (68)
Eugene P Nelson (68-69) MN
Thomas J Neuman (71-72)
Harold T Northen (70)
James L Norwood Sr (67-68) MS
Andrew J Obrien (70-71) MA
Donald L Ogelvie (68-69) AR
Patrick E Oleary (68-69) CT
Melvin L Olsen (70) MN
Dan W Olson (70)
Dennis L Olson (67-68)
George W Oplinger (71) PA
William G Orr (68)
Felix S Ortiz (67-68)
Donald L Otto (70-71) NV
August J Padalecki (69) TX
Edmond A Paradis (69) NC
Larry L Parkhurst (69-70) MO
Edward M Parkies (71-72)
John Pate (69-70) AL
Edward Patterson (71-72)
Richard V Patton (67-68)
Paul Pawlak (68-69) Australia
Eddie J Payne (69-70)
Robert Payne (69-70)

Ronald G Peabody (67-68)
Jorge Perez (70-71)
Walter Perez (70)
William V Perez (70)
James R Perkins (71-72)
Norman D Perry (70)
Dennis Wayne Peterson (68-69) NC
Patrick S Pickford (67-68) NH
Alan G Pidgeon (68-69) NC
John R Pierce (67-68)
Bob Pike (71-72)
Ernest Pimentel (71-72)
John O Plunkett (69-70) FL
Frederick Z Poliniak (68-69) NC
Donnie L Pratt (68-69) MD
Don Price (71-72)
Mike Pruett (69-70) NC
William D Puckett (69-70) TN
Arthur J Pue Jr (68-69) FL
Patrick Quill (68-69) WA
Stanley D Ralph (68) FL
Anderson Reed Jr (71-72)
Jerry W Reed (71-72)
Don A Reesor (71-72)
Michael W Reeve CA
Charles E Reimers (67-68)
Dave Reinheimer (68-69) MO
Richard W Reith (68-69) FL
David D Retlich (69-70)
Jerry D Reynolds (70)
Paul Rhodes
Gary M Rice (71-72)
Myron K Rice (68) NC
Jack L Richards (70)
James R Richardson (68-69)
John Richardson (67-68)
John H Richardson (68-69) AL
Oddis Richardson (68-69) MO
Bruce Riley (67-68)
Eugene Ripple (69)
David Roberts (70)
Gilbert Roberts (68-69)
Michael F Roberts (67-68) Australia
William T Roberts 69-70)
Phelix R Robinson (71-72)
Richard W Robinson OK
Michael T Roche (72)

Catarino Rodriguez (68-69)
Michael P Rodriguez (71-72)
Israel Roman-Diaz (67-68)
Wiley M Rone (70)
Randy J Roon (70) IL
Chris Ross (69-70)
Gregg A Ross (71-72) CA
Ernest F Rotermund (69-70)
Milton L Royal (69)
James A Ruiz (69-70)
Roosevelt T Russell (71-72)
David Salazar Jr (71-72)
Winston Neal Salsbery II (67-68) CA
Darryl E Sanders (68-69)
Robert D Sang (71-72)
Richard R Santos (69)
Dennis R Sartin (69-70) MS
Tommy C Saylor (69-70) NC
William Scarborough (69)
John W Schlichter (70)
John W Schlosser (68-69) OK
Gerald Scholzen (71-72)
George E Schorr (69) LA
David C Schutz (69-70) TX
Lawrence T Schwartz (71-72)
Jessie R Scott Jr (68) CO
King Scott Jr (71-72)
Alan W Searl (68-69) WI
Leroy R Seiv Jr (68-69) IN
Ronald L Sellers (71)
Courtney L Selley (68-69) OR
Ron L Sellins NC
Steven E Sellman (67-68) ID
Charles G Selman (70)
William Shackleford (67-68)
Lee A Shapanka (69)
Larry W Shaver (68-69)
Orin M Sheley (70) IL
Richard Shepherd (67-68) IL
David H Sherman (68-69) OR
James L Sherwood (68-69) AR
Paul S Sibert (67-68) GA
Arlen P Sieg (68-69) IL
Michael B Silverthorn (69-70) MI
Craig H Simmons (70)
Reginald A Simmons (69-70) TX
Stephen C Simmons (69-70) VA

Jim D Simpkins (71-72)
Eugene F Skelton (70) MI
Daniel R Skocelas (68-69) MI
Stirling Skolnik (68-69)
Charles E Smith (71-72)
Earnest Smith (68-69) IN
Jerry L Smith (69)
Jimmy E Smith (70)
Jimmy R Smith (70)
Keith A Smith (68-69)
Lester Smith (67-68)
Norman Smith (67-68)
Walter L Smith (70)
William Smith (67-68) WI
William C Smith (70)
Willie J Smith (68)
Alan H Sommer (69-70)
Paul S Sondey (67-68) NJ
Kenneth A Specht (68-69)
James D Speck (68-69) IN
David E Spicer (67-68) ID
Thomas M Spiller (70)
Michael L Stafford (70-71) TN
James Staggard (67-68)
James J Stallard (67-68)
Jimmie S Stallcup (71-72)
Alden R Stanley (67-68) MA
Robert Stanton (70)
Grady Luther Starks (68-69) NC
Robert Steele (67-68)
Mark D Steffens (67-68) WA
William A Stephens (67-68)
Donald L Stewart (68-69) KY
Virgil D Stone (69-70)
Billy J Stracner (69)
Randall Stubbs (71-72)
Samuel Suarez (71-72) NY
Joseph E Suazo (70) NM
Leslie G Sue (71-72)
David L Suggs (69-70) OK
David N Sullivan (69-70) MI
Jack E Sullivan (70-71) SC
Willie Sullivan (71-72)
James L Summersell (71-72) AL
Frank Syfor (71-72)
Wayne Sytkowski (71-72)
Andrew J Tarpey (68-69) FL

Henry Tate (67-68) MI
Gary Taylor (71)
James Taylor (71-72)
Newman Taylor (68-69) OK
Thomas L Taylor IA
Murden Temple (70)
Terry Templeman (69-70) GA
Francis Templeton (67-68)
Robert E Tenney (68-69) WV
David C Testerman (68-69) VA
Barton P Thompson (69) AZ
Charles Thompson
James L Thompson (69-70) WA
John W Thompson (69) MS
Aeril Thornton (69)
Dennis R Thurman (68)
Terry L Thurman (67-68) WA
David L Tinkler (68-69)
Larry T Trask (68-69) MI
Michael G Trent (70)
Alvin E Triplett (71-72)
Tom L Tripp (69-70) ID
Timothy J Turek (70) MN
Lyle Updike (70-71) WI
Gary L Vanetten (68-69) WI
David G Vankirk (69-70) MO
Wayne Vanvoorst (68-69) IA
James F Veal (68-69)
Paul N Veilleux (67-68) NH
George Vermilea (71-72)
David A Visnack (71-72)
Melvin L Waite (68-69) MI
Daniel L Wakefield (68-69) AZ
Allen I Walberg (69)
Granville Walker Jr (67-68)
James N Walker (69-70) SC
Rodney V Walker (71-72)
Thomas J Wall (71-72)
Edgar N Wallace (67-68) MI
J C Walton (70-71) GA
Gregory D Walz (69) IA
John S Ward (69-70) Viet Nam
Timothy D Ward (68-69) AZ
Joseph J Washart Jr (70) NJ
Lansing S Waters (71-72)
Terry F Weakley (70) OR
Alan R Webb (71-72)

David M Webb (69-70) NV
Charles E Webber (69-70) WI
Major P Webster (68)
Lawrence D Wedig (69-70) WI
Albert Werth (69-70) MI
James H Wertz (68-69) PA
Donald S West (67-68)
Chris A Westwood (67-68) WA
Mike Whatley (70-71)
Edward D White (67-68)
James L White (70)
John B White (68-69)
Dan Whybrew (70)
John Ed Wick (69) IN
Paul C Wilgus (70-71) CA
Brian S Williams (68-69) CA
Freddie Williams (69-70)
Jack Williams MO
Thomas S Williams (70)
Maurice H Wilson (68)
Paul A Wilson (71-72)
Ray E Wilson (70) AK
Douglas Wineglass (69) SC
Roger Winters IL
Robert F Wire (68-69)
William H Wiseman Jr (67-68) NC
Fred F Wohlfield (71-72)
James A Wojcik (71-72)
William P Wolf (70)
Burks A Wood (71-72)
Doug Woods (67-68)
Bob Wooley (67-68)
Robert L Worrall (69-70) TX
Tyrone Worthy (69)
Alfred B Wright (67-68)
Terry W Yenour (69-70) AL
William H Young (69)
Anthony J Zaikis (67-68) OK
Larry Zimmerman (71-72)

INDEX

II Corps, 33
III Corps, 34
A Shau Valley, 12, 49, 65, 66, 69, 82, 88, 132, 153, 157, 159, 169, 173, 183, 222, 223, 231, 234, 239, 309, 314
Advanced Individual Training, 30
Afghanistan, 311
Agent Orange, 302, 307
Aid Station, 57, 61, 62, 105, 132, 133, 136, 138, 139, 141, 143, 144, 159, 250, 251, 252, 260, 265, 276, 277
Air Force, 295
Airborne Div., 82nd., 34, 245
Airborne Div., 101st., 35, 37, 39, 62, 65, 92, 174, 207, 230, 237, 252, 254, 258, 259, 280, 283, 285, 305, 307
Airborne Div., 101st, A-Co. 2-501st, 11-14, 49, 62, 65, 91, 111, 228, 232, 296, 297, 309
Airborne Div.,101st, B-Co. 2-501st, 12, 14, 17, 64, 69, 82, 117, 121, 132, 187, 198, 207, 209, 237, 252, 252, 260-262, 269, 281, 304, 308
Airborne Div.,101st, C-Co. 2-501st, 50
Airborne Div.,101st, D-Co. 2-501st, 50, 111
Airborne Div.,101st, 1/ 502nd, 174
Airborne Div.,101st, 1/ 506th, 230, 245
Airborne Div.,101st, 2/ 327th, 174
Airborne Div.,101st, 3/ 187th, 230, 262
Airborne Div.,173rd, 304
Airborne, (Firebase), 231-234, 237, 238
American Airlines, 290
American Indians, 154
Anchorage, AK, 33, 288
Apache Snow, (Operation), 220, 229
Armendariz, Patrick, 40, 261
Army of the Republic of Vietnam, (ARVN) 36, 136, 167, 229, 253, 285, 307, 310
Australia, 62, 133, 254, 307
Ayala, "Doc," 278
Baldwin, Bob, 40, 48
Bamboo Vipers, 95
Bastogne (Firebase), 69,132, 330
Battle, Sgt., 72, 77, 78, 313
Bay City, MI, 18, 350
Beatles, The, 28
Bien Hoa, 34, 249, 252-255, 258, 275, 280, 282, 284, 289
Birmingham, (Firebase), 49, 69, 70, 82, 130, 132, 134-137, 141, 144, 150, 218-220
Boil, Executive Officer, (XO), 272
Bouman, Walt, 106,1506, 206

Boyd, (Firebase), 50, 54, 56, 69, 70, 132, 146, 149
Braniff Airways, 29
Branson, MO, 121, 198, 272, 337
Bronco, Landing Zone, (LZ) , 231
Bronson Hospital Neo Natal Care, 301
Brooks, Sgt., 225
Bush, George W., (President), 304, 331
Butts, Robert, 40, 117, 332, 333
Cam Rahn Bay, 33, 34, 109, 288, 372
Cambodia, 310, 359
Camp Alpha, 280, 282
Camp Eagle, 82, 89, 132, 139, 207, 212, 226, 252
Camp Eagle Field Hospital, 212
Camp (LZ) Sally, 37, 38, 40, 45-47, 56, 60-62, 64-66, 76, 134, 135, 148-150, 159, 171, 193, 208, 215, 243, 249-252, 259, 260, 265, 268, 272, 274, 275, 279, 280, 283, 288, 313
Campbell, Donna, 32
Campbell, Phillip, 32
Campbell, Stanley, 31, 32
Carrara, Wayne, 95, 97, 261
Chabitch, Jim, 301
Chalmette, LA, 194
Cherry, Corbin, (Chaplain), 79, 189, 194, 208
Chicago, IL, 11, 31, 290, 291, 354, 355
Chiew-Hui, 40
Christensen, William , 206
Chung ("Daisy"), 256, 257
Colombo, Bob, 269
Conscientious Objector, 25, 28, 283
Contrabecki, Al, 59
Cook, Captain "Doc," 132, 138, 139, 142, 144, 260, 265, 270, 277
Corpus Christi, TX, 299
Crossguns, Clyde, 70,168, 170, 190, 191
Culco Beach, (Eagle Beach), 101, 103, 251, 270, 271
Da Nang, 37, 41, 64, 81, 89, 251, 252, 259, 277, 279, 313, 346, 350
Daniels, Command Sgt. Major, 272, 275
Decatur High School, MI, 22
Decatur, MI, 24, 32, 127, 311
Defiance, OH. 315, 317
Delgiorno, Jim, 278
Dennis, Sgt., 54
Department of the Army, 29
Depierre, John, 208
Detroit, MI, 27, 40, 117, 328, 332, 333
Dillenbeck, Robert, 237

DMZ (Demilitarized Zone), 37
Dong Ap Bia, *see Hamburger Hill*
Dothan, GA, 189
Dotter, Edwin, 170
Dowagiac, MI, 26
Downs Syndrome, 302
Draft (military), 18, 23, 25, 41, 171, 238, 304, 311
Dragan, Phillip, "Flip," 326
Driver, John Cecil, 151, 152, 174, 177, 179, 190-193, 196, 209
Duchow, Frank, 105
Duke, Jim, 150-152, 162, 174, 208, 209, 264, 269, 314
Dumas, TX, 69
Dunkard Brethren Church, Hart, MI, 25
Durney, James, 177, 191
Eagles Nest (Observation post), 249, 271
Edwards, Mike, "Doc," 174, 191, 197, 198, 277
Ervin, James, 190
Farrell, James "Doc," 265, 339-341
First Cavalry Division, 23
Fisher, Dale "Gap," 40,128
Flory, Ann (Chabitch), 115, 201, 283, 290, 291, 293, 302
Flory, Bill, 23, 294
Flory, Bob, 81
Flory, Bonnie, 293
Flory, Dominiak, Elizabeth, 352
Flory, Esther, 315, 341
Flory, Joey, 81, 149
Flory, John, 293
Flory, June, 293
Flory, Lisa, 302
Flory, Paul, 293
Flory, Sandra, 293
Flory, Susan, 293
Flory-Hoekman, Rebecca, 203
Forbes, Ralph, 323, 324
Fort Knox, KY, 27, 29
Fort Lewis, WA, 33
Fort Sam Houston, TX, 29, 31, 32, 67, 68, 279, 287, 296
Fort Wayne Induction Center, Detroit, 27
Franzinger, Jim, 207, 210, 242, 269
Garber, IA, 275
German, Bob, 191
Germany, 208
Gibson Family, 312
Gibson, Mel, 341
Gipson, Clarence, 22, 327
Gobles, MI, 23

Goens Family, 312
Gothard Family, 312
Gould, Tim, 189
Graney, Pierce T.,10, 50, 56, 89, 90, 150, 151, 161, 200, 207, 208, 232, 337, 338
Great Depression, 18
Green Berets, 153
Green, Jimmy, 40, 47, 67, 69, 100, 110
Green, Richard, 227, 334
Grier, Doug, 189
Gulf of Mexico, 299
Gulf of Tonkin, 102, 104, 250
Gutenberg, IA, 314
Hallums, James, 50, 53
Hamburger Hill, 261, 262, 264, 269, 271, 272, 307, 309, 319, 338 *see also Hill 937*
Hanoi, 309, 314
Harris Family, 312
Hawaii, 216, 276
Hazen, Phil, 208, 269
Hefel, Dan, 85, 251, 270, 313
Heil, John, 308
Highway One, 101, 135, 271, 273
Hill 937, 153, 209, 234, 245, 247, 249, 252, 259, 261, 262, 264, 310 *see also Hamburger Hill*
Hiller, Leo, 270
Hilley, Frank, 40, 221
Hinery, Edward J., 262
Hoah, 210-213, 218
Ho-Chi-Minh, 115
Hoining, (Specialist), 255, 256
Hong Kong, 254, 255
Honolulu, 216
Hope College, Holland, MI, 302
Hope, Bob, 63. 64
Hudson, Joe, 40
Hue City, 37, 41, 43, 49, 56, 101, 117, 132, 135, 260, 271, 308
Hunt, Jim, 17, 227, 334-337, 343, 346
Hyatt, Charles, 168, 190, 191
International Date Line, 288, 289
Iraq, 172, 311
Ireland, 177, 178
Jack Daniels, (Whisky), 149, 188, 201
Jackman, Wilfred "Doc," 59
Jackson, Alan, 275
Jackson, Elmer, 316, 328, 329
Jackson, Michael, 179
Jeb Stewart, (Operation), 87
Jehovah's Witness, 25
Jessup Door Co., 26, 299
Jim Crow, Law, 313

371

Jimmerson, Bradley, 300, 308
Jimmerson, Cathy, 17, 300, 308
Johns, Jackie, 40
Johnson, Louis, 107, 261
Julien, Jim, 150, 200, 313
Julien, Ruth, 313
Kalamazoo, MI, 13, 19, 117, 207, 291-293, 300, 332, 337
Kansas City, MO, 207, 313, 337
Katrina, Hurricane, 194
Kaufmann, Bill, "Tiny," 190, 191, 205
Kemp Family, 312
Kimuchi Squat, 86, 185, 225, 274
Kissell, Dave, 105, 133
Kluch, Jake, 303
Kontrabecki, Al, 40, 155, 295
Kopystianskyj, Bohdan, 120, 187, 197, 272
Korea, Republic Of, 307
Korean USO, 545, 70, 253
Korean War, 18, 173
Kowloon, Hong Kong, 256
Krautscheid, David, 40, 90, 204, 206, 217, 338
Krautscheid, Pam, 207
Lake Cora, MI, 24
Lake Michigan, 109
Lansing, MI, 291
Laos, 49, 125, 309, 357
Las Vegas, NV, 303
Lawrence High School, MI, 61
Lawrence, MI, 61
Lee Family, 312
Louisville, KY, 27
McCammom, John, 278
McCoun, Irvin "Moose," 40, 111, 124, 127, 170, 188, 193, 197, 200, 201, 276
Mackinac Bridge, MI, 19
Malecki, Robert, 11, 15, 65, 232, 234-236, 319, 354
Manhattan, NY, 40
Marines, 90, 227, 276, 307, 346-350
Marks, John "Doc," 189
Marz Link, 64
Massachusetts Striker, (Operation), 153, 174
Massy, Ken, 301
Matelski, Bill, 133
Medal of Honor, 307
Mexico, 299
Military Records and Reserve Board, 196
Miller Beer, 303
Moak, Larry, 227, 334
Montagnard, 93, 133, 154, 183, 184
Motika, James, 187
Moving Wall, The, 127

MP (Military Police), 41
Muller, Larry, 278
Murray, "Doc," 265, 276
NCO Club, 56, 105, 250, 251, 259, 271, 272, 274, 284
Native-American, 70, 191
Navy, 82, 105, 107, 307, 340, 348, 349
Nevada Eagle (Operation), 153
New Orleans, LA, 194
New York, 95, 189, 295, 336
New Zealand, 307
Niagara Falls, NY, 40, 155, 295
Nieman, Gary, 174, 204
Noel, Chris, 146-148
Normandy, 305
North Central Airlines, 291
North Vietnam, 115, 116, 309, 314, 361
North Vietnamese Army, 52, 185
Oakland Army Terminal, 289
Oakland, CA, 288
Ogelvie, Don, 64
O'Hare Field, Chicago, 32, 291
O'Leary, Pat, 40, 70, 150, 151, 177-179, 191, 221, 237
Orangutan, 202
OTC (Officers Training School), 28
Overton Family, 312
Pabst Blue Ribbon, 272, 274
Panther II, (Firebase), 54 *see also Boyd*
Parks, Rosa, 313
Parson Business School, Kalamazoo, MI, 300
Patriot Guard, 172
Paw Paw, MI, 25, 27, 295
Pawlak, Paul "Doc," 31, 62, 178, 179, 265, 277
Peckinpah, Sam, 118
Penthouse magazine, 266
Pepper, Barry, 341
Perfume River, 82, 84
Peterson, Dennis, 278
Phisohex (Soap), 213, 214
Playboy magazine, 266
Pleasant Gap, PA, 40, 127
Pohl Bridge, 81, 82, 132, 135, 210, 240, 243
Portland, OR, 207
POW (Prisoner Of War), 303, 314
Pue, Art, 67, 96, 150, 161, 162, 179, 186, 187, 200, 217
PX (Post Exchange), 32, 148, 251
Quang Tri, 41, 260
ROTC (Reserve Officers Training Corps), 28
Reinheimer, David, 40, 64, 105, 177, 205,

206, 261, 318, 321, 337-339
Riley Family, 312
Roth Family, 312
Route #547, 49, 82
Saigon, 36, 34, 282
Saint Paul, MN, 177
Sally, (HQ Co.), *see Camp (LZ) Sally*
Salsbery, Neal, 46, 149
San Antonio Tech, TX, 297, 300
San Antonio, TX, 29, 299
San Francisco VA Medical Hospital Center, 208
San Francisco, CA, 290
Sault Locks, MI, 233
Saving Private Ryan, 305
Screaming Eagle newspaper, 263
Screaming Eagle patch, 35, 252, 296
Seiko watch, 288, 294
Shapanka, Lee, 120
Shorr, George "Top," 194, 195, 313
Silver Star, 117
Sir Tailors, 256
Slaughter Family, 312
Slaughter, Art, 312
Sneed, Carl, 249, 269
South Bend, IN, 291, 293
South China Sea, 33, 128, 350
Sowa, Jim, 81, 327
Special Forces, 35
St. Louis, MO, 40, 196, 261
St. Marys River, MI, 96, 233
Sullivan, Dave, 85
Summers, "Doc," 54, 61, 62, 161, 279
Tan Son Nhut Airbase, 34, 279-281
Tate, David, 304
T-Bone, (Firebase), 45-47
Tenny, Bob, 126
Testerman, David, 106,150
Thomas, James, 262
Thua Thien Province, 82, 309
Tie, (Interpreter), 184, 185
Time magazine, 307
Trask, Larry, 40, 332
Travis Air Force Base, 288, 289
Tulsa, OK, 80, 249, 314, 337
Tunnell, Freaman, 119
USO, 54, 62, 63, 70, 253
USS *Hope*, 313
Vaile, Donnie, 190
Van Buren Co. Library, Decatur, MI, 304
Vandalia, MI, 311
VC (Viet Cong) 36, 43, 260, 308
Vehgil, (Firebase), 39, 69, 71, 73, 132

VFW magazine, 234, 262
VFW Post 6248, 316, 327, 331
VHPA (Vietnam Helicopter Pilots Association), 227, 334
Vietnam, The Irish Experience, 177, 191
Waite, Mel, 40
Wakefield, Dan "Snake," 39, 47, 49, 98, 99, 127, 158, 177, 194, 271, 275, 305
Walsh, John, 150, 193, 197, 198, 200, 209
Welch, Gary, 40, 60, 106, 271-276
Weldon, Art, 198
Weldon, Denise, (Walsh), 198
Whip, (Firebase), 153, 161, 163, 166, 174, 177, 178, 181, 226
Wick, Ed, 124, 264
Withers, Russ, 323, 324
Withers, Vernon, 200
Wolf, Tobias, 305
Wooten, (Specialist), 72, 77, 78, 313
WWII (World War II), 18, 28, 172, 303, 316, 326, 328, 330
Yokota, Japan, 33, 288
York, PA, 174
Zaffiri, Sam, 319, 320, 338, 339